MAKING POWERFUL CHOICES

A Thirty Day Journey to a Life You Love

"What lies behind us
and what lies before us
are tiny matters compared to
what lies within us."

Ralph Waldo Emerson, 1803-1882

Powerful Choices Coaching is a registered trademark of the Powerful Choices Coaching, LLC.

Other brand names and product names are trademarks or registered trademarks of their respective holders.

©2005 Powerful Choices Coaching, LLC

Beaverton, Oregon 97005

All rights reserved. Partnered with Erickson College International.

Contents

Preface

My name is Marilyn Atkinson and I am the developer of **The Art and Science of Coaching,** an Ericksonian and Solution Focused coach training program now graduating over 500 people per year in eleven countries. I first met **Renee and Anthony Choice** and **Cara Beckett** when they were students in this program three years ago, and it has been my pleasure to watch then evolve into brilliant coaches, leaders, and trainers. **Larrye-Marie Heyl** was a later graduate and is just as talented and passionate.

Renee's passion is human development, and she combines profound sincerity with authenticity and enthusiasm. She has one of the most brilliant, systemic, and focused young minds on the planet today. Anthony, with his humor and pizzazz has a passion for success modeling. Cara is an exceptionally lucid writer, visionary, and creative thinker. Larrye is a great course designer, technical writer and trainer. Together they are a winning team with an extraordinary offering.

It is with pleasure that I recommend their outstanding and accurate book on solution focused self-coaching or for a coach to use with an appropriate client. The book provides a fun and comprehensive day-by-day framework for coaching in various ways: 1-on-1, group, or for yourself. It is wonderfully straightforward and clear. Renee and Cara move people into self assurance and belief with their electric metaphors. Anthony and Larrye support powerfully. Gentle, day-by-day inspiration makes self-coaching doable.

This thirty-day action plan champions the human spirit, and channels breakthrough with focused guidance. The book is filled with encouragement and trusts that people can truly shift gears when they have a clear aim. It both celebrates individuals in their capacity to move forward, and then shows the staircase with the easy steps and precise coaching questions and structures of professional Ericksonian Coaching.

The spirit of coaching is like the spirit of Christmas, generous and expectant that something wonderful is available. This powerful book makes it clear that what is truly wonderful is people's capacity, no matter what their history, to move past their old anchors and habits, lift their eyes to the horizon, and set sail into a transformed vision of their own future.

Written in the true spirit of Milton Erickson, the book is full of solution focused nuggets of pure gold. The authors have developed the ability to truly collaborate with their readers, as active participants. The day-to-day coaching plan organizes and simplifies clarifying questions that can truly assist people to move into momentum with difficult projects.

If you have an aim that compels yet eludes you, then open to the first chapter now. Keep moving, day-by-day, using thirty minutes per day, into the awesome first steps of an Ericksonian coaching experience. There is always more to be revealed...

Marilyn Atkinson, Ph.D.
Founder of Erickson College International
Vancouver, BC
April 2005

Acknowledgments

To our children - may they know their roots and find their wings to live their best life.

To our parents for giving us solid roots and wings to soar to our true purpose.

To Bill Harris of Centerpointe Institute for stimulating us to create a solid team.

To Wayne Ferguson for inviting us to be powerful.

To the Powerful Choices Coaching team for supporting us and being willing to co-create and pilot a number of the processes for our integration program. Special thanks to Thom Cathcart, Debra Ochoa, Diane Dreizen, and Yolanda Russell.

To Erickson College International for bringing us together through the Art and Science of Coaching.

To all the Erickson colleagues and coach graduates, for standing for what is truly important in this world.

And last, but not least, we are eternally grateful to Marilyn Atkinson for her influence, support, and encouragement to think in new ways and engage in highly effective thinking patterns. Marilyn Atkinson and Erickson have given us the integrated thinking systems to birth a product such as this.

The Powerful Choices Leadership Team
Cara, Renee, Anthony, and Larrye

Introduction

Welcome to the **Making Powerful Choices 30-Day Journey to a Life You Love,** and congratulations for making a powerful choice. Choosing to invest in yourself is unquestionably the greatest investment you can make!

We care about you living your best life!

Why? Because when you have the courage, commitment, skills and support to live your best life, you will naturally inspire others to do the same. And the more people that start living their best life, the less unhappiness and pain on the planet. And the less there is pain and negativity, the more energy that is available for making effective decisions and supporting everyone in getting what they want. And the more effectual the decisions, the higher the level of consciousness will grow in our complex and dynamic world. This helps both you and us!

Having invested in this workbook, we are sure you are clear that having a great life is a game worth playing, and the journey begins today!

If you are like us you have probably tried a lot of personal growth and self improvement programs. You might have spent thousands of dollars buying motivational tapes, self-help books, attending seminars and so on, looking for "the answer", but things still didn't happen for you.

You see, each of our Powerful Choices Leadership Team has had times in our life when things seemed completely hopeless, and we felt we couldn't see the light at the end of the tunnel. Ever have this experience?

Each of us has dealt with many overwhelming life challenges -- just a few of which include being a single parent, the death of a child, serious marital and partner problems, divorce, bulimia, depression, drug addiction, serious financial challenges, thoughts of suicide, ongoing inner turmoil, self doubt, anxiety, lack of fulfilling relationships, unclear purpose and meaning, victim identification, debilitating self talk, debilitating illness and so on.

You name it - we have likely experienced it, just like most people have!

Perhaps you have experienced a few of these things, or maybe more than a few. Maybe you're in a similar place where you're confused and just can't see how everything is going to fall together into place. Trust us, we have been there!

Nothing we tried seemed to work!

And then each of us, on our own timeline, came across a body of work through Erickson College International and Dr. Marilyn Atkinson that transformed our lives and has transformed the lives of hundreds of people that we have worked with since becoming certified coaches and trainers.

Today we are Erickson trained Solution Focused Coaches and Trainers, with an International Coach Federation (ICF) Professional Certified Coach (PCC) distinction and a HUGE passion for NLP (Neuro-Linguistic Programming).

We support people to re-program their mind for success, by transforming the way they think and act. This installs new and improved thinking patterns, beliefs, and habits into their beyond conscious minds, to help people attract success into their lives.

We have created the **Making Powerful Choices – 30 Day Journey to a Life You Love** for you. To support you, and anyone else you are participating in this journey with, to get from where you are to where you want to be.

About the Program

This 30-day program is a series of knowledge tools and coaching processes that teach you - by showing show you how to put into actual practice - certain key life principles and strategies—principles and strategies that will allow you to create the exact inner and outer results you want.

There is the possibility that some of you will feel overloaded. Be assured that one of the best ways to learn this is to overload the mind by giving you too much. We're doing that on purpose. We know you won't do all that we are giving you, and you won't do it perfectly. However, you will have a lot of transformational information to drop into your beyond conscious mind that will stick. Trust that this is the case. It will be available to you when you need it most.

We are purposely giving you more than you think you can handle in the 30-day journey, so if you are feeling a sense of saturation or frustration this is good. This is exactly how it should be. You may also feel a real sense of emotional tiredness where you feel drained. It's like saying, ***"Stop! I have already learned enough."*** If you feel this way, it's fine.

In fact, it is really good because it means you are starting to make some neuro-pathway connections. This process can be emotionally draining because you are re-wiring your neurology to recreate how you think.

Depending on where you are and how far you need to come in this direction, this journey can be an arduous process. So be gentle, trust the unfolding and go with the flow.

Just for the record, we believe you are a very resourceful person. Meaning, all the resources and all the answers to the questions you have exist within you. You are someone who has a vision for your life. By choosing to be an example of a person who is actualizing their vision, you are blazing the trail for yourself and for those you care about.

Living your purpose will make a huge contribution to the world - guaranteed!

About the 30 Days

This workbook was birthed out of our online audio program. It is important to realize that this is **not an exact transcript** of the online program or CD series, rather something to use by itself, with a coach one-on-one or in a group, or while listening to the CD program. When learning is alive for all the senses – visual, auditory, kinesthetic and experiential – integration is easier. If you use the book, CD series or group coaching and one-on-one coaching you will be sure to have a deep, profound and transformational experience.

This is a powerful and challenging unfolding. Each day we invite you to learn more about a significant activity that will help you reach your goal and live your best life. The questions and integration activities provide you with the necessary tools and readjustments so you are inspired, motivated and able to reach your goal.

You can use the 30 Days in whatever timeframe best suits your needs. You don't have to complete it in 30 days. Here are a few examples:

- Some people have told us that they work through the days during the week and take the weekends off to ponder and regain their energy. If you take this approach, think about how your life will change in just 6 weeks.
- Others tell us they like to work through the process every other day - taking 60 days to complete their journey.
- Other people say that working in a group coaching environment or with a personal coach is the best way to participate in the program because the conversation and additional coaching support provide deeper integration and further awareness.

The key to your success is to create a plan and stick to it! If you complete the course, and participate fully each day, and share the core principles with others, you will begin to have this be a way of life for you.

Using the Book Effectively

Before you start your journey to living everyday a life you love, we went to tell you a little about the structure of each day's work.

- We begin the day with a story, poem, or quote to set the mood and focus your mind on the topic or quality of the day.
- During the "training" portion of the day, we often invite you to ponder important questions.

PONDER:

When you see this text, take a moment to consider the question.

- Once you learn about the topic, we invite you to fully participate in the integration activity. This activity is extremely important for your success. And you may want to go through the activity more than once.
  During the activities you often see sections similar to this one:

ASK YOURSELF: What should I consider here?

This is an opportunity for you to answer the questions in your journal or in the space provided and fully integrate the information you have read.

- We finish each less with a strong encouragement for you to challenge yourself to keep moving forward and ask yourself what you are willing to do as you move forward to the next day.

Go For It!

We respect you for choosing the life you want. The purpose of this program is to support you in achieving what you want from your life. Your success is our success, so please email us at choices@powerfulchoices.net throughout the program and let us know how you are enjoying the book or other products such as the CD series.

The integration of this material is not something you do overnight, and it does involve some effort on your part - about 30-45 minutes per day, and can be done year after year with different goals and different areas of life. We are here to let you know that it is **very** possible. You **can** do it! And it is well **worth it**!

The more you integrate the proven methods in this program, the more you will start to take positive action, and the more you do this, the less you'll suffer in life and the better you will feel.

This program will make a difference in your life. We believe it will make as much of a difference in your life as it has made in our own.

Be sure to share your results along the way. And when people ask you why you seem so satisfied with your life tell them you have started making powerful choices.

With passion, respect, and joy,

The Powerful Choices Leadership Team -
Cara Beckett, Renee Choice, Anthony Choice, Larrye-Marie Heyl

Part 1: Set the Foundation

Your 30-day program starts with five days in which you build your foundation. A building with a weak or faulty foundation is not likely to withstand the day-to-day weathering or the major weather events that might occur during the life of the building. And so it is with your goals. If you fail to build a strong foundation for completing your goal and living your best life, then life's events - little or big - can greatly impact your stability in reaching your goals and maintaining them through time.

Architects know how to design a house with a strong foundation so it can withstand the "elements" through time. In these first five sessions we invite you to be the architect designing your own life. We share with you the secrets of building your foundation so you, too, can withstand the "elements" of life through time and live the life you love every day.

Journals

Before you begin your journey, get a journal so you can write and answer the questions in each exercise. Many exercises refer to previous ones.

The architect plans and creates a detailed set of blueprints that contractors use to build that house on a strong foundation. Your journal is your blueprint for building the foundation to reach your goal.

Five-Day Foundation Overview

The first five days of your journey are about setting a foundation.

Day 1 describes the advantages of taking 100% responsibility for your life. Rather than complaining, be creative enough to see each life event as an opportunity to learn and to expand your knowledge - and opportunity to achieve great success and growth.

To help you achieve your goals, **Day 2** describes how to become an Enlightened Internal Leader. You learn about the four stages of Enlightened Internal Leadership - Development, Intensity, Forward Motion, and Enlightened Internal Leadership - each stage getting you closer to getting what you want.

Often getting what you want means learning to accept that life sends us gifts and challenges in ways we may not recognize as beneficial. **Day 3** describes learning to go with the flow, getting back up when we fall, and recognizing the whole truth.

Day 4 describes the cycle of completion that involves several stages: Vision, Inspiration, Decision, Plan, Implement, Continue, Satisfaction Check, and Completion. You learn the key is flexibility and openness to alternative ways of getting what you want.

In **Day 5** we invite you to take a look in your closet of life - to clean out the old to make space for the new.

And once you have completed these first five days, you have a solid foundation on which to build the rest of your life - a life you love!

Are you ready?

Check out our readiness checklist:

CHECKLIST

- Open Mind
- Flexibility
- A journal to capture your thoughts and homework
- Life time - time set aside each day to do your life's work

Day 1 **Be Responsible and Accountable**

As we embark upon this profound 30-Day journey, it is valuable to consider the areas of your life where you are currently not as fulfilled as you might like.

Master's Tip Consider these three central rules to a fulfilling life:

- If something works, don't fix it.
- Once you know what works, do more of it.
- If it doesn't work, don't do it again - Do Something Different!

A Story

A Brief Tale

Madam C.J. Walker died a millionaire philanthropist, which in this day and age is not all together extraordinary. What made Madam Walker a financial phenomenon is the fact that she began life as the daughter of former slaves. Madam Walker was born Sarah Breedlove as the United States began the long healing process following the Civil War in 1867. Orphaned at age seven and married by age 14 she worked the cotton fields of the Mississippi Delta until her husband died two years later.

During the 1890s, Sarah began to suffer from a scalp ailment that caused her to lose most of her hair. She experimented with many homemade remedies and store-bought products. In 1905 after changing her name to "Madam" C. J. Walker, she founded her own business and began selling Madam Walker's Wonderful Hair Grower, a scalp conditioning and healing formula, which she claimed had been revealed to her in a dream.

Madam Walker promoted her products by traveling for nearly a year and a half throughout the southern states selling her products door to door. She would stop anywhere there was an audience, frequenting churches and lodges and other places that would allow her to demonstrate her scalp treatments.

Eventually she would establish a factory in Indianapolis, open schools, travel through out the Caribbean and donate huge sums to the various causes that moved her. By the time she died at her estate, Villa Lewaro, in Irvington-on-Hudson, New York, she had helped create the role of the 20th Century, self-made American businesswoman; established herself as a pioneer of the modern black hair-care and cosmetics industry; and set standards in the African-American community for corporate and community giving.

Personal responsibility, tenacity and perseverance, faith in herself and in God, quality products and "honest business dealings" were all elements of her success. But whenever she was asked how she was able to overcome what appeared to be insurmountable odds to get her business going, she would say, "I got my start by giving myself a start and taking 100% responsibility for my actions."

Get What You Want

Successful people don't make the same mistakes over and over again. The people that get what they want in life - be it getting into top physical shape, starting a business, making more money, increasing the quality of their relationships, traveling the world - basically live a satisfied life filled with peace, success and happiness. These people set goals and attain them by taking 100% responsibility for the outcomes of their lives. They see themselves **at cause** rather than **at effect**. They examine how their thoughts and actions produce their current results. And they adjust accordingly, so they can get back to moving towards the outcome they want.

A wise person once shared that for any result in life there is a certain way of thinking and acting that will produce the outcome you want. All you have to do is find out what it is, and be flexible enough to adopt it.

End the Blame Game

Have you ever blamed people or events for your present circumstance? Have you ever made a comment like one of these?

- *"I am overweight because my wife cooks these fatty meals or people always bring donuts to work."*
- *"I am in a terrible financial situation because my husband spends all the money."*
- *"The traffic made me late for work."*
- *"I am not getting a promotion at work, because no one sees my true potential."*
- *"I cannot do the things I want to do because my children take all my time."*
- *"My wife would never let me live my dream!"*

Perhaps you are someone that shames and blames yourself.

Consider if you ever heard yourself say:

- *"I can't because I am not smart enough!"*
- *"I don't have enough money to get started."*
- *"They won't take me seriously because I am a woman, a man, I am too thin, too heavy, too dark, too light, too young, too old."*

Consider that if you want to live your best life, you must stop shaming, blaming and complaining. It does not work! It is time to do something different.

Make a Genuine Effort

Consider that by taking responsibility and adjusting the way you think and act, you will transform and start to get what you want!

MASTER'S TIP Successful people take 100% responsibility for the outcomes of their lives. They recognize that every outcome is a direct result of how they think, act and respond to life's events.

PONDER: How do I currently take responsibility for my life? How do I currently not take responsibility for my life?

Have you heard the definition of insanity?

Insanity is continuing the same behavior over and over again and expecting different results.

Lots of people set goals:

- ***"This year I am going to lose 10 lbs."***
- ***"When I start this new job I am going to pay off all my bills."***
- ***"I am going to improve my marriage."***
- ***"I am going to build a better relationship with my son."***

Then they might make a tiny effort toward getting what they want. But when they discover reaching their goal is not as easy as they thought it would be, they go back to doing whatever they've always done. They set a goal, expect a different result, but do not make the necessary shifts in their thoughts and actions to achieve their goals.

Unsuccessful people persistently complain about their lives by blaming and shaming themselves and others. They seem to think it is easier to blame and complain, and remain in pain, than to look into **how** they create what is currently happening in their lives.

On the other hand, successful, happy, and peaceful people create their lives by taking responsibility. They think and act differently than complainers. They look for ways to turn problems into challenges and challenges into opportunities. If you want your life to be different in some way, if you really want to achieve your goals, you have to think and act differently than you've done before. As we said earlier, if it doesn't work for you, don't do it again - **Do Something Different!**

Take an Accounting

Where are you currently not as satisfied as you might like?

Consider that hidden in this area is a persistent complaint, reaction, or a way you are blaming or shaming yourself or others in this area.

Consider that this is a huge opportunity to choose new thoughts and behaviors that will start to get you what you want.

- Are you overweight?
  Just suppose this is an opportunity to think and act like a healthy person to get to the weight you want.
- Are your finances are in bad shape?
  Just suppose this is an opportunity to think and act like a wealthy, abundant person and to have the financial situation you want.
- Are you wanting to meet a special someone?
  Just suppose this is an opportunity to think and act like an attractive, friendly person that is a magnet for that special someone.

Being Responsible and Accountable

INTEGRATION CHECKLIST

Things you will need

Your journal

A quiet space to think and write

Integration-Related Activity

It's time to break out your homework to set the foundation for living your best life. You get what you want by doing what works.

1. Consider all the areas of your life in which you have less than fully satisfied **right now.**
2. Rate each of the following areas on a scale from 0 to 10:

   0 = no satisfaction and 10 = complete satisfaction.
3. Please add any areas that are important to you to the list

.

SATISFACTION RATING	AREA OF LIFE
	Physical Environment
	Health & Fitness
	Work & Career
	Financial Situation
	Life Management Skills
	Personal Growth & Development
	Friends
	Family
	Fun and Recreation
	Relationships & Romance
	Communication Skills
	Personal Character
	Emotional Well Being
	General Quality of Life
	Spiritual

Select your top three areas of dissatisfaction right now. Organize them in order of priority.

Most dissatisfying: ______________________________

Second most dissatisfying: ______________________________

Third most dissatisfying: ______________________________

Remove Dissatisfaction

In the following exercise you select one area of dissatisfaction to complete the process. To improve your life, we recommend that you complete this process for each of the three areas you just listed. If you get important information from this process, use it on other areas in which you feel dissatisfaction.

1. Select the area of dissatisfaction you want to remove: _______________

2. Write down all the persistent complaints you have in this area.

3. Reconsider your list from Step 2.

   Be certain you are satisfied that your list addresses **all** your persistent complaints in this area of your life.

   Is there any possible complaint you left off the list?
   If so, add it to your list now.

4. For each complaint in Step 2, first list the complaint and then answer each of the following questions as thoughtfully and thoroughly as possible.

   Complaint: ______________________________

   - ☐ What are all the pay-offs or benefits I get for keeping it like this?

   - ☐ What costs do I pay for keeping it like this?

   - ☐ How does my current thinking create my dissatisfaction?

   - ☐ How do my current actions maintain my dissatisfaction?

   - ☐ What am I pretending not to know?

   - ☐ What do I really want?

- ❒ What is important about getting what I want?

- ❒ Look at what you wrote for your previous answer.
  What is important about that?

- ❒ Once again, look at what you wrote about importance.
  Ultimately, what is important about that?

- ❒ How do I need to think to get what I want?

- ❒ What beliefs do I need to have to get what I want?

- ❒ What actions will get me what I want?

- ☐ What one action can I take to begin to improve my satisfaction in this area?

- ☐ When will I take this action?

- ☐ On a scale from 0 (low) to 10 (high), how committed am I to taking this action?

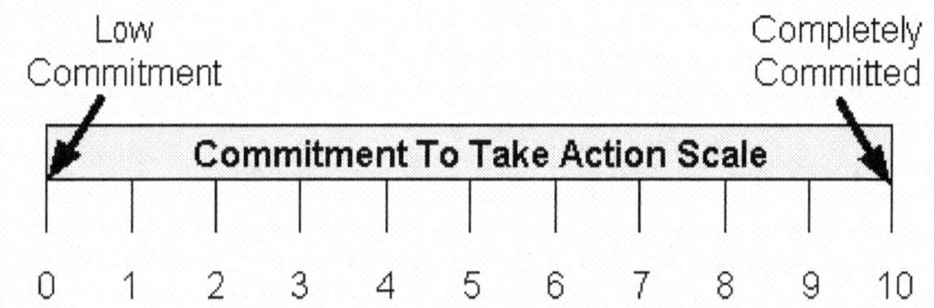

- ☐ If you are lower than a 10, just suppose you were to move your commitment up one number; what might you do differently?

After you complete Step 4 for each complaint you wrote down in Step 2, compile the list of actions you can take to improve your satisfaction in this area of your life:

Action	When I Will Take It

Be Responsible and Accountable NOW

Knowing that as you continue to take action your level of dissatisfaction decreases, what would it take for you to take at least one action now to declare your commitment to eliminating your dissatisfaction and claiming the life you love?

Imagine yourself successfully taking action. Notice how you look. Notice how you feel.

Make a commitment to take at least one action **today**! Your life is worth it. You are worth it!

Day 2 **Become an Enlightened Leader**

There are four stages to achieving any goal:

1. Development
2. Intensity
3. Forward Motion
4. Enlightened Internal Leadership

A Story

A Brief Tale

The Holy Now

-Annie Dillard, For the Time Being

There were no formerly heroic times, and there was no formerly pure generation.

There is no one here but us chickens, and so it has always been: a people busy and powerful, knowledgeable, ambivalent, important, fearful and self-aware; a people who scheme, promote, deceive and conquer; who pray for their loved ones, and long to flee misery and skip death.

It is a weakening and discoloring idea that rustic people knew God personally once upon a time -- or even knew selflessness or courage or literature -- but that it is too late for us. In fact, the absolute is available to everyone in every age.

There never was a more holy age than ours, and never a less. There is no less holiness at this time -- as you are reading this -- than there was the day the Red Sea parted, or that day in the thirtieth year, in the fourth month, on the fifth day of the month, as Ezekiel was a captive by the river Chebar, when the heavens opened and he saw visions of God.

There is no whit less enlightenment under the tree by your street than there was under the Buddha's bo tree. There is no whit less might in heaven or on earth than there was the day Jesus said "Maid, arise" to the centurion's daughter, or the day Peter walked on water, or the night Mohammed flew to heaven on a horse.

> In any instant the sacred may wipe you with its finger. In any instant the bush may flare, your feet may rise, or you may see a bunch of souls in a tree. In any instant you may avail yourself of the power to love your enemies; to accept failure, slander, or the grief of loss; or to endure torture. Purity's time is always now.
>
> Purity is no social phenomenon, a cultural thing whose time we have missed, whose generations are dead, so we can only buy Shaker furniture. "Each and every day the Divine Voice issues from Sinai," says the Talmud. Of eternal fulfillment, Tillich said, "If it is not seen in the present, it cannot be seen at all."

Today's conversation is about being present in the moment now, and allowing yourself to be an Enlightened Internal Leader.

Have you ever started down a path to get what you really want - vowed to start eating healthy, stop smoking, exercise daily, or to take on a new challenge like building a house, writing a book, starting a new business or getting married?

And while on your path, have you ever said, ***"WHOA! This is a lot harder than I thought it would be!"*** Or did you ever question if you could do it, or fall down with exhaustion or frustration and say, ***"I can't do it! This is just too hard."***?

To achieve any goal there are four different stages you must go through. In each stage you learn and achieve. And if you keep going, eventually you will get what you want and reach the realm of what some people call mastery and what we call **Enlightened Internal Leadership**.

When you understand what to expect and have a feel for each stage, you are more likely to keep going when it feels really tough. Consider that anything worth doing is worth doing badly in the beginning. And if you keep going, it will get easier.

Development

The first stage is **Development.** You create and develop a vision of what you want, get inspired about it, and say, ***"YES, I will do this!"*** In this stage, you *may be* unconsciously incompetent for what is to come - not fully aware of how challenging it might be to take action on your goal. For example, if you set a goal to exercise at the gym daily, you may not realize that you don't know how to use the exercise equipment or how challenging it is to get back in shape. Or if you have a goal to improve your financial situation, you may not realize that you don't know how to invest your money effectively.

During the Development stage, consider being prepared for some surprises and challenges. And remember, if it can be done in the world, it can be done by you - you just need to figure out **how.** When you begin to realize it is hard to start making changes or take on big goals, you have entered the second stage.

Intensity

In the **Intensity** stage you are aware consciously of how incompetent you are or how difficult reaching your goal may be. For most of us, this stage is challenging - really challenging. In fact, this is the stage where a lot of people quit. They may think, ***"This is too hard. I'll never be able to do it".*** However, if you continue, there is fast learning and growth at this stage. Think about it - the less a person knows about something, the greater the room for improvement and the faster progress can occur.

Forward Motion

After the intensity stage you enter the third stage: **Forward Motion.** You know you have forward motion when you start thinking ***"Yeah, this is getting easier!"*** Your thoughts, skills, and actions support achieving your outcome. However, they are not yet consistent or habitual. You are consciously competent in this stage, but you still need to concentrate to make progress towards your goal.

Enlightened Internal Leadership

The fourth stage is **Enlightened Internal Leadership!** When you reach Enlightened Internal Leadership, your thoughts, skills, and actions associated with your goal are habitual or automatic. Maintaining the habit or finishing the project feels natural and easy. In this stage you are unconsciously competent - able to flow with the project or have the habit as a new part of being - a part of who you now are.

Master's Tip No matter who you are, you will likely experience resistance. Expect to experience resistance!

In the first few stages, especially the second stage, **Intensity**, resistance shows up. And if you get what you want, you must move through all the stages of learning and achievement.

Resistance

What's resistance? Resistance is defined as a force that tends to oppose or retard motion, a process in which the ego opposes the conscious recall of anxiety-producing experiences.

For example, resistance is the feeling you have when it seems tough to achieve or even work toward your goal, and you just want to quit. You encounter resistance when you want to cheat on the diet, skip the workout, go shopping or just stop doing whatever it is that seems so hard.

We resist when we leave our comfort zone because we unconsciously and habitually relate the old way of doing things with security. Resistance comes up because it seems to be easier to keep doing things the old way.

Have you ever heard that little voice in your head that says, ***"This is too hard. Just go back to doing things the way you used to. That would be way more comfortable!"*** That little voice is resistance.

When you feel resistance, be aware of it and what it is trying to accomplish for you; and then keep moving towards your goal. Leaving old habits and achieving goals take commitment. Consider that if it is the **right** goal for you – something you really want instead of something you think you **should** want – overcoming the resistance to achieve it is worth it! See resistance as an old friend that is just trying to keep you safe and secure, but is not very fun to hang out with anymore. Keep going in spite of it!

Your friend, **Enlightened Internal Leadership**, is waiting to connect with you on a deep level. And, so you know, this part is already a true friend, just waiting for you to reconnect.

Become the Enlightened Leader of your Life

Integration Checklist

Things you will need

Your journal

A quiet space to think and write

Integration-Related Activity

In Day 1 you looked at the level of satisfaction in your life. Now it is time to take a step towards living a life you love.

Create a Goal

1. Pick a goal that you plan to work on in this program.
2. Pretend for a minute that you are at the end of this journey, the journey of achieving your goal. Envision that you have gone through the four stages to get exactly what you want in this area. For example, maybe you are 10 lbs. lighter, you have stopped smoking, you've started your own business and it is running smoothly, you have more energy and feel much healthier, you have paid off all your bills and are now ready to invest your money for a secure future - whatever it is for you, you have accomplished it.
3. Now that you can see yourself as having already achieved your goal:

   Ask yourself: What do I look like?

   Ask yourself: What am I saying to myself?

Ask yourself: What are my friends/family members saying about me?

Ask yourself: How do I feel?

4. Looking back from this future, having already achieved your goal:
   - What did you experience in the **Development** stage?

     In this stage you had an idea and decided to take a stand and to go for what you wanted. When you **decided** powerfully to go for it:

Ask yourself: What did I say to myself? "I am…."

Ask yourself: How did I feel in this stage?

Ask yourself: What actions was I taking to support myself?

Ask yourself: What helped me move to the next stage?

- ☐ What did you experience in the **Intensity** stage?

  In this stage you persevered through the challenging parts and managed yourself extraordinarily well, in spite of the temptation to return to your old way of thinking and acting. You handled the inner and outer stress powerfully even when you did not know what you were doing.

Ask yourself: What did I say to myself? "I am…."

Ask yourself: How did I feel in this stage?

Ask yourself: What actions was I taking to support myself?

Ask yourself: What helped me move to the next stage?

- ☐ What did you experience in the **Forward Motion** stage?

  In the forward motion stage things started to get easier as you began to get wind in your sails. You said to yourself, ***"I can act with consistency. I can be accountable."*** In this stage you realized that you could trust yourself to follow through powerfully to get what you wanted.

ASK YOURSELF: What did I say to myself? "I am...."

ASK YOURSELF: How did I feel in this stage?

ASK YOURSELF: What actions was I taking to support myself?

ASK YOURSELF: What helped me move to the next stage?

- ☐ What did you experience in the **Enlightened Internal Leadership** stage where you knew that the leader within was guiding you to be, do, and have what you want?

  In this phase you naturally and easily integrated the skills and habits into automatic thinking and behaving. Rather than the mind focusing on the next best action to take, your Enlightened Internal Leader is calling forth your greatness so every choice aligns with the truth of who you really are.

  This is a place where you naturally accessed the source of the internal flame and ignited the fire within that illuminated the path that has sustained your accomplishment.

Ask yourself: What did I say to myself? "I am...."

Ask yourself: How did I feel in this stage?

Ask yourself: What actions was I taking to support myself?

Ask yourself: What has helped me remain in this stage?

Be an Enlightened Leader for Yourself NOW

Knowing that as you continue through the stages you eventually reach Enlightened Internal Leadership, what would it take for you to be an Enlightened Leader for yourself **now**?

What would it take to declare your commitment to Enlightened Internal Leadership and claim it now?

See yourself filled with wisdom, capability, and an enlightened frame of mind. See the bright light within lighting the path of your inspiring future!

Day 3 **Overcome Resistance**

Often getting what you want means learning to accept that life sends us gifts and challenges in ways we may not recognize as beneficial. This session describes overcoming resistance, forgiving yourself, learning to go with the flow, getting back up when you fall, and recognizing the whole truth of who you are.

The Comfort Zone
Author Unknown Author

I used to have a comfort zone where I know I couldn't fail.
The same four walls of busy work, were really like a jail.
I longed so much to do the things I'd never done before.
But I stayed inside my comfort zone and paced the same old floor.
I claimed to be so busy with the things inside my zone,
But deep inside I longed for something special of my own.
I couldn't let my life go by just watching others win.
I held my breath and stepped outside to let the change begin.
I took a step and with new strength I'd never felt before,
I kissed my comfort zone goodbye and closed and locked the door.
If you are in a comfort zone afraid to venture out
Remember that all winners were at one time filled with doubt.
A step or two and words of praise can make your dreams come true.
Greet your future with a smile
Success is there for you!

Master's Tip "Success is the ability to go from one failure to another without any loss of enthusiasm." Winston Churchill.

If during this journey you momentarily fall back into your old way of doing things, or feel drawn toward your old way of being, before feeling frustrated, angry, or depressed, forgive yourself. Yes, forgive yourself! There's nothing you can do about a past thought or behavior, so let it go, get back on purpose, and take action toward what you want!

Conscious Incompetence

The **Intensity** stage is the phase of conscious incompetence. And conscious incompetence means exactly what you think it means - you are consciously aware of your own emotional, intellectual, directional, relational or spiritual ineffectiveness in some area. You wake up to the fact that there is a lot about the area that you don't know and that you want to know! And that's a challenge for anyone.

Your first step is to recognize that where you are at any moment in your journey is the perfect place to be. And the thoughts and feelings you are having are natural.

Nobody enjoys feeling incompetent or having to truly concentrate to make the internal shifts required to change. It may sound cliché, but:

Master's Tip "Change is hard - it takes commitment".

Life Happens

You learned in Day 2 that if you continue to take action towards what you want, it does get easier - **guaranteed**! At times we all want to take our ball and go home...

- ...when the game gets tough.
- ...when we're really tired.
- ...when someone says something about us that we don't like.
- ...when an emergency takes us away from the game.

In each case, there is a key to success:

- Handle the issue.
- Take a break.
- Ignore or learn from the ignorant statement.
- Attend to the emergency.

And **always** come back to the field and continue the game where you left off.

Life happens! That's the "Rated G" version of a tired cliché; but clichés exist because there is truth in them. Life does happen. Deal with it and get back in the game.

Remember the three central rules to living a fulfilling life that you read about in Day 1:

- If something works, don't fix it.
- Once you know what works, do more of it.
- If it doesn't work, don't do it again - **Do Something Different!**

CONSIDER: Where are you currently not as fulfilled as you might like to be?

Perhaps an even more important question is this:

PONDER: What do I get out of not thriving in this area?
Who do I get to be?
What do I get to do?
What do I have at the end of the day?

CONSIDER: How painful will your life be if you continue to do what doesn't work?

Think about it.

- Do you really want to pack around those extra pounds for the rest of your life?
- Do you really want to struggle financially for the rest of your life?
- Do you really want to be without companionship until you die?

PONDER: What would my life be like if I were to live my entire life without achieving my goal?

PONDER: How bad will my life be if I don't get back on the field of play now to begin the journey - doing what works to get what I really want?

PONDER: Am I really prepared to go through my whole life without ever achieving this goal?

Sometimes, as we take the risk to go for what we really want in life, all we need to move past resistance is to know that we are okay - safe and secure.

Now ask yourself the most important question of all.

PONDER: What do I really want?

Appreciate Yourself

Consider appreciating yourself for what is working, for what you have done well. As soon as you have taken some action toward your goal, any action, one of the best ways of honoring yourself is to appreciate yourself for making the effort and taking that step, that action - even if you have yet to achieve the ultimate results you want.

Appreciate yourself for playing a big game, and then remind yourself of how painful life might be if you don't achieve your goal. And think of how great your life will be once you've worked through the resistance!

If you feel like you want to quit or you make a choice or two that momentarily takes you off track, don't fall into the "blame and shame" game. That approach doesn't work.

Did you ever know a high school athletic coach or teacher who tried to shame you or someone else into action? Perhaps that coach mistook your passion for anger or your lack of preparedness on a certain day for apathy. Did it work?

Shame - the UN-motivator

In case you have any doubt that shame is **the un**-motivator, let's test the theory. Let's see if shaming and blaming yourself works to motivate you.

Say to yourself, "Come on... stop being so lazy."

Go ahead, say it out loud. People often talk to themselves in the car or at their computer. And, if someone can hear you, they may think it's the voice in their own head saying that same thing. So try it.

Say to yourself, "Come on... stop being so lazy."

Now say it like you mean it!

Now try these phrases to motivate yourself:

- **Be tough!**
- **Stop cheating yourself!**
- **Don't be a loser!**
- **Try harder!**
- **Stop being such a baby!**

How does that feel? Seriously, what happens when you say these things to yourself? Do you feel more motivated?

Now try saying these phrases and take on a defeatist tone.

- **See, I knew I couldn't do it!**
- **I'll never make it!**
- **This is too hard. I can't do this!**
- **Everyone else has more power than me!**
- **I am not smart enough, pretty enough, or strong enough!**
- **I am not as good at this as others!**
- **Oh, it doesn't matter anyway.**
- **Who cares if I keep doing the same old thing?**
- **No one is really harmed by my smoking, drinking, overeating - It hasn't killed me yet!**

When you say these things to yourself, do you feel better about yourself? If any of these phrases are part of your self-talk, remember that your self-talk is often an attempt to stop you from getting hurt just in case you don't achieve your goal.

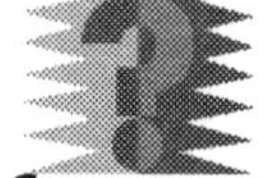

CONSIDER: How does this talk affect you?

- Does it really keep you safe and secure?
- Does it move you toward an inspiring future, or does it keep you stuck in the past?
- Does it empower you or disempower you?
- Does it add to your life energy or take away from it?
- Is it an act of self-love or self-sabotage?

Become a Curious Scientist About Your Life

There is a strategy that you can use to help you through negative self-talk and to help you overcome resistance.

Imagine that you are a **curious scientist**, witnessing your life. Notice that I didn't say a **mad** scientist, because being a **curious** scientist is not about being crazy or angry but rather about observing yourself.

When you start to feel bad, put on your curious scientist hat and just observe yourself by noticing what causes you to feel bad. Pay attention to the inner thoughts you have that cause you to yell at yourself or someone else, or get depressed.

As a curious scientist, observe your life without judgment. Don't advise yourself or call yourself names. Simply gain knowledge about how you think and act.

PONDER: What did I do inside of myself that took me off track?

And then continue to take action toward your goal.

Here's an example of how your self-talk might sound when you're in the curious scientist mode. In fact, you might even try saying these out loud:

- **Hmmm, isn't it interesting that I behaved like that?**
- **How did I do that?**
- **What did I do inside of myself that created this feeling or action?**

Even if you are not exactly sure how you did what you did, *own* that you did it and continue to be curious without judging yourself. Keep asking yourself the questions:

PONDER: What was I thinking that caused me to do that?

PONDER: How might I adjust my thinking to get what I want?

Begin your Journey

Now that you know how to take curious scientist posture with your life, would you like to know the most powerful way to overcome resistance? The answer is simple:

MASTER'S TIP Start the journey toward Enlightened Internal Leadership with Enlightened Internal Leadership.

This answer may sound crazy; but suppose you began your journey with a mindset of integrated wisdom, recognizing that the part of you that is resisting is just trying to keep you safe and secure.

When you begin your journey by thanking that resisting part of you for playing it's role and letting it know that you're okay, then you can stay on track toward your goal. And you discover that all of your goals are much easier to achieve.

The time to be an Enlightened Internal Leader is now - at the beginning and throughout the journey - not at the end! Be an Enlightened Internal Leader now!

Resistance Tips

So let's look at what techniques you learned to help you overcome resistance and go with the flow.

- You learned the value of forgiving yourself.
- You experienced that taking a negative tone with yourself doesn't help you on your journey to Enlightened Internal Leadership.
- You learned to think like a curious scientist as you master negative inner dialogue.
- You began to imagine what it is like to begin your journey as an Enlightened Internal Leader.

You've probably heard the old joke:

Question: "How do you get to Symphony Hall?"

Answer: "Practice, Practice, Practice!"

Believe it or not, some people read each day and only think about practicing or doing their homework. They never set pen to paper or put the knowledge into action, and then they complain that the program doesn't work!

To achieve your goals, you must do the work!

So find a quiet place and complete the integration exercise. You'll be glad you did!

Overcoming Resistance

INTEGRATION CHECKLIST

Things you will need

Your journal

Approximately 4 feet of floor space OR a clean area of a table or desktop on which you can lay out four pieces of 4.25"x5.25" paper.

Integration-Related Activity

The goal of this activity is for you to thoroughly understand each stage of learning and integration to clarify what you can expect in each stage. With this knowledge, you can create a masterful plan on how to achieve your goal - no matter what stage you are in.

Integration Space Exercise

The following exercise is an integrating thinking space exercise that is a variation of an exercise originally developed by Dr. Marilyn Atkinson of Erickson College International, www.erickson.edu.

NOTE. If you do not have the floor space available, sit at a table or desk and use the tabletop or desk space in front of you. If you remain sitting, just follow the instructions and in your mind, pretend to take a step while moving your hand to each of the papers.

1. Cut a piece of paper into 4 equal sections.
2. Label the four paper sections with the four key developmental stages of learning and integration.

1 Development	3 Forward Motion
2 Intensity	4 Enlightened Internal Leadership

3. Place the papers on the floor to create a line with each of the papers approximately one foot apart in the order of the cycle, as shown:

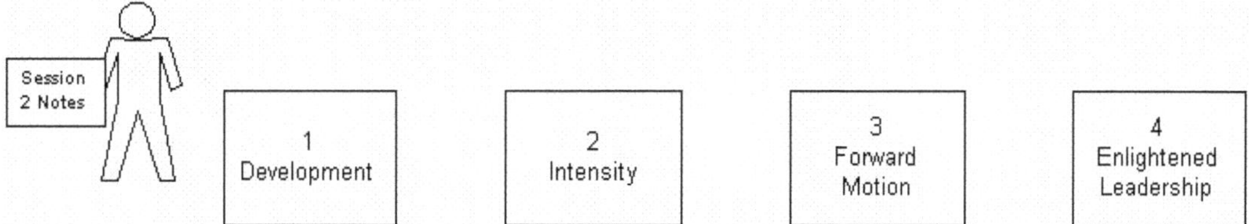

4. Stand up and take your answers from Lesson 2 with you. Stand at the end of the line, the place closest to **Development** and turn your back to the papers.
5. Take a deep breath and relax, knowing that this journey will be fun and enlightening.
6. Take one step backwards, stepping into Stage 1 - **Development**.

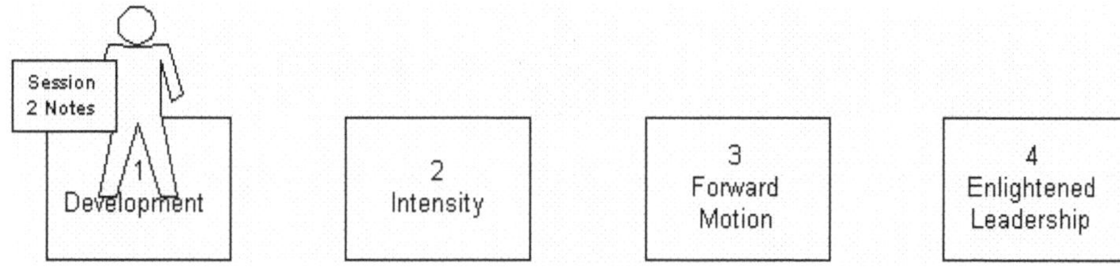

In this phase you evaluated powerfully and then decided to go for your goal. This may be the stage you are in right now.

A. From your Session 2 worksheets, read aloud what you wrote about this stage.

B. Close your eyes and **feel** this stage.

- Notice what you can realistically expect here.
- Sense how your body feels and notice all the things that are going on internally and externally.
- Notice your level of motivation, excitement, and clarity as you anticipate the next step.

7. Take one step backwards, stepping into Stage 2- **Intensity.**

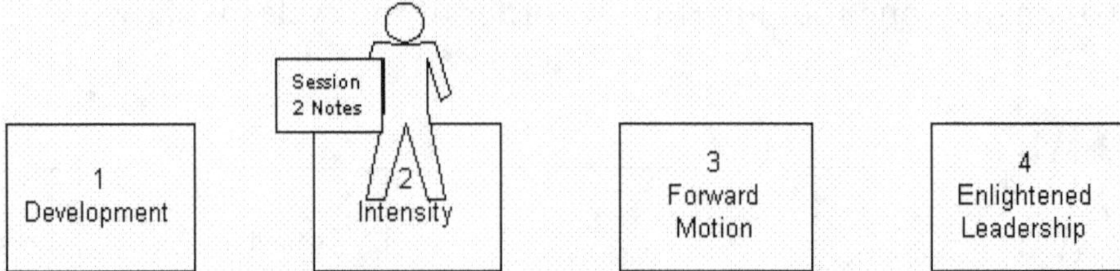

This is the phase in which you are likely to experience resistance.

In this phase you maintain steadiness and focus through the taxing parts and operate extremely well under stress or inner struggle, even when you may not know what to do.

A. From your Session 2 worksheets, read aloud what you wrote about this stage.

B. Close your eyes and **feel** this stage.

- Notice what you can realistically expect here.
- Sense how your body feels and notice all the things that are going on internally and externally.
- Notice your level of motivation, excitement, and clarity as you anticipate the next step.

8. Take one step backwards, stepping into Stage 3 - **Forward Motion**.

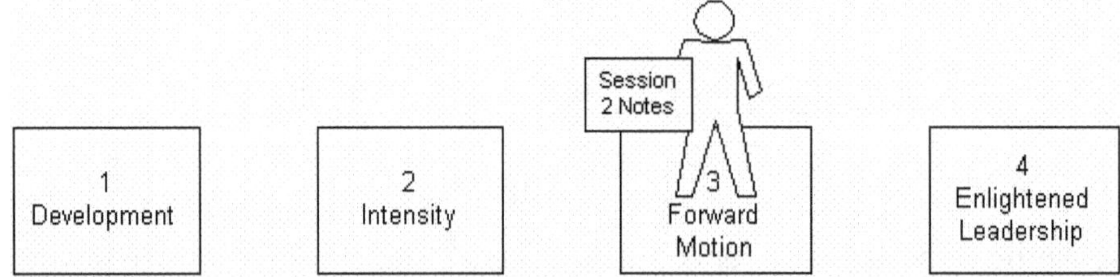

In this phase things get easier, and you demonstrate that you can trust yourself and create routines and competence in this area. You could naturally be integrous with your world and be held responsible to follow through.

A. From your Session 2 worksheets, read aloud what you wrote about this stage.

B. Close your eyes and **feel** this stage.

- Notice what you can realistically expect here.
- Sense how your body feels and notice all the things that are going on internally and externally.
- Notice your level of motivation, excitement, and clarity as you anticipate the next step.

9. Take one step backwards, stepping into Stage 4 - **Enlightened Internal Leadership**.

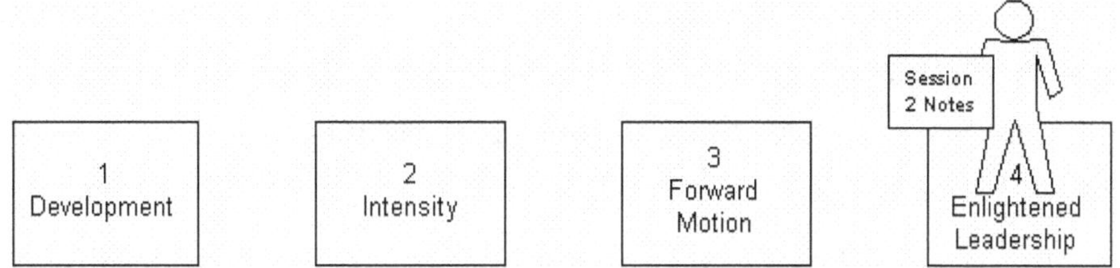

In this phase you demonstrate reliability and focus naturally and easily. Rather than emphasizing doing, you are relaxed and focused more on who you are being. This is a place of integrated wisdom, flow and Enlightened Internal Leadership. You sense, visualize, and identify with the quality of Enlightened Internal Leadership.

A. From your Session 2 worksheets, read aloud what you wrote about this stage.

B. Close your eyes and **feel** this stage.

- Notice what you can realistically expect here.
- Sense how your body feels and notice all the things that are going on internally and externally.
- Notice your level of motivation, excitement, and clarity.

10. Turn around, and looking from the eyes of **Enlightened Internal Leadership** in each step, gradually step back through the phases to development.
    - How does already having and starting with Enlightened Internal Leadership impact or transform the Forward Motion stage for you?
    - How does already having and being able to start with Enlightened Internal Leadership impact or transform the Intensity stage for you?
    - How does already having and being able to start with Enlightened Internal Leadership impact or transform the Development stage for you?
11. Ask the older, wiser, enlightened leader you, who has already achieved **Enlightened Internal Leadership**, to inspire the younger you of today. Invite today's you to act with **Enlightened Internal Leadership** - every step of the way!

When you start with the mindset of **Enlightened Internal Leadership** now, you can overcome any resistance.

Ask yourself: How might I integrate the mindset of Enlightened Internal Leadership through time?

Take a moment now to write down your experience in your journal.

Overcoming Resistance Always

Imagine if you honored whatever came into your life as being "okay". Imagine embracing even those events that seem far less than ideal - perhaps even embracing what you might label as "bad things" happening to you.

Make a commitment to dance with resistance by going with the flow, and accepting that even the darkest cloud has a silver lining - if we look hard enough!

Knowing that releasing and accepting what is happening would make your life less stressful, what would you be willing to do now? Would less stress and more satisfaction in life be worth stepping back and seeing the glass as half full when you feel like it is half empty?

What action might you take to remind yourself to dance with resistance, to go with the flow of life, to be okay, and see what you can learn so the future is filled with a life you love?

Day 4 **Complete the Cycle**

This session is about the cycle of completion. To complete any life project, you go through several stages.

A Story

A Brief Tale

Bits & Pieces - March 1997

Economics Press

Novelist Sinclair Lewis was supposed to deliver an hour-long lecture to a group of college students who planned to be writers. Lewis opened his talk with a question:

"How many of you really intend to be writers?"

All hands went up.

"In that case," said Lewis, "my advice to you is to go home and write."

With that, he left.

The cycle of completion starts when you become dissatisfied with your current state and you begin to build a strong foundation for change. By setting an intention and focusing your attention, you begin to move towards mastery, or what we call enlightened internal leadership.

A friend calls this the I AM foundation. Start with intention, add attention, and you have mastery.

I		A		M
n		t		a
t	+	t	=	s
e		e		t
n		n		e
t		t		r
i		i		y
o		o		
n		n		

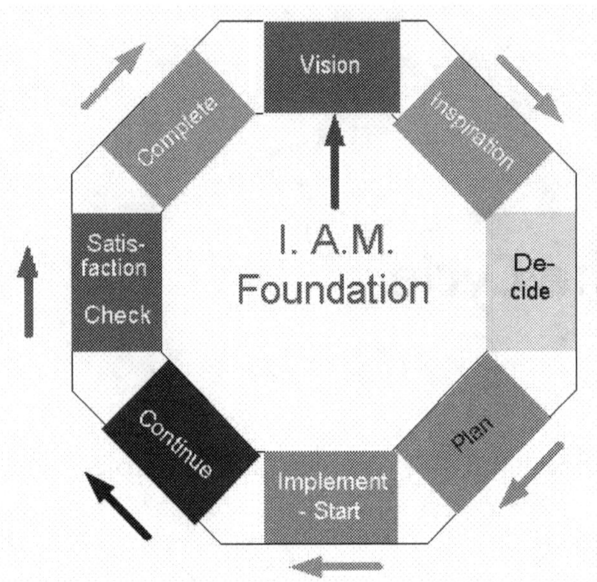

- Vision
- Inspiration
- Decision
- Plan
- Start to Implement
- Continue
- Satisfaction Check

and

- Completion

We'll discuss these stages in just a minute. But first, think about this:

How many people do you know who have decided to do something, told others they were going to do it, and, for whatever reason, did not follow through and do it? Or do you know people who start something and leave it half-done when it gets difficult or uncomfortable? Or how about people who complete a project, but the process was horrible and they complained all the way through? Or how about people who are still working on a project they started 15 years ago and likely will never be done?

Do you recognize any of these patterns in your own life?

All projects, all goals, all habit change processes start somewhere and end somewhere - either incomplete or complete.

If they end as incomplete, then, for some reason, you did not reach your goal. Perhaps the goal was something you thought you "should" do, or something that was not important right now, or something that scared you so you made excuses not to do it. Perhaps you let the rest of your life take over, or you are still working on it and will likely never finish it.

Even completed goals and projects have different outcomes. Perhaps you completed your goal, but not to your satisfaction. Or perhaps you completed and got what you were really going for, ending strong. You reached your goal, finished the project and made the internal habit shift - and enjoyed the journey!

To succeed at something and enjoy the journey, you must go through all the steps of the cycle of completion - Vision, Inspiration, Decision, Planning, Starting, Continuing, and Completing Strong with consistent satisfaction checks along the way.

- **Vision** - What do I want? If I had it already, what would I see, hear, feel?
- **Inspiration** - Why? Who else is impacted? How does it fit?
- **Decision Point** - Yes! I choose this.
- **Plan** - How might I make it happen? What's within my control to do now? What is my contingency plan? How can I make this plan even more powerful?
- **Start to Implement** - What action creates the greatest gain? What am I willing to do right now? What do I need to do first? Second? Third?
- **Continue** - How do I know I am on track? How can I keep going? How can I deepen my commitment? How can I maintain my focus?
- **Satisfaction Check** - How can I make this more satisfying for me? How can I make this journey more meaningful?
- **Completion** - How will I know when I've got it? What are the visions, actions, and feelings that tell me I've finished the ride of a lifetime?

Let's look at these phases of the cycle of completion.

Vision

Your goal starts with a vision beyond your current state! Being dissatisfied with where you are right now, you begin to have a vision of what you really want in the future - not what someone wants for you. You envision something that is linked to your inner truth and linked to an image or an idea of what it would be like to have it.

Inspiration

If this image, idea or vision is "right", it triggers massive **inspiration**:

"WOW! That's great, I really want to be, do or have that - be a parent, be married, go to Italy, run a marathon, learn an instrument, start that business, go back to school to learn a new trade, have that car, remodel my house, and so on."

Decision

When you see it in your mind's eye and the vision is important enough to inspire you, it is natural to make the decision to **Go For It!** You hear a passionate and powerful voice inside of you shouting:

"Yes! I choose this! This inspires my life. I am doing this!"

MASTER'S TIP "Once you make a decision to do something, the Universe moves itself to help you."

When you say yes to something, when you decide on it, then your mind is free to begin to find ways to have it happen.

Plan

After your vision inspires you to create it and you make a decision to do it, you need a plan.

PONDER: How can I make this vision happen? What are the first steps, the small things I can do right now, to get myself in action?

You do not have to wait until everything is perfect before you begin - things are never perfect in the beginning. No one expects someone to be a perfect swimmer the first time they get into the pool. Remember the stage of high intensity and the high probability of feeling consciously incompetent when you start? You can't learn less in life, you can only learn more. It will get easier. You will get better.

Start to Implement

Have you seen the movie Field of Dreams with Kevin Costner? The key concept in the movie is: "If you build it, they will come." - meaning, get into action, begin-to-begin-to-begin and the Universe will get behind you.

The first prerequisite to completing anything is starting! So where do you start? You start with a plan. You create your ideal plan and then look at it and decide if there is a way to make the plan even more meaningful for yourself or for others.

As soon as you have the beginnings of the "most meaningful plan" in place, take immediate action on the thing that will create the greatest gain. For example, your greatest gain may be fast results or the biggest step towards your goal.

PONDER: What small steps am I willing to take right now?

PONDER: What do I need to do first, second, and third to begin to make this vision a reality?

As you are in motion with your plan, consider a plan B, so to speak. Create a contingency plan so you have a fallback position.

MASTER'S TIP *"Always prepare for the worst, but expect the best."*

Sometimes the events don't line up in the way that you hope, and the key is to be flexible and open to other possible ways of getting what you want. Always do your very best, and then surrender. The Universe has a bigger idea for you than you could ever have for yourself.

Continue

Discomfort is often part of the process of putting your plan in action. Consider that it wouldn't be a worthwhile goal if it didn't make you a little uncomfortable. So, if you are not just a little uncomfortable every day, consider that you not stretching yourself enough to reach your potential.

As you continue, it is important to be clear that you are on track toward achieving your goal.

PONDER: How will I know that I am on track?

PONDER: What is my evidence that I'm moving toward what I really want?

Satisfaction Checks

Build in satisfaction checks.

PONDER: On a scale from 0 to 10, how satisfied am I with this journey?

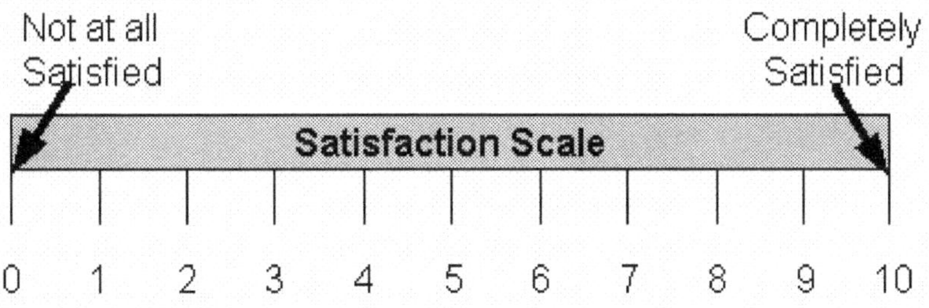

PONDER: How can I make what am I doing even more satisfying?

Completion

Finally, you must finish. The question is:

CONSIDER: ***How will I know I've got what I wanted?"***

One way to know is to answer these questions:

PONDER: What will I see?

PONDER: What will I hear and feel once I've achieved my goal?

Sounds simple, right?

Completing strong and moving on to the next inspiring vision is extremely important, but many people get caught up in not completing anything.

Some people, perhaps unconsciously, equate not finishing with the best way to avoid failure. If you don't complete anything, then no one can judge your work.

Do you have incomplete projects? Perhaps a painting you started, an unwritten screen play, pants that need sewing, a house project that is incomplete, or a new idea you have been wanting to discuss with your supervisor?

To help keep you inspired while you're planning and taking action to achieve your goal, try out the feeling of completion, the feeling of having already achieved your goal!

Ah, the feeling of completion. Imagine it! See yourself finishing strong! Doesn't it feel good?

Completing the Cycle

INTEGRATION CHECKLIST

Things you will need

Your journal

A quiet space to think and write

Integration-Related Activity

In this integration activity, you look at your cycle of completion. This can take quite a bit of time and you may want to come back to this exercise several times to revise it.

IMPORTANT INSTRUCTION **PLEASE SET ASIDE AN UNINTERRUPTED BLOCK OF TIME**

The first time through, go with your first answers. Have you ever taken an exam, answered the question, gone back later and changed it, only to find that your first answer was correct?

As you work through these questions, just let the answer come to you. Go with the flow of your thoughts. You can take another look at it later.

Vision

The first step on the cycle of completion is your vision.

WRITTEN ACTIVITY **IN JUST A FEW WORDS, WRITE IN YOUR JOURNAL THE ANSWERS TO EACH OF THE FOLLOWING QUESTIONS.**

ASK YOURSELF: What is my vision? What is it that I want?

ANSWER: My vision is ...

Ask yourself: If I had already achieved this, if I already had what I wanted, what would I see around myself?

Answer: I would see ...

Ask yourself: What would I feel as I enjoyed having achieved this goal?

Answer: I would feel...

Ask yourself: What would I hear as I enjoyed having achieved this goal?

Answer: I would hear...

These notes form the basis of your vision.
When you visualize, this is a starting point!

Inspiration

Inspiration is **why** we do what we do.

Ask yourself: Why is it that I want this goal? What's the reason I want to do this?

Answer: I want this because ...

Ask yourself: What's important about that?

Answer: It's important because ...

Ask yourself: Who else will benefit from my achieving this goal?

Answer: Others who benefit are ...

Ask yourself: How will they benefit?

Answer: They benefit ...

Ask yourself: How does that affect my life and theirs? How does it fit?

Answer: It affects my life ...

Answer: It affects their life ...

Answer: This all fits together ...

Wow! Now you have some Powerful Reasons for making a Powerful Choice to take action on what you want!

Decision

It's time for a decision. Now is the time to ask yourself if you are ready to commit to making this choice. In the long run, life is just a series of choices.

When you commit, you say ***"Yes - of course!"*** to making a choice - you've decided!

Ask yourself: Am I ready to commit?

Answer: Yes - I'm Ready!

If you're not, go back and take another look at your reasons. If you are ready, write a big, bold ***"Yes - I'm ready!"*** in your journal. Shout **Yes** to the sky! Feel it deep inside you!

Ask yourself: How would I say **Yes** to something I have always wanted?

Feel that **Yes** inside you.

Plan

Part of commitment is taking action as soon as you make the commitment.

Ask yourself: What is one action I can take, today, before I go to sleep tonight? How can I start? What's the first action I need to take to get started?

Answer: My first action is ...

Ask yourself: What other changes are in my control to make in my life immediately? What else can I do to get started?

Answer: Other actions I can take are ...

In the planning process, you start your plan by deciding what you can do immediately. And since humans never do anything without a reason, part of a successful plan is to look at how this goal is meaningful to you, to look at your reasons for **wanting** this goal, and see the meaningfulness in taking action to get started right now.

Consider the long-term gain as you decide which action creates the greatest gain for yourself and others.

Suppose you decide the best thing you can do is to go "gun ho" with your exercise program, and you exercise so much you injure yourself and then can't exercise again for a week. Was that really the action with the greatest gain?

Ask yourself: Which action can I take that will create the greatest gain?

Answer: The action that creates the greatest gain is ...

Ask yourself: What action will I need to do second?

We're just talking about broad categories of action here. No need at this point to get down to the nitty-gritty of exactly which action you'll take. Think of the broad categories. What might be the second step of your plan?

Answer: The second step of my plan is ...

Ask yourself: What is the third step?

Answer: The third step of my plan is ...

You may need to break your plan down into more steps. If so, just go ahead and do so.

Answer: Other steps for my plan include ...

Stay on Track

Part of accomplishing any goal is to make sure that you stay on track. Otherwise, we get distracted by the latest and greatest new thing to come along.

Ask yourself: What is my plan for keeping myself on track?

Answer: To stay on track, I plan to ...

When the going gets tough - and almost all of us have a point where it does - what will you do to keep yourself motivated and on track?

Ask yourself: How will I inspire myself to keep going?

Answer: I plan to stay inspired by ...

Now is a good time to consider if there is a way to deepen your commitment. For example, if the reason you are getting into shape is so you can provide a better life for your children, for some people, this might mean something as simple as a picture of your children placed inside your gym bag. Others may need something else to deepen their commitment, such as a planned activity in which the children can participate.

Ask yourself: Is there a way to deepen my commitment, to remind myself every day of why I am doing what I'm doing?

Answer: I can deepen my commitment by ...

Be Satisfied

We won't continue to work on a plan that is not satisfying our needs. Satisfaction checks are an important part of developing a solid plan.

Ask yourself: What would create satisfaction for me?

Answer: I know I am satisfied if ...

Ask yourself: Is there a way to make my accomplishment something even more satisfying?

Answer: I would be thrilled if ...

Measure your Success

Finally, a great plan has methods to measure if you carried out the plan. So another part of the plan is to consider how you know that you've completed your goal.

If you're getting into shape, is your measurement of completion when you weigh a certain weight, can play a certain sport, or is it something more nebulous, like being able to play soccer with your kids?

Ask yourself: How, exactly, will I know when I complete this goal?

Answer: I'll measure my success by ...

Ask yourself: What will I see when I achieved this goal?

Answer: I'll see ...

Ask yourself: What will I hear when I achieve this goal?

Answer: I'll hear ...

Ask yourself: How will I feel when I achieve this goal?

Answer: I'll feel ...

You've now completed your integration work for today. We go into more details on planning later. Be sure to come back and add to your answers anytime you feel the need. Plans, goals and dreams are not set in stone. They change as we progress.

Complete the Cycle NOW

Through each of the steps, see yourself filled with grace, skill, capability, and an enlightened leader state of mind. See the bright light from within!

Knowing, as you continue through the process, that you will eventually reach your goal, what would it take for you to powerfully declare your commitment to reach your goal by following through to completing strong?

Day 5 Make Space for the New

You've heard the phrase, "Out with the old, in with the New!"
Is there anything weighing you down that you need to complete?
This session is about making space for new habits, new ideas, and new goals.

Master's Tip Make space by making a choice:

- **Do it!**
- **Defer it!**
- **Delegate it!**
- **Delete it!**

A Story

A Brief Tale

Obstacles? Deal With Them Now

The Sower's Seeds **by Brian Cavanaugh, T.O.R.**

An old farmer had plowed around a large rock in one of his fields for years. He had broken several plowshares and a cultivator on it and had grown rather morbid about the rock.

After breaking another plowshare one day, and remembering all the trouble the rock had caused him through the years, he finally decided to do something about it.

When he put the crowbar under the rock, he was surprised to discover that it was only about six inches thick and that he could break it up easily with a sledgehammer. As he was carting the pieces away he had to smile, remembering all the trouble that the rock had caused him over the years and how easy it would have been to get rid of it sooner.

Take a look in your closet. Is yours so full you have to issue an avalanche warning if you want to pull out a pair of pants? Have you seriously thought that you had better not buy anything new because you have nowhere to put the new items?

If you have a closet full of old clothes, a shed full of unused fishing gear, a shelf packed with old books, or a brain cluttered with incomplete agreements, broken promises, past resentments, unresolved emotional trauma, or past unproductive processes - it's pretty hard to make space for something new.

If you're wondering what cleaning and clearing yourself on all levels - physically, emotionally, intellectually, socially and spiritually - has to do with achieving your goals - the answer is: Plenty!

If you want something in your life - new friends, a new career, a new bedroom set, a new attitude on life, new knowledge, a new car, a new relationship - you must clear out the old and make room for the new on all levels.

Master's Tip If the mind, the heart, and the other "book shelves of your life" are full, it is almost impossible to have room for the new things that the future might bring.

- If you want new friends in your life, but your schedule is packed with other commitments, it will be pretty hard to have this happen.
- If you want a new romance, but you are still thinking about and angry with your ex-wife from 15 years ago, you will repel any possible candidates with your cluttered brain. Women will walk away saying that you are still attached to someone else and emotionally unavailable for them.

Have you ever walked down the street and saw someone you knew, but did not want to run into because you had something incomplete with him or her? Maybe you owe this person money, didn't show up for a date, had a disagreement in high school, or had some other misunderstanding. Perhaps you even went out of your way to avoid connecting with this person by crossing the street or pretending you didn't see him or her. This scenario is an example of something incomplete that can control your life.

Master's Tip "Incompletes" weigh you down!

Every incomplete thing in your life - a broken promise or agreement, a personal relationship with unstated resentments or appreciations, or forgiveness that needs to occur - clutters your mind, weakens your focus, and draws you away from what is most important to you.

If you have something weighing you down, it is time to complete it! If you don't, you might as well be standing at the curb tied to the lamppost because you can't cross the street when the crosswalk sign changes to **walk**!

MASTER'S TIP To embrace the future, you must let go of the past!

CONSIDER: How many things do you need to complete?

- Do you have unpaid debts, a disorganized garage, overflowing junk drawers, missing or broken tools, disorganized tax records, filing left undone, family pictures not put in your album, a disorganized desk or office?
- Do you have incomplete personal relationships, promises that have not been kept or renegotiated, or things you have not forgiven?

Whatever it is that might be holding you back, take care of it. Do it right now! If you continue to put it off, it continues to hold you back by leaking negativity into your life.

Releasing past hurts, anger, resentment, and fear definitely supports you in succeeding faster and easier.

Complete your incompletes

Whatever incompletes you have on your list, you have four choices of how to get them off your incomplete list:

Do	Defer
Delegate	Delete

Do it

It may feel great to "Just do it!"

If it takes less than 15 minutes to do, do it immediately. If it takes longer, create a plan to get it done and put it on your schedule.

Delegate it

If you can't do it yourself or don't want to do it because it is not the best use of your time, delegate it to someone else. And delegate it now!

Defer it

If you still want to take care of it yourself, but are clear that it takes longer than you want to devote to it at the moment, defer it.

If you do defer it, schedule it on your "To Do" list for when you do have time to devote to completing it. Once the task is on your list, you can take it out of your mind. You have a plan, so you can relax.

Delete it

If you've had a task on your mind for a while, you may want to delete it. Perhaps you realize it doesn't need to be done. Or maybe it was something you thought you "should do" but is not really important to you. Sometimes just getting rid of stuff makes life simpler.

And deleting can be freeing in addition to an excellent clearing process. If you dumped all that old fishing gear you haven't used for 15 years, would you really miss it? How about those old resentments that keep you stuck in the past?

Decide now

Make what you think is the right choice about those incompletes in your life.

PONDER:

Will this choice add to my life or keep me stuck in the past?

Will it clear the way for me to live a bright future?

Does this choice empower me, or disempower me?

Defer it, delete it, delegate it, or just do it. Whatever your choice, take care of whatever might be holding you back.

Making Space

INTEGRATION CHECKLIST

Things you will need

Your journal

A quiet space to think and write

Integration-Related Activity

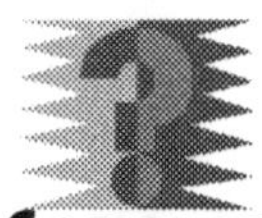

CONSIDER: What's holding you back?

Your Unfinished Business

Here are a few examples of unfinished business that might hold you back by tying up emotional energy that you could be using to achieve your goals:

- An unpaid bill from the past.
- A feeling that you should have done something you didn't do.
- A person whom you are avoiding or would never like to see again.

WRITTEN ACTIVITY Take the time now to write out a list of all the unfinished business in your life - of all the situations you are avoiding. Consider all areas of your life - your physical environment, relationships, work or career, health and fitness, financial situation, and all other significant areas.

Once you have written your list, you can take a walk thorough your life with this list handy. You can look at all the things holding you back, and make a choice of how to handle each of them. And make space for the new!

WRITTEN ACTIVITY Review your list and choose now!

In your journal next to each item on the list, write one of these words: do, delegate, defer, or delete.

- **Do** - especially if it takes 15 minutes or less.
- **Delegate** - Decide who else can do it and delegate it to them.
- **Defer** until some future date - just schedule it now so you can release it
- **Delete** - Decide to never worry about it again.

Taking care of your unfinished business brings you peace of mind.

People or Situations Holding You Back

Your worst unfinished business, the incomplete situations that tie up emotional energy, is often related to the people in your life.

ASK YOURSELF: What people and situations would I like to delete from my mind and heart?

WRITTEN ACTIVITY Start a second list for people or situations holding you back. Be sure to put plenty of space between the items.

One way to clear the emotions around these types of situations, so that you can delete them, is to come up with three different meanings or interpretations of the event.

For example, suppose you are still burning inside because you feel your brother didn't help you enough with a project, even though you told him how desperately you needed help. What are three different interpretations of the situation?

Your current interpretation might be that he didn't care enough to help. The truth might be that he's sick, is getting treatment, and just isn't able to help you right now. It might be that his girlfriend just dumped him and he's so emotionally wrecked that he can't function. Maybe he's got a new job that's taking all his time.

As soon as you can see three other possible interpretations of the situation that is bothering you, the emotional impact is lessened. You can delete that old situation from your mind and your heart, and free up that emotional energy.

Written Activity In your journal write three possible interpretations for each of the people situations that really are bothering you.

Make Space NOW

As you make space in your life for new things, see yourself filled with grace, skill and capability. See the bright light from within!

Knowing that as you free up space your world can be filled with new events and new wonder, what would it take for you to make space **now**, to declare your commitment to moving through your lists - doing, delegating, deferring, or deleting **now**?

Part 2: **Vision and Inspiration**

Now that you have a strong foundation for reaching your goal, it is time to move on to being inspired about how to reach the goal.

The next phase of the 30-day program is two days during which you become inspired and build a vision of your dream.

The architect has a vision of the house or building. He determines how to build it on a solid foundation and then enjoys the next phase of designing the home - the details that make it structurally sound and buildable.

As you continue to be the architect of your life, creating the blueprints for success, we share with you the secrets of design - how to be creative and envision a life that is so wonderful you are inspired to build it - one day at a time.

Journals

We said at the beginning that your journal is your blueprint for you to reach your goal. And your success depends on how good your blueprints are.

What should be in it now? This is a checkpoint - a time to encourage you to complete the exercises you might have skipped - or to repeat ones you think may help you clarify your goal.

2-Day Inspiration Overview

The first five days of your journey was about building a foundation. We are taking 100% responsibility, learning what it takes to be an Enlightened Internal Leader, overcoming our resistance, becoming familiar with the steps to take to complete a cycle, and finally making the space for new things in our lives. Now it is time to step up to the plate and "Live our Dreams".

These next 2 days are for visions and inspiration. It is time to clarify your unique calling and learn about your contribution to yourself and others.

Day 6 invites you to consider that your sole responsibility on the planet, the only thing you are really here to do, is to **Live your best life.** And to do that, we have you ponder some questions in **Day 7** that help you to clarify what purpose you have in life - what you are, do, or dream you can be, and ponder what you can offer the world.

Are you ready?

CHECKLIST

- Be sure you have your journal.
- Set a time aside each day to do your life's work.

Day 6 **Live Your Dream**

This session is about living **your** dream - not someone else's.

Commitment
by W.H. Murray

Until one is committed there is always hesitancy, the chance to draw back, always ineffectiveness. Concerning all acts (and creation) there is always one elementary truth, ignorance of which kills countless ideas and splendid plans; that the moment one definitely commits oneself, then providence moves too.

All sorts of things occur to help one that would never otherwise have occurred. A whole stream of events issues from the decision raising one's favor all manner of unforeseen incidents and meetings and material assistance, which no man could have dreamt would have come his way.

I have learned a great respect for one of Goethe's Couplets:
Whatever you can do, or dream, begin it. Boldness has genius, power and magic in it.

Decide what you want! Chances are, it wants you! Your goals and desires are waiting to gravitate towards you - once you decide what you truly want.

You Matter

If you don't recognize this already, be clear that you are here for a reason and that your life really matters. **You Matter**! You have a true purpose, a calling, and a significant offering in this world. And following this deep inner knowing - your life's calling - is your gift to the world.

Your offering may be to share your art with the world, be an exceptional mother, provide medical support to those who are dying, discover something amazing or inventive, or support others in clarifying and living their dreams! What ever it is - **You Matter** - your offering matters.

You are not here to live someone else's dream.

Consider that the things you really want in life - not the things you think you should want, but the things you really **do** want - the things that you know are the "true you", such as the healthier body, the more abundant mind, the richer relationships, the deeper spiritual connection, the more fulfilling work, the bigger contribution to the planet, is what you are meant to go after.

MASTER'S TIP Don't seek success or fame in the world, but rather seek significance.

Seek a significant offering that inspires you and also inspires others to become more of who they really are.

Your Significant Offering

Consider the possibility that your sole responsibility on the planet, the only thing you are really here to do, is to **live your best life** - to be, do, and have all the things you dream about. Through this way of living, you inspire your children, your significant other, friends, family, colleagues, your community, and your country to do the same.

A wise friend once said, "The universal currency, meaning the way Spirit pays you, is through ideas." When you live your best life, when you do the things that occur to you, that call you, you are living your most significant offering. And this way of living gives others permission to do the same.

PONDER: If it didn't matter what other people thought, what would you try? What would you let go of? How would you behave?

If you knew that no one would criticize you and you didn't have to be modest, how would you describe your best self?

If you had no fear at all, what would you let yourself offer the world?

Consider that in your heart you are clear on what you are meant to offer the world. What is that offering? This is your calling. This is why you are here!

Choose to Live Your Life Purpose

When you feel your purpose calling you, it is very important that you start to move in that direction. What you want also wants you! When you make a powerful choice to live your purpose and go for what you really want, uncanny things start to occur.

Reread the poem by W.H. Murray from The Scottish Himalayan Expedition at the beginning of this Day. It sums it up perfectly.

Master's Tip "Whatever you can do, or dream you can, begin it. Boldness has genius, power, and magic in it." - Goethe

List what Inspires You

Start by writing down the things you really want that inspire you. These are not things you think you "should want" but rather the things you really do want. If these desires are your deepest truth, they will be linked to your calling, your offering to the world. Of course what often stops people from expressing their true desire is that they don't think they can make a living doing what they love to do.

If what you love to do is be generous, consider how Oprah Winfrey gives away millions of dollars worth of gifts and services every year! It is possible to make a great living doing what you love - you simply have to risk it.

Once you are clear on what you want, open your mind to infinite possibility.

If your dream really was true right now, start to imagine what you would feel, see, and hear

Ponder: How would your daily actions be different than they are now?

Ponder: How would you see others in your life and the opportunities that are available to you?

Ponder: What do you think your friends and the ones you love would say about the new you?

Are you ready to play for a minute?

Just relax and pretend for a moment that the Universe is caring for your life with love, and that the Universe wanted for you exactly what you wanted from it.

Ponder: How would you feel if you absolutely knew that the Universe was in your corner and really wanted you to live your best life, your most significant offering?

Pretend that this is true, and take on that feeling now.

Visualize The Impact

As you look at your ideal life, visualize your offering to the world.

Ponder: What am I doing?

Ponder: Who am I working with?

Ponder: Where am I working? Just imagine yourself in action.

Ponder: As I imagine myself living my calling, what value am I offering to the world?

Ponder: Who is impacted by my offering?

Now visualize your financial situation. Simply be honest with yourself around what you want - considering the fact that you are living your calling.

Ponder: What is my income?

Ponder: What is my net worth?

Ponder: How is my cash flow?

Ponder: What does my home look like? And where is it? What does the inside of it look like? Walk through your perfect home in your mind's eye.

Now imagine your relationships with your friends and family.

Ponder: What is the quality of my family life?

Ponder: What are the qualities of those friendships?

Ponder: Who am I being as a friend?

Ponder: Who are the type of people I attracted to be my friends?

Ponder: How is my romantic life?

Now imagine your physical, emotional, and spiritual being. Visualize your connection to the Universe.

Ponder: How is my spiritual connection?

Ponder: What am I doing that is keeping me connected?

Visualize your body.

Ponder: What does it look like?

Ponder: How well is it functioning?

Ponder: What is my body able to do?

Ponder: How is my emotional life?

Ponder: What do I feel throughout the day?

Ponder: How do I handle challenges that arise?

Notice how you spend your free time.

Ponder: What do I do that creates fun in my life?

Ponder: How much time do I have to spend with family and friends? What do we do together?

Ponder: What types of vacations do I take?

Ponder: What types of fun or creative projects do I enjoy?

Notice yourself as part of a community.

Ponder: How do I participate in my ideal community?

Ponder: What do I offer others?

Ponder: What do they offer me?

Ponder: What do I do to help others? How often do I participate in these activities?

From the perspective of trusting something bigger than yourself:

Ponder: What new ways might I start to move toward my most fulfilling and significant life?

Living your Dream

INTEGRATION CHECKLIST

Things you will need

Your journal

A quiet space to think and write

Integration-Related Activity

In this activity you list the things you want in life. Having a list helps you clarify where your journey is taking you.

You are going to create a list of the things you want. Then you play with this list as you notice what comes up. Remember to just keep writing.

ASK YOURSELF: What is one thing I want? What else? Fill in the table.

ONE THING I WANT	MORE THINGS I WANT

In the life I really want - the life my highest self knows I am meant to live...

- My friendships would be...

- My family connection would be...

- My career would be...

- My financial condition would be...

- My body and health would be...

- My romantic life would be...

- My thoughts would be...

- My actions would be...

- My emotions would be...

- My spiritual connection would be...

- My contribution would be...

Ask yourself: If I didn't have to be modest and knew that no one would judge or criticize me, how would I describe my best self?

Ask yourself: If anything was possible and it didn't matter what other people thought, what three things would I let myself want?

-
-
-

Ask yourself: If anything was possible and it didn't matter what other people thought, what would I stop doing?

Ask yourself: If I had no fear at all, what would I allow myself to offer the world?

Consider that your spirit is crystal clear on what you are meant to offer the world.

Ask yourself: What might that offering be?

Ask yourself: What internal shifts might I need to make to be the person my spirit knows I am meant to be?

Ask yourself: What do I yearn to do?

Ask yourself: What do I yearn to feel?

Ask yourself: Who do I yearn to be?

Ask yourself: What do I yearn to contribute?

Life Purpose Statement

Now create a Life Purpose Statement with a version of an exercise originally created by Arnold Patent.

- List two unique qualities that are you, such as compassionate, cooperative, loving, enthusiastic, creative, energetic, fun loving, patient, and so on.

  ________________ and ______________________

- List one or two ways you enjoy sharing those qualities when interacting with other people. For example maybe you enjoy supporting, teaching, or inspiring people, or making them laugh!

  ________________ and ______________________

Your Perfect World

Consider: If it were a perfect world right now:

Ask yourself: What would this world look like?

Ask yourself: How would people interact with one another?

Ask yourself: How would people act?

Ask yourself: What would be the ultimate condition - the perfect world as you would see it and feel it?

For example: Everyone is fully self-expressed and enjoying life. Everyone communicates effectively with one another. People are participating in the sustainability of the planet and recycling. Everyone acts with compassion and forgiveness.

Now combine your answers to the three questions into one statement. For example:

My purpose is to share my creativity and enthusiasm, to support and inspire people to become fully self-expressed and enjoy life.

or

My purpose is to act with compassion and love as I teach others to participate in the sustainability of the planet.

or

My purpose is to be fun-loving and kindhearted as I coach people to communicate effectively with one another.

or

My purpose is to use my creativity and enthusiasm to support and inspire others to freely express their talents in a harmonious and loving way.

Write your statement here:

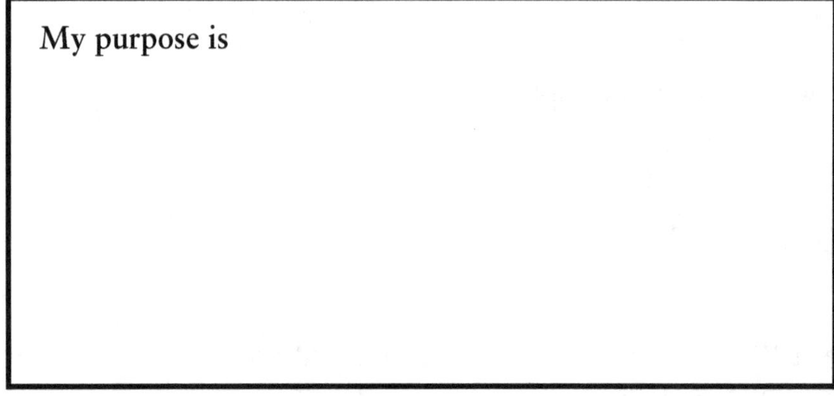

Once you have your purpose statement, check to see if your current goals for this program fit with this purpose statement.

Ask yourself: Does my goal support me in living my life on purpose?

If not, it is time to re-create the goal you have for this program.

Live YOUR Life On Purpose NOW

Imagine if you read your Life Purpose statement every day - several times a day and lived with that purpose. Would you be inspired?

What action might you take to remind yourself to live your life on purpose, to share your gifts and support others in living the life they loved so that together you could create the perfect world?

Day 7 **Make It Happen**

In Day 6 we talked about your significant offering in life. It's now time to go further.

Here's the premise: We are all, right now, living the life we choose.

This choice, of course, is not a single, monumental choice. No one decides, for example, "I'm going to move to L.A., and in five years I will be a waiter in a so-so restaurant, planning to get my 8-by-10's done real soon so that I can find an agent and become a star," or "I'm going to marry a dreadful person and we'll live together in a loveless marriage, staying together only for the kids, who I don't much like, either."

No. The choices I'm talking about here are made daily, hourly, moment by moment.

Do we try something new, or stick to the tried-and-true? Do we take a risk, or eat what's already on our dish? Do we ponder a thrilling adventure, or contemplate what's on TV? Do we walk over and meet that interesting stranger, or do we play it safe? Do we indulge our heart, or cater to our fear?

The bottom-line question: Do we pursue what we want, or do we do what's comfortable?

For the most part, most people most often choose comfort - the familiar, the time-honored, the well-worn but well-known. After a lifetime of choosing between comfort and risk, we are left with the life we currently have.

And it was all of our own choosing.
-- Peter McWilliams

Remember that your most significant offering, the only thing you are really here to do - is to **Live Your Best Life** - your authentic, value-based life.

Why is this your most significant offering? Because when you choose to live authentically who you are and from your values, you inspire others and give others permission to do the same.

Ponder Your Life

In this session we ask you to do some pondering.

Pause after each question and take time to explore it with your heart and mind. Answer the questions inwardly. And notice your honest responses.

PONDER: What is the one thing that you feel **must** happen in your life? As you consider this question, also ask yourself: "Why is this important to me?"

PONDER: If you achieved this intention, what would that lead to?

PONDER: What is the ultimate purpose of that for you?

PONDER: Who else will benefit from this? As you consider this ask yourself again "Why is this important to me?"

Consider Your Willingness

Knowing what your heart and mind just revealed to you:

PONDER: Are you willing to live your purpose, your significant offering?

PONDER: Are you willing to do whatever it takes to live this purpose?

In this example of pondering, we linked something you really want in your life to your values.

PONDER: Did you feel the impact?

PONDER: Do you feel inspired to actually find a way to have this happen?

Values Motivate You

I bet you said **YES** because a value is what is important to you. Your values represent your unique and individual essence. Living from your values is the ultimate and most fulfilling form of expressing and relating. Your values act as your **life compass**, pointing out what is true for you. So when you honor your values on a regular and consistent basis, life is good, life is fulfilling.

MASTER'S TIP Consider that everything you do, you do for a reason.

That reason usually relates to your values. The values that motivate you also help you to evaluate your actions or the actions of others. If someone does something that upsets you, it is likely you're upset because something you value was violated. And sometimes we do not recognize that we have a value until it is violated.

Let's go back now to that purpose you thought about earlier.

Your values are important to you. So when a goal you set is deeply linked to your core values, you are much more likely to follow through and to make your goal happen!

Think about fulfilling each of your present goals. What value is linked to each goal? If you aren't certain how to answer this:

PONDER: What's important about this goal to me?

IMPORTANT EXAMPLE **VALUES AWARENESS PROCESS**

Let's suppose your goal is to get fit.

What's important about that?

Getting fit means getting healthy.

Now ask the question again.

What's important about getting healthy?

Getting healthy means I'll be able to do things with my kids, like play ball, and I'll be around longer. I'll feel better, too!

So ask one more time: Why is that important?

It's really important to me that I can give my kids the best life possible. To do that, I need to be able to keep up with them, and not set a bad example of being unhealthy and out of shape.

Now look at your list of goals and try this "values awareness" process out on one of your own goals. Once you know the value behind your goal and are clear that it is compelling enough to move you into action, you can draw on this energy whenever your old friend Resistance shows up!

Values are the future you are moving into. Resistance has to do with a belief that was created in the past and that you think keeps you safe, even though the truth is: it doesn't.

When the mind is lifted to the level of value, old limiting beliefs begin to fall away. When you are clear why your goal is worth doing, worth working for, you'll be unstoppable.

If something comes up and you find it difficult to carry through with your goal, remember to focus on the value. Whenever we have something that is really important to us, we find ways to make it happen!

Making it Happen

Integration Checklist

Things you will need

Your journal

A quiet space to think and write

Integration-Related Activity

The goal of this activity is to clarify the values associated with your goal. With this knowledge, you can more readily step into action.

Values Clarification Exercise

As you just learned, it is very important to look at your goal from a higher perspective. This perspective means you clarify the higher good of your goal and verify that it fits with your calling.

Written Activity Write out your most important goal for this program.

Ask yourself: What's important about this goal to me?

Ask yourself: What is the higher value this will serve? That is, what will I really get once I have achieved this goal?

Ask yourself: And ultimately, what is important about that?

Ask yourself: Does this goal fit within my life purpose?
Does it support my life purpose in some way?
Is this something I really want, or something I think I should want?

Ask yourself: Is this a compelling enough reason for me to actually follow through on my goal? If not, what adjustments might I need to make so the goal is even more inspiring to me?

Once you are sure your goal is one you really do want and that it powerfully aligns with your purpose and life values, it is time to create your dream - on paper!

Many of us have rather vague goals. For instance, we want to be the **best** lawyer in New York City. This is not a measurable or specific goal until you set criteria to determine who is the **best** lawyer in NYC. For example, to determine the **best lawyer in NYC**, do you consider:

- Billable hours?
- Billable rate?
- Number of clients successfully defended?
- Depth of knowledge about the law in general, or a certain area of the law?

Clarify Your Goal

The Goal Clarification exercise that you are about to do is 30 questions that help you see the depth and detail about what it really means for you to achieve this goal. When you are finished, you should have complete clarity on your goal.

This is your opportunity to be open, honest and direct with yourself. Champion yourself to follow through and have exactly what you want.

Many of these questions you can answer with a simple **Yes** or **No**.

IMPORTANT INSTRUCTION **PLEASE WRITE THE FIRST THING THAT COMES TO MIND. COMPLETING THIS EXERCISE IS NECESSARY BEFORE YOU CONTINUE YOUR 30-DAY JOURNEY.**

You can always come back to this exercise. It is useful to read your responses back to yourself when you are done. In Day 8 you examine some of this information, so it is important to take time to do this exercise now.

Goal Clarification Exercise

Did you know that your mind doesn't know how to process a negative? If, for example, you were to say to yourself: "I don't want to put on weight in 2005", guess what you see in your minds eye?

How about this one: ***"I don't want to be poor in 2005?"*** Do you see poverty?

Make it easy for your mind, and phrase your goal in the positive!

Clearly State Your Positive Goal

1. Look at your goal. Is your goal stated in the positive? Does your statement focus on what you want rather than what you don't want?

   State your goal in the positive now.

My goal is

Own control

2. Look at your goal, on a scale from zero to 10, how much is your goal under your direct control?

   Your goal must be something you can do something about. Wanting someone else to stop smoking is not something you can do much about! You can decide that you want to have clean air available for your lungs at all times. That's a very different outcome than telling your spouse to stop smoking. You might decide instead, to ask that they smoke outside, purchase a new air filter for the house, or take other action that would make sure you get what you want - clean air.

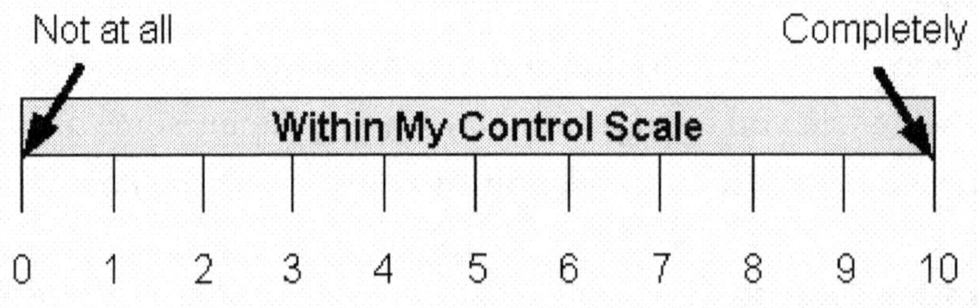

3. What can you do directly to get this outcome?

4. What isn't under your direct control?

5. What can you do to help yourself achieve your goal?

6. What can others do to help you achieve your goal?

7. How might you invite or persuade others to support you?

8. Who will you ask to support you?

9. What can you offer that would encourage them to want to help?

10. When will you ask?

Be Specific

Your goal needs to be specific. It should state exactly what it is you want.

11. What Specific Measure will you use to measure your achievement?

    Example:

    - I will have $10,000 in my bank account.
    - I will have 25% body fat.
    - I will have 10 new clients.

12. When and where, specifically, do you want this?

    Examples: In my US bank account on September 30, 2005

    On the scale on July 1, 2005

    By August 15, 2005

Evidence

Now it is time to clarify how you will know that you achieved your goal.

13. If you had already achieved your goal, what would you have?

    What tangible evidence would prove you have your outcome?

    Examples:

    - If you want to improve your marriage, how will you know that you have done this?
    - If you want a great new career, how will you know it is the best one for you?
    - If you want to have more fun, how will you know you are doing this?

    Even if you are not certain what the evidence is, what is your best guess?

14. What standard is the most important standard to measure yourself against when working towards your goal?

    Examples:

    - Your level of relaxation
    - The number of actions you take daily
    - The amount of trust you feel in yourself and the Universe
    - The amount of fun you are having
    - The degree to which you are operating from an enlightened leader state of mind
    - Your inner knowing of who you are, balanced with people's feedback.

15. Does the evidence you are using to prove you've reached your goal really measure the achievement of the goal? If not, what adjustments might you make?

Size

16. Is this goal the right size? How do you know?
    Is it achievable for you?

17. Is your time frame the right size? How do you know?

Ecology

18. How does achieving this goal fit in with your **ideal** life?

19. How does the work required to reach the goal fit in with your current life?

20. How will this goal affect your family? Your finances? Your health?

21. When you see yourself in the future, having achieved this goal, how does this feel? What do you see? What was the cost? What was the really big gain?

22. Is there anything you would not do in order to achieve your goal? What principles would you **never** violate in reaching your goal?

Fit

23. What is the 'goal within the goal'? What will this goal get for you?

24. Does this goal fit together with other goals in your life?

25. What does having this outcome do for you? Would having this outcome serve you well? Would it fit with who you really are?

26. Why wouldn't you want this outcome?

27. What might prevent you from achieving this outcome?

Resources

28. What resources do you already have to help reach your goal? What additional resources might you need?

	Have	**Need**
Objects		
People		
Role Models - People who have already done this or something similar or a hero you use to inspire you.		
Personal Qualities		
Money		
Skills		

Planning

29. What are the specific mini-outcomes and steps you need to achieve to reach your goal?

    Example: If your goal is to weigh 140 lbs in 6 months and you are currently 20 lbs away from your goal, you might have specific mini-goals:

    - To eat 5 fruits and vegetables a day
    - To eat 3 servings of lean protein,
    - To drink 8 glasses of water a day
    - To walk 2 miles at least five mornings a week
    - To meditate every day for 15 minutes.
      This is the basis of your plan to achieve your goal.

30. How might you stop yourself? And what is your plan for dealing with this?

Make it Happen NOW

Imagine if you accepted whatever comes into your life as okay. Imagine embracing even those events that seem far less than ideal - perhaps even a bit of what we might label as **bad things** happening to us.

Make a commitment to go with the flow, to accept that even the darkest clouds have a silver lining if we look hard enough!

Knowing that releasing and accepting what is happening would make your life less stressful, what would you be willing to do now?

Would less stress and more satisfaction in life be worth stepping back and seeing the glass as half full when we feel like it is half empty?

What action might you take to remind yourself to go with the flow of life, let it be okay, and then see what you can learn so the future is filled with a life you love?

Part 3 **Decision**

Now that you have built a strong foundation for reaching your goal and created a vision to help you reach it, it is time to make a decision to go for it.

The next phase of the 30-day program is four days during which you make a powerful decision to reach your goal and declare that decision in writing.

The architect determines how to build the house on a solid foundation and then enjoys the phase of designing the home - the details that make it structurally sound and buildable. The next phase is to start construction.

As you continue to be the architect of your life, creating the blueprints for success, we share with you the secrets of construction - how to be decisive and support yourself in building your dream - every day of your life.

Journals

By now your journal has a lot of pages filled. Remember your journal is your blueprint for you to reach your goal.

What should be in it now? It's time to take another look. Check out your blueprint and make certain that you have completed all the details - done the exercises you might have skipped or put extra effort into ones you might have found challenging.

4-Day Decision Overview

The first five days of your journey were about building a foundation. The next two were about inspiration and vision, learning to live **your** dream.

These next four days are for decisions. It's time now to powerfully make a choice - to decide to reach your goal.

In **Day 8** we invite you to be specific about what you want and why it is important to you. Then you declare your desire by writing it down - the power of the pen and the written word will amaze you! And once you know exactly what you want, we invite you in **Day 9** to make visualizing it a daily event.

In **Day 10** we invite you to focus your mind on exactly where you are heading. Clarity around your destination means less wandering along the way and quicker results. And to help keep you focused, in **Day 11** we encourage you to engage in daily meditation as well as reading about people who might inspire you or provide clues for you on how to most easily reach your destination.

Are you ready?

CHECKLIST

- Be sure you have your journal.
- Set a time aside each day to do your life's work.

Day 8 **Write It Down**

This session is about the Power of the Pen - the value of written goals.

Have you heard of Alice Henry (1857–1943)?

Diane Kirkby wrote a biography about this intelligent, formidable woman of great energy who was a pioneer in both the Australian and American labor movements early this century. She fought for the rights of millions of women in both countries.

After a childhood largely spent in the Australian bush, Alice Henry became a journalist in Melbourne, where she witnessed the growth and upheavals of the Australian labor movement and consequent experiments in state regulation of industrial relations. During her 28 years in America she became a prominent figure in the Women's Trade Union league and campaigned for the rights of wage-earning women using her powers of 'pen and voice' as a writer and lecturer.

Alice Henry knew her life's purpose and she used her skill as a journalist to put her plans in action. She truly knew the Power of the Pen!

We've been talking about your calling, your purpose, and your deep inner knowing of what you can offer the world to live your best life. Today you are going to learn a specific method to turn this purpose into goals that you can make real.

Be Specific

Start by focusing your mind on exactly what you want. Be specific.

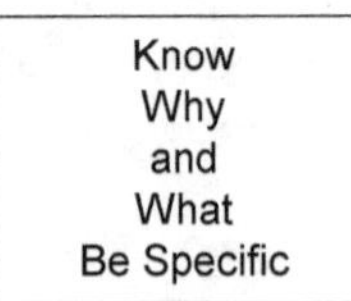

You do not need to understand how to do it yet.

Just be clear on what will support you in living your best life.

You do not need to know the how!

It is not sufficient to say, "I want to be healthy or wealthy or smart." You need to be specific about what you want. For example:

- "I want to weigh 140 lbs and have 25% body fat in exactly 6 months." or
- "I want to have $100,000 in my savings account exactly one year from today." or
- "I want to learn how to build my own airplane and build one that meets all regulations in exactly 24 months."

It's important in this step to be clear on exactly how you would know if you got what you wanted. What evidence would you have? If you had already achieved your goal, what would you have?

Relate Goals to Value

The second step in the process relates to the values awareness process we discussed in Day 7 - clarifying why achieving this goal is important to you. This is a very important part of the process! And, once you know why your goal is important, you must be sure it links to a core value.

Remember the questions:

- What is important about this goal?
- If I achieve it, what would having that lead to?
- Ultimately, what is the purpose of this for me?
- Who else will benefit from this?

Look at your answers.

PONDER: Is this a compelling enough reason for me to do what ever it takes to do this?

Sometimes in this step of the process you realize your reasons are not compelling enough for you to do what it takes. If so, go back to step one and clarify what you really want.

Master's Tip You are not on this planet to do what you think you should do or what others want you to do. You are here to live your best life on your terms.

Once you know what you want and have compelling reasons to make it happen, move on to Step 3.

Write Down Your Goal

Step 3 is when you use the Power of the Pen.

Writing your goal down on paper helps make it real! It's as though we have an invisible circuit in our brain that says, "If you don't care enough to write this down, you don't really want it."

S	M	A	R	T
p	e	c	e	i
e	a	h	a	m
c	s	i	l	e
i	u	e	i	d
f	r	v	s	
i	a	a	t	
c	b	b	i	
	l	l	c	
	e	e		

Write out a clear, concise statement of your goal. Make sure your goal is **SMART**: Specific, Measurable, Achievable, Realistic, and Timed for completion.

Have you heard of the study done years ago with a Harvard graduating class where only 3% of the graduates had written down their financial goals? The study powerfully demonstrated that twenty years later, the 3% that had written down their goals not only achieved their goals, but also were significantly happier and were worth more than the other 97% of the class combined! Isn't this amazing?

Process Review

So let's quickly review the process:

Step 1 - Be specific about what you want.

Step 2 - Relate your goal to your values. Make sure your reasons are compelling or return to Step 1.

Step 3 - Write it down!

Remember you have a calling, a purpose, an offering that is linked to you living your best life! When you create definite goals and write them down, you are making the abstract concrete - the formless takes form so you can actualize it in the world.

Master's Tip Consider your goal to be a dream with a deadline.

When you write down a goal that is linked to something that is important to you and that represents you living your best life, you are a thousand times more likely to achieve it.

If the reasons you want the outcome are not compelling enough for you to actually do it, don't write it down.

Now let's add a little twist to Step 3. You've written down your goal.

Create Mini-goals

Take a look at what you just wrote down and make a list of all the "baby-steps" you can take to achieve it. We'll call these sub-goals, or mini-goals, which lead into your bigger goals.

Example

Written goal: I want to start my own business and be making a million dollars in one year.

Now you need a series of smaller, more easily achievable steps that support you in getting there. Each of those steps should also be **SMART** - specific, measurable, achievable, realistic and timed with a date for completion.

In the business example, you might have mini-goals like these:

- I will have my business plan created in one month.
- I will have investors in place in two months.
- I will open the doors for business in 3 months.

As you achieve each mini-goal, you get closer and closer to achieving the big goal. And achieving the mini-goals indicates that you are on track to getting what you want.

Tips for Success

So you've made it through the three steps:

1 - Being Specific about what you want

2 - Relating your goal to your values, and finding compelling reasons to achieve it

3 - Writing it down!

Now we have three tips that can be the "difference that makes a difference."

TIP #1: Get a Goal Book to track your goals and the progress you're making towards them.

If you don't have a date assigned to your mini-goals or some method to track your progress, there is a very strong possibility that you will get off track or never take action at all!

We live in a busy world. Without a deadline, we often find other things to do. The urgencies of life speak louder than your goals - the baby is crying, the phone is ringing, the bills need to be paid, there is a meeting to attend, a dinner to go to. We can find loads of interruptions and detours on the way to our goal, right?

The way to stay motivated is to have written goals with mini-goals and deadlines, and a clear "compelling reason why" you want to achieve your goal - and a way to keep yourself on track, which leads us to the next tip.

TIP #2: Read your written statement aloud!

Twice daily, read your goal with passion - once in the morning and once in the evening. Read with laser-tight clarity that this is the future you are moving into.

And when you read it, feel and believe that you will achieve it. See yourself already having what you want.

Then, directionalize your mind and focus on your goal. Do your best everyday to make it a reality, and then give it over to the Universe. Remember, the Universe can dream a bigger dream for you than you can dream for yourself.

TIP #3: Be Flexible!

Remember that sometimes getting from here to there looks different than we thought it would. Be open and flexible to dancing with the Universe instead of against it, as you continue to move towards what you want.

In conclusion, the Power of the Pen is enormous. Write your goals down, and say them out loud with passion.

MASTER'S TIP In the words of Napoleon Hill: "Whatever the mind of man can conceive and believe it can achieve."

Writing it Down

INTEGRATION CHECKLIST

Things you will need

Your journal

A quiet space to think and write

Integration-Related Activity

The goal of this activity is for you to engage the Power of the Pen.

IMPORTANT INSTRUCTION **BE SURE TO HAVE YOUR ANSWERS FROM SESSION 2.**

Writing Exercise

Today's the day you say **Yes** to your goal with every fiber of your being. You are going to write out a clear, clean, concise statement of your goal.

WRITTEN ACTIVITY **WRITE OUT YOUR GOAL**

S	M	A	R	T
p	e	c	e	i
e	a	h	a	m
c	s	i	l	e
i	u	e	i	d
f	r	v	s	
i	a	a	t	
c	b	b	i	
	l	l	c	
	e	e		

Write exactly what you want.

Be sure it is **SMART** - specific, measurable, achievable, realistic and timed for completion.

Now, look at what you have written and by sure you have used powerful language that creates certainty.

For example, it is one thing to "**want**" and another to say, "I will have, or I choose to have, I decide to have." So "I want to have fifty thousand dollars in the bank, by this coming Christmas" becomes "I will have fifty thousand dollars in the bank by Christmas!"

Create Three Mini-Goals

In your journal, write out at least three mini-goals that are **SMART** and that support you in achieving this goal. Be sure each mini-goal has a timeline. And again, use powerful language.

Scripting your Life

You are going to write a story or a **script** of what your life will be like once you achieve this goal. The reason we do this is related to how your brain works. The more you imagine yourself already having the goal, including how you feel, what you see and what you hear, the better your visualizations get. And the better your visualizations, the more likely you are to achieve your goals.

This part of the exercise is a script that, as you read through it, helps you visualize having achieved your goal.

Write your script

In your workbook write out a description of your life with your goal accomplished. This description should be as real as possible. For example, some people like to describe how they would live a complete day with their goal achieved. Other people, who are after a specific possession, might describe what it would be like to be using that possession.

TIP: Use a whole page or more. Go overboard with describing how good it will be to have this goal achieved.

There's a theory of attraction that says you attract to yourself whatever you feel good about. When you read this script, it is your chance to feel really great about achieving your goal.

Write the story of the amazing future you are moving into. Enjoy the process and take the time you need to write a detailed description of your life after having the goal, how you will feel once you've achieved it, how your life will look, what you'd be hearing and saying, and add all the details that make this description seem real. Don't forget to add the date by which you will have this goal!

Handling Objections

You may find that some objections come up as you write this script. That's great! This is your beyond conscious mind coming forth with important things to consider. Write these down on a separate sheet of paper, and make sure your script shares how you overcame these challenges.

Okay, it is now time to write the story of the amazing future you are moving into. Please enjoy the process.

Read your Script

Now read your script aloud, in front of a mirror. Make this a daily practice.

Every time you read this script, you should be automatically feeling great, just as good as you would feel if you had achieved your goal.

Write it Down NOW

Imagine if you read your story every day - several times. Imagine embracing any objections and seeing them as things to consider so you don't get bogged down on your journey.

Make a commitment to read your story frequently.

Knowing that writing and reading about having achieved your goal helps you achieve it, how might you remind yourself to visualize success daily and move to a future filled with a life you love?

Day 9 **See it Coming**

This lesson is about the power of visualization, about seeing what your future will be like once you achieve your goal.

A Story

A Brief Tale

IMAGINE
John Lennon

Imagine there's no heaven.
It's easy if you try.
No hell below us. Above us only sky.
Imagine all the people. Living for today...

Imagine there's no countries.
It isn't hard to do.
Nothing to kill or die for. And no religion too.
Imagine all the people. Living life in peace...

Imagine no possessions.
I wonder if you can.
No need for greed or hunger. A brotherhood of man.
Imagine all the people. Sharing all the world...

You may say I'm a dreamer. But I'm not the only one.
I hope someday you'll join us. And the world will be as one.

John Lennon invited each of us to imagine a better place, where "the world will be as one." Today we invite you to imagine your world with no obstacles and no roadblocks - just a clear path to your goal.

Master's Tip Albert Einstein said, "Imagination is everything. It is the preview of life's coming attractions."

Visualization or mental rehearsal is a way to success because it keeps you focused on what you want and supports you in knowing that your goal is something within your control to achieve.

The power of positive imagery is not just some popular illusion or wish. It is a key factor in every action and result we have.

Michael Gelb and Tony Buzan say, "Most of us visualize on a daily basis, but we often do it unconsciously and in a negative fashion." We call it *worrying.*

And what happens when we worry? We tense up, disrupt our normal breathing, and psycho-physically prepare ourselves for failure. What if, instead, you used positive visualization to prepare yourself for success? Consider the impact of transforming the energy that supports your worrying into fuel for making your dreams come true!

In Day 8 you wrote some steps to achieving your goals. But what if you saw, on the movie screen of your mind, pictures of yourself already having achieved your goal and could easily see the steps from getting from where you are to where you want to be? Would that be motivating?

Many wise philosophers have said that whatever you can conceive, or dream, you can have. The secret is to visualize.

Master's Tip "A vivid imagination compels one's whole being to obey it." - Aristotle

Visualization is a widely-used technique for improvement in music and sports. Jack Nicklaus, one of the world's greatest golfers, won't even pick up a club until he has a clear visualization of exactly how the ball will fly through the air and where it will hit the ground. "I never hit a shot, not even in practice, without having a very clear, in-focus picture in my head."

Visualization is one of the greatest secrets of success and is very different from daydreaming because it demonstrates **how** you achieve the desired results versus having it appear like magic.

I remember playing lawn darts with my friend's son when he was little. I'd never played before, and he had. He couldn't understand it. Time after time, my dart would go exactly where I wanted it. But once I'd taught him to visualize seeing himself throw the dart effectively and then see it land where he wanted it, he could put his dart anywhere he wanted!

Visualization works best when you see yourself going through each of the steps to your outcome, achieving what you want in full color, life size, and in action - just like a great movie. The best visualizations are the ones where you can see all the steps and it's so real you are convinced it is happening, right now!

This vivid mental rehearsal uses the neural pathways that are involved in doing the activity. And if you focus on a skill you actually create micro movements in the muscles that support you in doing that skill in reality! Amazing, isn't it? This is simply how the brain works!

As you create your movie and watch it over and over again, you activate the creative powers of your deeper knowledge system and direct your brain to attract what you want. This focusing creates a magnetic pull and you begin to attract the people, resources, and opportunities that you need to achieve your goal. And you learn later in your 30-day journey that focusing also programs your Reticular Activating System, the part of your brain that tries to make sense of all the sensory input you receive, to notice resources that were always there, though unnoticed!

Perhaps you are not a person who easily sees pictures in your head. This is perfectly okay! The truth is that at least 80% of us do not see clear pictures! You can just **think** about it and you get the same benefit as those that actually see the image.

Visualization Practice

How do you visualize? It's easy. Let's practice.

- Relax.
- Begin to imagine already having your outcome.
- Imagine seeing, hearing, and feeling perfection.
- Imagine it exactly how you want it to be and use all your senses.
- Make the image big, bright, in action.
- Now add sound, feeling, and smell. The more senses you access internally, the more powerful the experience and the deeper the imprint. So fill in as much detail as possible.
- Once you have a clear outcome in your mind, begin to focus on the process.
- What steps did you take to reach the desired result? Play an internal movie of how you achieved the goal finishing with the exact outcome you want.

Try this now. See yourself being successful every step of the way.

In Day 8 you wrote your goals and mini-goals. Now it's time to practice achieving them. See yourself practicing daily.

MASTER'S TIP Perfect practice in mind makes perfect execution, and repetition is the key! The more you visualize or mentally rehearse the outcome, the more skilled you become and the more likely you are to live it.

To increase the effectiveness of the visualization, consider combining your visualization with reading your written goals. The combination of written goals, passionate speaking, and visualization is extremely powerful.

And to add even more power, you can also use external pictures, images, and symbols associated with your goal!

Image Board Power

Some people build collages, or image boards, with pictures cut out from magazines. Make these collages or image boards colorful, with as many pictures as you can find of your dream. Then, put that image somewhere you see it everyday.

Inner and outer imaging works!

When NASA was working on putting a man on the moon they had a huge picture of the moon covering the entire wall of their main construction area. Everyone was clear on the goal and they reached that goal two years ahead of schedule.

You see it in real life when you first see it as an image.

All things happen first in mind, then in reality.

Writing it Down

INTEGRATION CHECKLIST

Things you will need

A creative mind

Your journal

A quiet space to think and write

Integration-Related Activity

The goal of this activity is for you to play with the power of visualization so you can become better skilled at visualizing your life with your goal complete.

With effective visualization, you create a masterful inner picture that supports focusing your mind to attract what you want.

Learning to Image Exercise

It is time for us to play with the power of visualization.

The following exercise gives you practice with imaging. The better and more skilled you are at imagining, the better the visualization and the more benefit you receive.

- Imagine you are holding half a lemon. Now take a bite of it. Can you taste how bitter and sour it is in your mouth. Is your mouth watering like you have just bitten into a lemon?
- Imagine the taste of your favorite treat. Mmmm - notice how great it tastes. Feel the texture on your tongue. Can you taste it? Can you see a picture of yourself enjoying your favorite treat?
- Imagine a larger-than-life size, purple elephant with yellow polka dots. You probably see the elephant, at least for a moment. It's easier to see larger images. Change the elephant to a pink elephant with purple fringe around its trunk and running down its legs. Change it again to a yellow elephant with blue ears, a pink trunk, and a candy cane hung from its tusks. See how easy it is to visualize?

- Visualize your front door. You've walked through the door many times. Visualize it as if you were walking right though it. What color is the door? What color is the door handle, and how is it shaped? Do you have to step up as you walk in? What color is the floor inside the door? What color are the walls?
- See a picture of the chair, and then see a picture of yourself sitting in the chair. Imagine yourself sitting down in your favorite chair. Feel how the chair would feel against your body. Let yourself sink into the chair in your mind. Feel the sense of relaxation you feel when you sit in your favorite chair.
- While still in this imagining, add in the sound of the phone ringing, or the TV playing, or both. Hear voices talking around you, just as if you had friends or family around you. Imagine the faces of your loved ones. Practice feeling how you would feel if they were actually in front of you. This visualization is a combination of feeling, seeing, and hearing.
- Build your image of having achieved your goal. First, what would you be seeing? Then, add in what you would be hearing, and then add in what you would be feeling.

See It Coming NOW

Imagine your goal achieved and imagine yourself living your life with it achieved. This is the future you are moving into.

Make a commitment to visualize your goal daily to set the attractor factor into play.

What action might you take to remind yourself to visualize your goal daily so your future is filled with a life you love?

Day 10 **Focus Your Mind**

This session is about focusing your mind.

I have a dream

Martin Luther King

Note. 210,000 gathered at the Washington Monument in August 1963 and marched to the Lincoln Memorial, where the high point of the day was this speech by Martin Luther King. He had written it in longhand the night before and did not finish it until 4am.

I say to you today, my friends, that in spite of the difficulties and frustrations of the moment I still have a dream. It is a dream deeply rooted in the American dream.

I have a dream that one day this nation will rise up and live out the true meaning of its creed: 'We hold these truths to be self-evident; that all men are created equal.'

I have a dream that one day on the red hills of Georgia the sons of former slaves and the sons of former slave owners will be able to sit down together at the table of brotherhood.

I have a dream that one day even the state of Mississippi, a desert state sweltering with the heat of injustice and oppression, will be transformed into an oasis of freedom and justice.

I have a dream that my four little children will one day live in a nation where they will not be judged by the color of their skin but by the content of their character.

I have a dream today.

I have a dream that one day the State of Alabama, whose governor's lips are presently dripping with the words of interposition and nullification, will be transformed into a situation where little black boys and black girls will be able to join hands with little white boys and white girls and walk together as sisters and brothers. I have a dream today.

I have a dream that one day every valley shall be exalted, every hill and mountain shall be made low, the rough place will be made plains, and the crooked places will be made straight, and the glory of the Lord shall be revealed, and all flesh shall see it together.

This is our hope. This is the faith with which I return to the South. With this faith we will be able to hew out of the mountain of despair a stone of hope. With this faith we will be able to transform the jangling discords of our nation into a beautiful symphony of brotherhood. With this faith we will be able to work together, to pray together, to struggle together, to go to jail together, to stand up for freedom together, knowing that we will be free one day.

This will be the day when all of God's children will be able to sing with new meaning:

My country, 'tis of thee,
Sweet land of liberty,
Of thee I sing:
Land where my fathers died,
Land of the pilgrim's pride,
From every mountainside
Let freedom ring.

And if America is to be a great nation this must become true.
So let freedom ring from the prodigious hilltops of New Hampshire.
Let freedom ring from the mighty mountains of New York.
Let freedom ring from the heightening Alleghenies of Pennsylvania!
Let freedom ring from the snow-capped Rockies of Colorado!
Let freedom ring from the curvaceous peaks of California!
But not only that; let freedom ring from Stone Mountain of Georgia!
Let freedom ring from Lookout Mountain of Tennessee!
Let freedom ring from every hill and molehill of Mississippi.
From every mountainside, let freedom ring.

We let freedom ring, we let it ring from every village and every hamlet, from every state and every city, we will be able to speed up that day when all of God's children, black men and white men, Jews and Gentiles, Protestants and Catholics, will be able to join hands and sing in the words of the old Negro spiritual,
'Free at last! Free at last! Thank God almighty, we are free at last!'

As we have said many times before, all things are created twice - first in mind, then in reality. Just as we see, hear, taste, touch, and smell in the outside world, we also recreate those same sensations in our mind by "**re-presenting**" the world to ourselves using our five senses inwardly.

Many years ago I read a quote by an unknown author:

Master's Tip "Watch your thoughts, they become your words.
Watch your words, they become your actions.
Watch your actions, they become your habits.
Watch your habits, they become your character.
Watch your character, it becomes your destiny."

When you think of this course, there are many aspects to it. And your choice of how you view, act, and re-act to the information determines your destiny.

For example, you could place your attention on the time it takes, the energy required, or the scheduling you have to do. In other words, you concentrate on what many people consider the **negatives** or the challenges associated with the course for you - the things you wished were not present, the time it takes, the feelings that come up, the time you need to face something about yourself that you know is true but wish were not true.

On the other hand, you could choose to concentrate on the **positives**, such as the long-term benefits of investing the time and showing up powerfully to do the work. You could think about how great it is to be in charge of your thinking and acting, where you are no longer side-swiped by feelings you have trouble dealing with or bounced around by life's events.

Focus Forward

Do you remember those seats in station wagons that faced backward so you could look out of the rear view window? They allow you to see where you have been, what you are moving away from - which can be interesting for a while. But wouldn't you rather be in the driver's seat of your life, focusing on where you are going - on getting to your destination, rather than living life looking out the back window?

Thinking of this course as a journey, you can use your mind to be a passenger and watch what you are moving away from or you can put yourself in the driver's seat and have your thoughts move you towards your purpose.

When you are focused on moving away from something, as a passenger looking back, you often end up concentrating on what you want to stay away from, what you are scared of, what you are anxious about, what you are troubled by, what you are angry about, what you are uncomfortable with - basically all the things you want to avoid.

It probably won't surprise you to learn that we often take a passenger position in our lives - most of our thoughts are unconscious and happen without us even being aware of them.

Be in the Driver's Seat

You can learn to be the driver in your life - to use your mind consciously, deliberately, on purpose, with intention. And your driving skills - how effectively you move towards your destination - determine how you feel and the results you get in life.

If you spend your life taking the passenger role with your mind, letting your mind wander, thinking about the negative things in your past or what you don't like about your life, you often have unpleasant feelings - like feeling disheartened, angry, anxious, annoyed, panicky, resentful, jealous, hostile, discouraged, or even physically ill. Wow! Think about that! When we think about the negative aspects of something, negativity creeps into our entire being. Consider that this is the single-most cause of self-destructive behavior, emotional pain, and suffering.

It's true that even in the driver's seat, where your mind is consciously choosing your thoughts, you can have unpleasant emotional experiences. For example, if you live your life "looking in the review mirror" at the annoyances behind you, you are more likely to get into an accident. While you might avoid what is behind you, when you continually look back, you can easily collide with what is in front of you.

The Power of Thought

We don't usually think of thoughts as things. However, consider that your thoughts are very powerful and they might be things. Every time you think of something, you make a representation or **re-presentation** of it in the form of an image, sound, or feeling. And this thought creates an emotion - anxiety, happiness, sadness, love, frustration, exhilaration, peace - inside your mind, which influences how you think and act, and ultimately determines what you have in life.

Let's test this theory about our thoughts.

Think of yourself when you were really young coming home from school. As you walk through the door, you can feel the warmth of the oven and smell the scent of your favorite meal. Do you remember that? Just let your mind go back there for a moment and enjoy it. What was cooking? Was it fresh bread, a favorite casserole? Maybe pizza or roast beef? Whatever it was, think of it.

Okay, now come back to the present. Did you notice what happened?

Your thoughts -- in the form of a picture, a smell, or a taste -- created an experience; and all of the positive thoughts that were associated with that experience came with the pictures. Did you notice that you started feeling good? Perhaps you remembered sitting around the table with someone, leaning back in your chair, telling stories, and laughing.

Okay, let's try the test again.

This time think of a time when you sat down at the dinner table and you were served something you didn't like, something that for you smelled and tasted yucky!

Experience that time now. Remember how you didn't want to eat it. Did you make a big fuss? Maybe the taste was not at all enjoyable. Notice what that feels like in your body.

Okay, come back again to the present.

This memory was likely a very mild experience, but was there a part of you that didn't feel good when you visited that moment - a part that said, ***"Auk, I don't want this."*** that created a less-than-perfect feeling in your body?

Negative Images

Let's continue to play with this concept for a moment. Think of a time that you were unhappy or a moment when you were definitely not feeling on top of the world. Have it?

Notice what you were thinking about in that moment.

Perhaps you were thinking of how disappointed you were in your husband because you didn't want him to do what he did.

Or, perhaps you remembered when you couldn't pay your bills because you didn't have enough money.

Or, did you think about how your career wasn't fulfilling because you made the wrong choice with your education.

Or, how you didn't want your puppy to be sick?

Or, how you didn't want to look stupid in public?

Or, how you didn't want your boss to criticize your work?

Recall what you were thinking about in that moment.

Now think about what message you were sending your mind and what message your mind was ultimately sending you. That message was most likely about what you did not want to be, do, or have in whatever was happening in that moment. And it wasn't stated as something you did not want, it was something that you were moving away from. Right?

For example, consider the statement, ***"I just want to get my desk organized!"*** The motivation behind this goal is based in moving away from the clutter on the desk.

PONDER: How does your body feel? Where in your body do you feel this?

Positive Images

Now think about a time you felt great - a time you felt fully alive, on top of the world, completely joyful.

Notice what you were thinking about then.

Were you thinking about what a beautiful day it was?

Or how much you loved your child?

Or how lucky you are to live where you live?

Or how beautiful your wife or husband was?

Or how wonderful it felt to float in the ocean?

Or how great it was to be with your family?

Or how you could purchase your dream car?

What was the message or image you generated in your mind? Was it positive? Was it about what you loved about your life in that moment? The positive images you created in your mind informed what you felt and how you acted in that moment. And as you remembered that time, your response was a positive experience - perhaps feeling relaxed, loving, friendly, fulfilled, or alive. Am I right again?

PONDER: How does your body feel? Where in your body do you feel this?

MASTER'S TIP Your mind is a very powerful instrument. As Steve Covey says in 7 Habits of Highly Effective People, "Everything is created first in mind and then in reality."

Think of the computer you use or the chair you might be sitting in. Some genius created this in his mind. He had an idea, a spark of inspiration around what he wanted to create and then took action to make it a reality. The mind creates a blueprint of what is possible, and if you continue to place your attention on the blueprint, intend to make it real, and take action accordingly, what is possible translates into reality.

Focus on Positive Thoughts

Remember the traveler with his clean shoes in his bag and his aching feet? Talk about painful! Placing attention on the rocks when relief is at hand. Consider that the way to move past suffering and into goal achievement is to concentrate on what is available to you and to put your attention on driving your mind toward what you want.

Have you ever noticed how we steer horses and dogs? They go the way we make their heads and eyes go. Study after study shows that our bodies - and our lives - go where our minds go. If you place your attention on the rocks you definitely find them because they are all around you.

When we place our mind on what we want, that's where we go. With this in mind - literally- it is vitally important to take action to drive your mind towards what you want by concentrating on your desired results rather than on what stands in your way or what you don't want.

Try this. Say to yourself: ***"I don't want to be poor."***

What happened? You created an image in your mind of being poor, right? Our minds do not register negatives. Even though your words were intended to have you moving away from poverty, your brain saw yourself in poverty. And to top it off - your brain takes that image, thinks it is what you want, and starts to make it happen, even if this is not your intention. Talk about self-destruction rather than creation!

Think of your mind as a **go-get-it** device working in conjunction with the Universe. When you put your attention on something, your mind and the Universe think you want more of it and they work together to find ways to create it for you. And, the more attention you put on something framed in the negative, the worse you feel and the more likely you are to attract it into your life. Now there's a vicious cycle.

As you are doing your best to run away from a big boulder called poverty, an important question is: Where are you running to? What do you really want?

If your answer is: ***"Well, of course, I want to have money!"***, notice that your original motivating factor was moving away from being poor. And the way the mind and the Universe work, you are more likely to create poverty in your life than wealth because you are putting your attention on the poverty.

Focus Study

A friend told me about a study to find out how Anthony Robbins and Donald Trump were focusing their minds when it came to money and wealth. Each was asked what they wanted, and both said they wanted to be wealthier. However, when asked why wealth was important, Mr. Robbins answered that if he had more money he could contribute in a bigger way. He was "moving toward something". Donald Trump's answer was that he was poor as a child and didn't want to have that experience ever again! Mr. Trump was "moving away from poverty". The fascinating thing about this is the analysis of the financial history of the two gentlemen. Anthony Robbin's wealth has consistently increased through time while Mr. Trump's has ridden a financial roller coaster throughout his career. Isn't this amazing?

Let's look at a more subtle example. Suppose you say, "I want to lose 20lbs." Your attention is on what you want - losing 20 lbs. You create an image in your mind of being 20 lbs lighter. You've put yourself in the driver's seat but are looking in the rearview mirror. The energy behind this goal is moving away from those 20lbs. The big boulder this time is that extra 20 lbs you want to run from. And sometimes the final result is that you do lose this weight, but then you relax and put the weight back on. Can you relate to this at all?

If you are focused on being a certain weight and the energy behind it is about something you really do want, re-present the concept to your mind. Drive your mind toward your destination! Put your attention on moving toward the new, lighter you.

You might wonder why someone would spend time thinking about what they don't want or focusing on the negative. Like Mr. Trump, often a past trauma or experience is a powerful memory and we think: "I don't ever want to experience something like this again!" Consequently, you go out of your way to avoid the hurt again. The irony here is that to avoid the hurt you spend time watching out for it. And when you put your attention on it, you unconsciously create it and end up feeling bad. This is a terrible cycle - so how can we end it?

While the answer is simple, the implementation takes tremendous commitment and self-awareness.

Notice Your Thinking

The key to ending the negative-thought cycle is to notice when you are thinking or concentrating on the negative, when your mind is placing attention on what you don't want, or when you are running from a big boulder.

And how might you notice that?

First, notice when you have negative feelings such as anxiety, self consciousness, depression, insecurity, despair, animosity, annoyance, suspicion, anger, stress, shame, loneliness, envy, and so on. Then stop, take a curious scientist posture and notice your mind's thoughts.

Ponder: What am I thinking about?

Ponder: Are my thoughts framed in the negative?

Another way to tell is to listen to your inner and outer dialog. Is there any **negation** when you are speaking? Are you focused on moving away from something or focused on what you don't want? When you hear yourself say -

I am troubled by ...

I am disappointed by...

I want her to stop...

I don't want him to...

I am angry about...

or any time you hear yourself say

Not, no, don't, avoid, bad -

STOP! You are concentrating on negative desires.

Again, take the curious scientist posture and notice what you are doing inside of yourself. Remember that the negative views in your mind are often associated with negative experiences from the past, so be patient with yourself and gently keep guiding your mind back to a positive view of what you want.

Listen Attentively

As you listen to the words of your inner and outer dialog, notice the tone, pitch, and speed of your speaking. It often changes when you are putting your attention on something negative.

Try this the next time you feel bad. Stop and then be curious with yourself: *"Hmmmm... I am feeling badly. What am I thinking about?"*

PONDER: What do I really want in this situation?

Notice the motivation behind what you want.

PONDER: What is the true intention behind what I want?

PONDER: What is the energy behind what I want that is motivating me?

PONDER: Am I moving toward something or away from something?

When you feel that your intention serves the highest good and is best for yourself and everyone involved, then put yourself in the driver's seat with your mind - immediately!

PONDER: What is within my control to start being, doing, or having right now?

The energy behind what you do determines your success through time. So check out your intention.

Move Toward Your Desires

Only you know if you are moving more toward what you want or away from what you don't want. Only you know your **true** intention. The better you feel about the intention behind what you want and the more you concentrate on it through time, the more likely you are to get it and the better you will feel.

If you notice that your mind has taken the passenger position, moving away from something, or you notice you are in the driver's seat, but spending most of your time cursing in the rearview mirror, gently invite your mind back to what you are aiming towards.

MASTER'S TIP Looking forward while you drive will transform your life.

Training yourself to drive your mind rather than taking the passenger position may seem like a monotonous or perhaps rigorous process, but consider the long-term value.

A Mind in Training

Let's review the steps one more time:

1. Notice when you have a negative feeling in your body - depression, anxiety, anger, loneliness, dread, annoyance, distress, insecurity, or whatever other negative feeling you might have.
2. Be aware of what you are paying attention to or concentrating on in the moment.
3. Invite your mind to think about what you **do** want in the situation.
4. Notice the true intention behind what you want.
   Is it who you really are?
   Are you moving toward something or away from something?
   If you were at your best right now, how would you think and act in this situation?
5. Determine what is within your control so you can start to get what you want now.
6. Take action on whatever is within your control. And do it **now**!

If you notice you have a negative feeling come up again, repeat the process. Be patient with yourself and gently guide your mind back to positive thoughts. You didn't learn to drive comfortably in one lesson! But I bet now you can drive without thinking about it much. The same is true with being the driver of your mind.

Factors in Change

Changing your thoughts to what you want doesn't necessarily mean you automatically feel better. There are a number of factors that affect the change. Here are the top five.

- **How much are you in the present moment?** You have to be in the present moment, not thinking about what you wanted in the past and didn't get.
- **How much do you want it?** The more you want it, the better you feel.
- **How much is within your control?** The more it is within your control, the better you feel.
- **How much is your true intention who you really are?** The more your intention reflects who you are and the greater good, the better you feel.
- **How much are you moving toward what you want, instead of moving away from something you don't want?** The more the energy behind what you want is moving toward something, the better you feel.

When your mind is in the present moment, what you want is something you **really** want, your true intention is who you are and it is within your control to get it, you will feel fantastic and are unstoppable in moving towards a bright future.

Master's Tip Build the muscle of focusing your mind effectively today. Your quality of life depends on it!

Writing it Down

INTEGRATION CHECKLIST

Things you will need

Your journal

A quiet space to think and write

Integration-Related Activity

The goal of this activity is for you to notice how you are currently using your mind and then to learn to focus your mind on the positive. With this knowledge, you can create a masterful plan on how to reach your goal powerfully.

IMPORTANT INSTRUCTION **BE SURE TO HAVE SOME TIME TO WRITE.**

Focusing Exercise

Consider that what you learn in this session is the most important of all the sessions because how you focus your mind is the key to living a life you love.

WRITTEN ACTIVITY **WRITE DOWN FIVE TIMES IN YOUR PAST WHEN YOU FELT BAD ABOUT YOURSELF OR SOMEONE IN YOUR LIFE, OR TIMES WHEN YOU WERE IN A FORM OF MENTAL, EMOTIONAL, SPIRITUAL, OR SOCIAL GRIEF.**

Perhaps you felt bad about a family member, a friend, a boss, a romantic partner, or the world in general. Perhaps your cat passed away, you failed an exam, you got a divorce, the war happened, the election happened, your car stopped running, or you lost your job. Just think of 5 times you were in pain - mental, emotional, spiritual or social grief - and write them down now.

Now look at your list and think about each of these events.

Ask yourself: What was I putting my attention on in each moment?

Ask yourself: Was I focused on what I wanted or didn't want?

Ask yourself: Was I moving towards something or away from something?

Written Activity Now write down five times in your past you felt really great about yourself, or someone in your life or times you felt mental, emotional, spiritual, or social enjoyment.

Perhaps you felt great about a family member, a friend, a boss, a romantic partner, or the world in general. Maybe the event was your wedding, when you found out you had a new job, when your first child was born, when you bought plane tickets to Spain, when you bought a new car you knew you could afford, when you got an excellent grade in school, or fell in love.

Now think about each of these events.

Ask yourself: What was I putting my attention on in each moment?

Ask yourself: Was I focused on what I wanted or didn't want?

Ask yourself: Was I moving towards something or away from something?

Ask yourself: What was I doing differently with my mind in the times you felt good?

Ask yourself: Was there an obvious difference in my two answers with respect to how I was focusing my mind and how I felt?

Ask yourself: What's the learning in this?

Handling Challenges with Ease

1. Write 3 difficult situations you handled successfully.

   - ❐
   - ❐
   - ❐

2. Write 3 difficult situations you handled less well.

   - ❐
   - ❐
   - ❐

3. Next to each item you just wrote down, rate yourself from 0 to 10 on how clearly you knew what you wanted.

   0 = You didn't know what you wanted because you were completely focused on what you didn't want or you were moving away from something

   10 = You knew what you wanted and were completely focused on getting it and were powerfully moving toward something.

When considering your rating:

Ask yourself: What did I notice here?

Most people realize that if they are focused on what they don't want in challenging situations, they are likely to handle the situation poorly. However, if they focus their mind on what they do want, and take action accordingly, they can handle any difficult challenge.

Master's Tip You have to focus on what you want if you are ever going to get it.

Focus on Your Goal

Think of the goal that you have for this 30-Day Journey.

Ask yourself: How much of my energy is focused on moving towards something I do want?

Ask yourself: How much of my energy is focused on moving away from something I do not want?

Rate yourself on a scale from 0 to 10

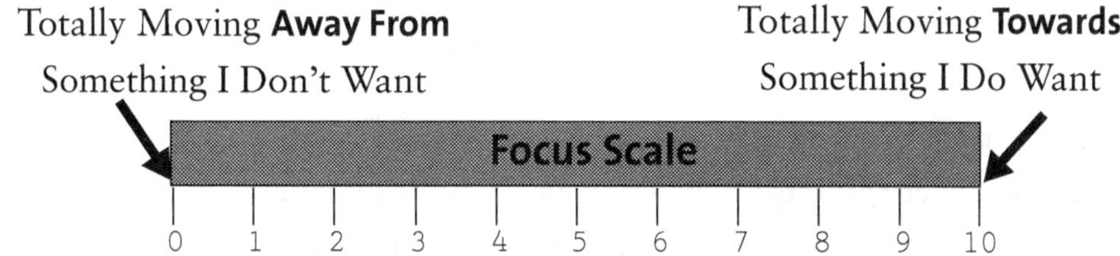

If you are less than a 10, notice your rating.

Ask yourself: What might I do differently to move my number up one notch so that I start to shift the energy towards something that inspires me?

Focus on Your Focus

Now it is time for some very important fieldwork.

Throughout the next week, carry a piece of paper with you.

- Every time you notice yourself focusing on what you do want, make a note of it.
- When you notice yourself focusing on what you don't want, also make a note on your paper. Then, stop and ask yourself, ***"What do I want?"*** and gently change your focus. Also ask: ***"What is within my control to start to get what I want?"*** and take action accordingly.
- At the end of each day note how many marks you have in each area.

Consider continuing this fieldwork for at least a week to clarify how you are currently using your mind.

Here's to focusing on and moving towards what you want, and making powerful choice after powerful choice.

Focus Your Mind NOW

Imagine if you were able to focus your mind so that whenever a negative thought came to mind, you could immediately refocus to take action on what is within your control.

Knowing that what you want and focusing on it starts a magnetic pull to bring you incredible success and happiness, what are you willing to do now?

What action might you take to remind yourself to focus on positive thoughts, and take action towards your goal to live a life you love?

Day 11 **Meditate and Read**

This session is about accessing the resources within and learning from the genius of the people who have gone before us.

A Story

A Brief Tale

Thinking Makes It So

Anthony de Mello, One Minute Wisdom, Image Books, 1985

"Nothing is good or bad, but thinking makes it so," the Master said.

When asked to explain he said, "A man cheerfully observed a religious fast seven days a week. His neighbor starved to death on the same diet."

Meditate daily

Unlock your wisdom and inner resources by making meditation a daily routine. This practice has worked for millions of years and when part of your daily practice, it helps you live your life on purpose every day, in every way.

Ideally, spend at least 30 minutes of your day in meditation. However, even giving yourself five minutes at the beginning and end of each day supports tapping into the flow of life.

Master's Tip Meditation is a wonderful way to connect your mind, body, and spirit to things beyond your conscious mind.

Self-discovery comes from giving yourself time with yourself. In the quiet of meditation you can tune into the deep inner truth of your life. And your brain can access unconscious resources.

Many people find that meditation helps them reach a large collective unconsciousness that holds many answers. Regardless of your beliefs, meditation helps you achieve goals as you tune into the Universe of greater ideas already at work.

Begin to Meditate

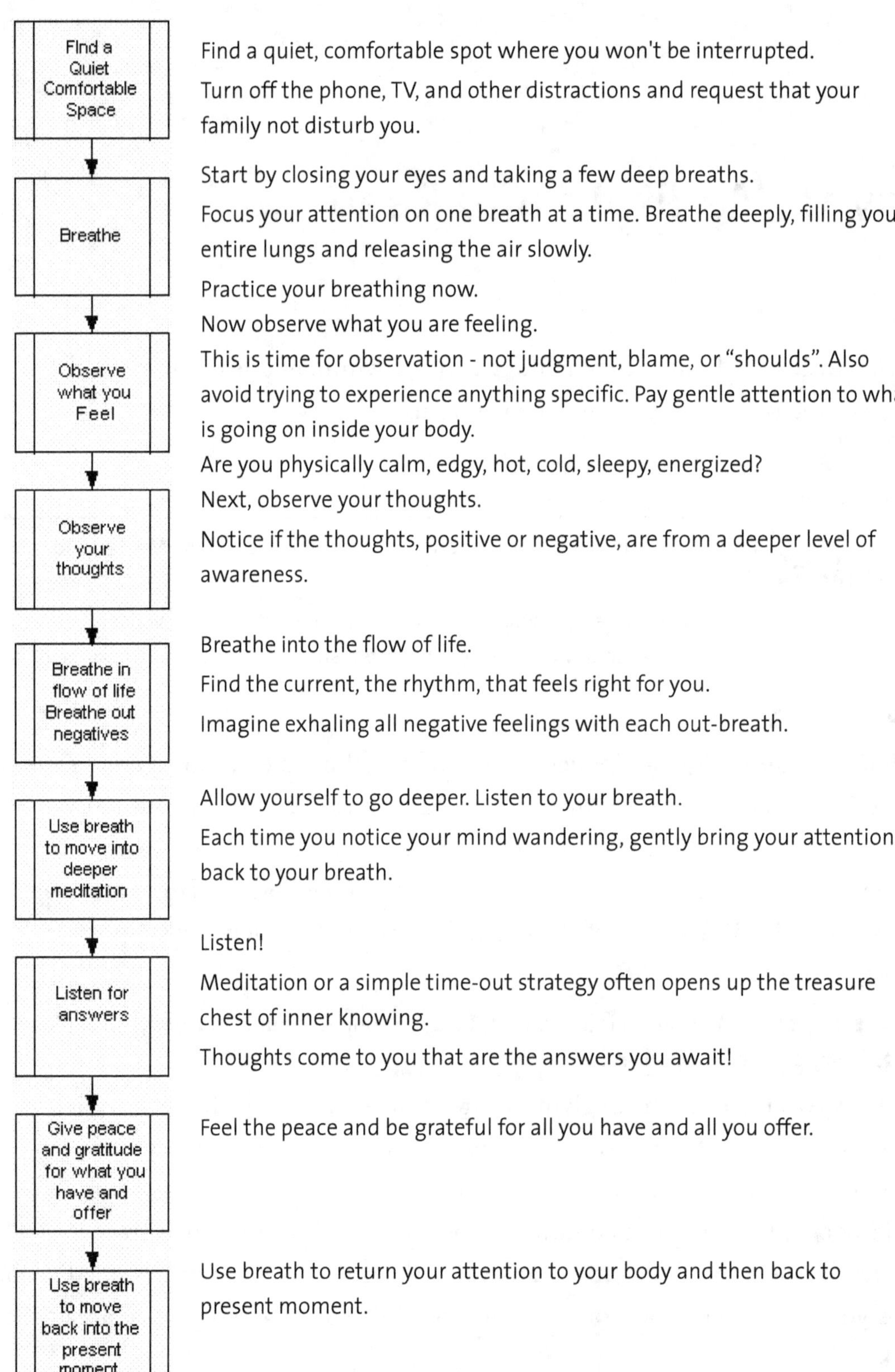

Find a quiet, comfortable spot where you won't be interrupted.

Turn off the phone, TV, and other distractions and request that your family not disturb you.

Start by closing your eyes and taking a few deep breaths.

Focus your attention on one breath at a time. Breathe deeply, filling your entire lungs and releasing the air slowly.

Practice your breathing now.

Now observe what you are feeling.

This is time for observation - not judgment, blame, or “shoulds”. Also avoid trying to experience anything specific. Pay gentle attention to what is going on inside your body.

Are you physically calm, edgy, hot, cold, sleepy, energized?

Next, observe your thoughts.

Notice if the thoughts, positive or negative, are from a deeper level of awareness.

Breathe into the flow of life.

Find the current, the rhythm, that feels right for you.

Imagine exhaling all negative feelings with each out-breath.

Allow yourself to go deeper. Listen to your breath.

Each time you notice your mind wandering, gently bring your attention back to your breath.

Listen!

Meditation or a simple time-out strategy often opens up the treasure chest of inner knowing.

Thoughts come to you that are the answers you await!

Feel the peace and be grateful for all you have and all you offer.

Use breath to return your attention to your body and then back to present moment.

A few years ago I was really lost, fussing and stewing for months around making a decision; and I still didn't know what to do. I remember asking for guidance around making the right choice, and knew I needed to start a meditation practice that supported accessing the truth. When I took up meditation, the decision was easy. I came to the understanding that the truth is beauty and the beauty is truth, and as soon as I awoke to this, I knew the best decision to make.

Meditation is very powerful. The answers may come in different ways and on different timelines, but they do come - if we listen. Sometimes we're directed to call a certain person, read a certain book or live from a certain value.

Read about Enlightened Leaders

In addition to meditation, it's useful to add 30 minutes of reading to your 30 minutes of meditation every day. We don't mean reading the latest thriller, romance novel, or the newspaper! We mean reading inspirational books about people who achieved what you want, or about ways to get what you want.

Master's Tip A reading time investment helps keep you focused and accessing the best information from the masters.

Many people have gone before us, leaving maps and guides to model some of the best known and most proven wisdom, information, methods, strategies, and secrets that have ever been recorded. All we have to do is apply these universal principles to our own life, in our own way. Reading supports you in doing this. Apply the principles you discover in your life. The results will be miraculous.

Invest in Meditation

If you really want to live your best life, investing 30 minutes in reading uplifting material and 30 minutes in meditation is a small investment for the gains you'll make, the insights you will have and the connection you will feel. These two 30 minute periods will help you achieve that magnetic pull, pulling your dream towards you! And if 30 minutes seems too challenging with your current schedule, start with 10 minutes.

Meditating and Reading

INTEGRATION CHECKLIST

Things you will need

Your journal

A quiet space to think and write

Integration-Related Activity

The goal of this activity is to begin to develop the habit of meditating and reading daily.

It takes 21 days to develop a habit, and the way to track how well you are doing is to write it down. With this knowledge, you can create a masterful plan that incorporates meditation and reading into your daily life.

Meditation Focusing Exercise

The only way to meditate is to do it!

MASTER'S TIP Schedule meditation into your day and make it a priority.

You can meditate for one long period, or several short periods, whatever works best for you and your schedule.

Create a quiet, comfortable place where you will not be disturbed. Turn off the phone, TV, and other distractions. Request that your family not disturb you.

Focusing techniques

The method of focusing on your breath is an excellent method for beginners. Some people prefer to count their breaths, some time their breaths with counting. There is no right or wrong way.

Some people meditate by focusing their attention on a candle flame, or silently repeat a mantra inside their head to focus their attention. You know you are meditating when your normal rapid flow of thoughts slows down and stops.

When a thought does come to you, notice it, observe it, and let it go without getting caught up in the content of the thought, or the emotion it brings. Meditation is a time of calmness.

Activity Before Meditation

For some people, it can be helpful to exercise before meditation.

Exercise releases many of the stress hormones that excite us and make us easily agitated or aggravated. The flow of oxygen-enriched blood from exercise also helps. We're not suggesting that you run several miles or go straight from the boxing ring to meditation time. Too much exercise can have you too stimulated to meditate.

A Personal Practice

Meditation is a deeply personal practice. It is a practice, because we meditate, over and over, rather than meditating just once.

The main benefits of meditation come from regular daily practice.

Track Your Progress

To build forward motion and create a habit, keep track of how often you meditate, and for how long.

You might want to use a chart similar to the following one.

DATE I MEDITATED	LENGTH OF MEDITATION	DATE I MEDITATED	LENGTH OF MEDITATION

Reading Habits

Before we finish this exercise, let's remember that there are many benefits to reading about the techniques that other people use to succeed.

Why reinvent the wheel when there are many books that can tell you how to reach your goal effectively and efficiently?

Ask yourself: What five books, that could help me achieve my goal, have I been intending to read but, for whatever reason, have not yet done so?

-
-
-
-
-

Ask yourself: Just suppose a miracle happened and I naturally committed to adding reading related to my goal to my daily practice, what might I be doing differently?

A Tracking System

Keep track of how often you read, and for how long.

You might want to use a chart similar to the following one.

DATE	TIME	WHAT I READ

DATE	TIME	WHAT I READ

Break State Meditation

You now know that it is useful to build in moments of consciousness into your day, preventing stress from affecting you and increasing your energy and focus.

There are many ways to connect to the moment **now**. One of the easiest ways is to connect to the body while focusing all your senses inward.

Let's try this active break-state meditation together.

1. Begin by concentrating on the feeling of your right foot.
   How does the shoe feel against your foot? Or your socks?
   Feel your toes, each one touching the next.
   How about the feeling in your right ankle?
   And how does the sole of your foot feel?
   And the top of your big toe?
   Reach out with your right foot and tap the floor.
   Feel how your foot feels when you tap the floor.

2. Now concentrate on the feeling of your left foot.
   Feel the shoe feel against your foot. Now your socks...
   Feel your toes, each one touching the next.
   How about the feeling in your right ankle?
   And how does the sole of your foot feel?
   And the top of your big toe?
   Reach out with your left foot and tap the floor.
   Feel how your foot feels when you tap the floor.

3. Feel how your hands feel.
   Reach with one hand and touch the other.
   Really concentrate on how it feels to touch one hand with the other.
   With your hands together, lift your hands and touch your face, feeling with great attention exactly how your face feels to be touched, and how your hand feels to be touching.

4. Slowly run your hand over your hair, or through your hair. Really concentrate on how your scalp feels, as your hair and the scalp are touched.

5. Bring your hand down and over your eyes.
   Close your eyes, and feel how they feel to be closed, with a hand resting over top of your closed eyes.

6. Slowly bring your hand down over your throat, and rest it in your lap, feeling the touch of your hand and the movement of air against your skin.

For an instant calming effect, this simple exercise or a variation of it, can be performed anywhere at any time.

Meditate and Read NOW

Imagine if you pampered yourself every day by giving yourself the gift of connecting to the Universe and connecting to the wisdom of the ages!

Make a commitment to move towards peace and calm by adding meditation and reading into your life daily.

Knowing it would lead to less stress and more satisfaction in life, would you be willing to take time daily to practice?

Now, knowing that meditating and reading provides you answers on how to get exactly what you wanted in life, what are you willing to do today to start meditating and reading? What action might you take to remind yourself to gift yourself both meditation and reading time?

Part 4: **Plan**

Now that you have built a strong foundation for reaching your goal, created a vision to help you reach it, and made a powerful choice to go for it, it is time to plan your journey.

The next phase of the 30-day program is three days during which you create a plan of the actions that take you to your goal.

The architect has a solid foundation, has designed the home, and decided to build it. It's time now to determine the phases of construction so the house will be completed on schedule.

As you continue to be the architect of your life, creating the blueprints for success, we share with you the secrets of being the construction coordinator - determining what must be completed first and then how to proceed. For example, you must have the walls done before the roof is put on.

Journals

Your journal continues to fill up. Your blueprint is becoming better defined so you can reach your goal.

What should be in it now? It's time to take yet another look. Check out your blueprint and make certain that you have completed all the details - done the exercises you might have skipped or put extra effort into ones you might have found challenging. Make sure you are ready for construction of your goal.

3-Day Planning Overview

The first five days of your journey were about building a foundation. The next two were about inspiration and vision, learning to live **your** dream. Then you spent four days learning how to make your decision powerful and compelling. These next three days are for planning. It's time now to specifically plan how you are going to reach your goal.

In **Day 12** you learn to create a plan, step-by-step. We invite you to build your staircase to success, putting in landings so you can stop and enjoy the view as you climb to the top and reach your goal.

In **Day 13** you learn to let go when things aren't going exactly as you planned. No blueprint is perfect - so when the flaws of your plan surface, learn what you can and forge ahead.

In **Day 14** we invite you to reward your small successes - to play a bit along the road to your destination, so you continue to infuse energy and desire into reaching your destination.

If you've ever built a home, you know that there is much joy in watching the foundation be poured, the walls go up, and the plumbing or electrical wiring complete. With each stage the house is closer to completion, but there are a lot of stages along the way.

As you journey up your staircase, sit a bit at each landing and ponder on how wonderful the view is from where you have already climbed.

Are you ready?

CHECKLIST

- Be sure you have your journal.
- Set a time aside each day to do your life's work.

Day 12 **Climb Your Staircase**

This session is about reaching your goal by climbing to it one-step-at-a-time, taking breathers at landings along the way.

If you want to read something inspirational, consider the real life story of the beginnings of human exploration of space with "Apollo 13" and "The Right Stuff".

When Neil Armstrong landed on the moon he declared,
"That's one small step for man, one giant leap for mankind."

The corks came out when the "eagle landed" and the citizens of the world celebrated and marveled at the accomplishment. Everyone at NASA knew that the moon was only one stop in a journey to reach the furthest galaxy; and yet, reaching earth's nearest terrestrial satellite was clearly no less an accomplishment than landing on Mars.

How might you make your goal happen? What is within your control to do now? If it doesn't happen exactly as you would prefer, then what is your contingency plan? How can you make this journey even more meaningful for you and for others?

Significant offerings, or what some see as big successes, are built from a series of smaller accomplishments. Once you break down your goal into **doable** chunks, you can begin to accomplish the small tasks you determine lead to achieving your larger goal.

Take Small Steps

The small successes are like steps towards your big goal and help you to live your life on purpose. One of the important keys to getting what you want is to have planned a series of smaller accomplishments, or steps, that lead you to your goal.

Think of a staircase. Each step leads to another. The reason we have staircases is because having a staircase makes reaching the second floor possible! Without the staircase, it's an awfully large step!

Climb Your Staircase

Your plan is your staircase to your goal. Be aware, however, that looking at the staircase is different than climbing it. Creating the perfect plan to move forward is not the same as taking the action itself. While research, preparation, and detailed planning are very important, some people get so bogged down in the planning that they do not take action and climb the staircase plan they created.

Ever seen a really long staircase, one that just goes up and up? It seems like a lot of work to climb a set of stairs like that, doesn't it? You get tired legs and possibly a little winded.

Create Landings

The great thing about long staircases is that they usually have landings - points where you can stop and rest, then get going again.

Break your plan down into mini-goals that are like the landings on the staircase. Each mini-goal then breaks down into action steps. Each action step, once accomplished, leads you higher. When you've accomplished enough action steps, you'll be at a landing, where you can stop, take a breather, and check out the next set of stairs, or your next set of actions to lead you to the top of the stairs, your goal.

Landings allow us to evaluate where we've been and where we are going. They provide an opportunity to stop and take stock.

PONDER: Is our plan working?

PONDER: Are we on track to getting the goal?

PONDER: Are we as close as we want to be at this point?

PONDER: How might we climb the stairs more effectively and efficiently?

PONDER: Is there a way to make this better, faster, easier?

PONDER: Can the steps be made easier to take?

MASTER'S TIP Each step is a little success that builds to the achievement of our goal!

Climbing Your Staircase

INTEGRATION CHECKLIST

Things you will need

Your journal

A quiet space to think and write

Integration-Related Activity

The goal of this activity is for you to modify your plan into small action steps that lead you to accomplish your big goal and complete your 30-day journey successfully. With this knowledge, you can create a number of masterful mini-plans to move you forward to Enlightened Internal Leadership.

IMPORTANT INSTRUCTION **BE SURE TO HAVE YOUR WORK FROM DAYS 4 AND 7.**

Planning Exercise

In this session you learn how to create more details in your plan.

By now, you have started on your plan and possibly realized that it's not always easy and that more structure can and does help you make progress.

Manage the Unknown

As you are aware, a good plan breaks down the things you don't know how to do into smaller steps, thus allowing you to figure out how to accomplish them. For example, if your goal is to make a million dollars, but you have no idea how to do it, you're unlikely to make it a reality. Small, doable steps are the key to reaching large, in some cases quantum-leap, goals.

When planning to make your million dollars, for example, you could be meticulous and specific very small, individual steps, such as go to the bank, pay the bills, deposit the check, and so on. However, consider that, because you already know how to do this, it would likely be counter-productive.

Typically the most effective use of a plan is to describe the process to complete the things you don't know how to do to, thus forming the pathway, a staircase, or a road map to achieve your goal.

Create Doable Steps

Start with the big chunks. For example, to make the million dollars, you need a business!

Then break your plan down further. For example, your first step might be to decide on which kind of business you want. Your second step might be to research the opportunities available for a business that aligns with your purpose and life calling, and that matches the lifestyle you really want.

Build on Past Work

Consider using the work you did in sessions 4 and 7 to move into a more detailed plan. In this previous work you described resources that you have, so now you can build a plan around accessing the resources you don't have.

Sometimes a plan is quite broad and this can work for some people. Other people need more structure; they need to be able to see exactly which internal and external action steps they must take today and tomorrow and the next day so they can stay on track.

Be honest with yourself and create the system that supports you best. You know, or your deep knowledge system knows, the perfect approach for you. So follow your inner knowing and do what works, not what you think you **should** do.

Creating the plan that works for you will elegantly support you to move around any resistance that might come up without sabotaging yourself.

Write your Plan

It is time now to create your steps and fill in your planning pages.

The following planning page allows you to see all the steps to your success so that they take form in front of you!

Fill out the planning form and then move on to completing the accountability index. Both these exercises provide you with important information.

Planning Page

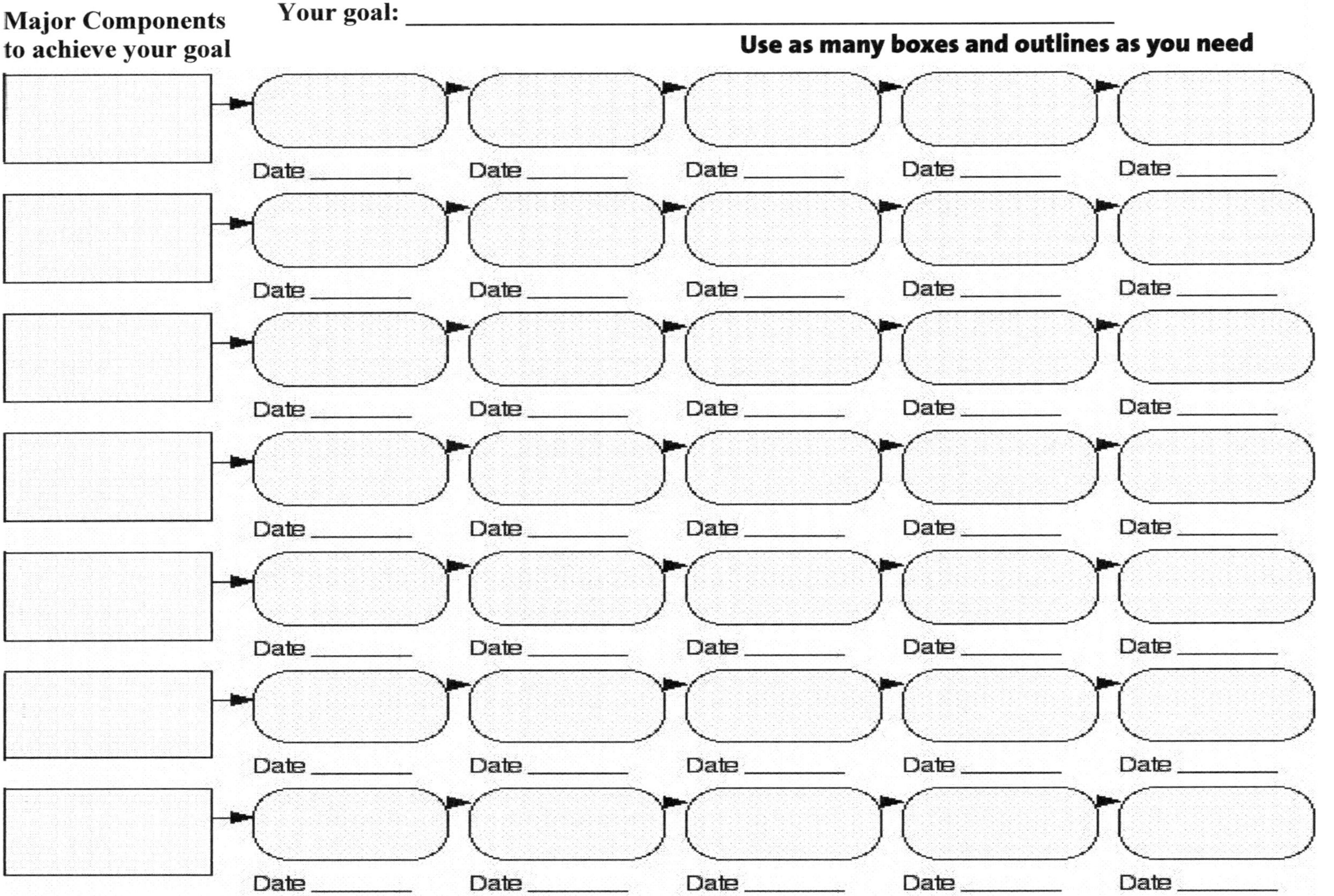

Accountability Index - A Bonus Exercise

This 15-statement scaling interview supports you in clarifying how powerfully you are holding yourself accountable to do what it takes to get what you say you want. Use a scale from 1 to 5:

1=Never True	2=Sometimes True	3=Often True	4=Usually True	5=Always True

Record your answers so you can calculate your score at the end.

Rating	Rate each statement as it applies to your Goal.
	I have a set of clear, well-articulated goals that are framed in the positive.
	I have planned clear steps, outcomes that will lead to my goal.
	I have planned how and what I will do to reach my outcome.
	I am doing the things I know I should do.
	I am stopping myself from doing things that I know I shouldn't do.
	I decided today what I would do to move towards my outcome.
	I did what I said I would do today.
	I have and will continue to plan my day, including setting an intention with a priority for my day.
	I control my day; my day does not control me.
	I discipline myself in small things so I can have success in large things.
	I have a plan to measure my attitude and who I am being throughout the process of reaching my goal and I measured my attitude today.
	I have a plan for measuring my activity and progress towards my goal and I measured my progress today.
	I have a plan for measuring my results and I measured my results today.
	Every day I check that my purpose, vision, and values link to my goal.
	Every day I make sure my day's activities, attitude, and results lead towards my vision.
	Total Score

Score Your Accountability

Add up the total number of points for all 15 questions.

- **Below 20 points**: Hmmm. What are you resisting? It is time to determine what you want from life, and then start planning how you might get it. Start by going within and asking yourself in an open, honest and direct way:

  Ask yourself: What do I really want out of this program?

- **21-39 points**: You are obviously trying hard, but are not moving as fast as you could.

  Ask yourself: Am I clear on what I really want from this goal or my life overall? If not, what might I need to let go of to allow myself to get clear? What gift might I need to give myself that produces the clarity I want?

- **40-59 points**: Good, and there is room for improvement. You are probably moving toward your goal at an effective rate.

  Ask yourself: How might I support myself to be even more effective so I am unstoppable at getting what I want?

- **60-75 points**: WOW, great job! You are definitely on track with your outcome and are almost guaranteed to get it. Keep going for the perfect score.

  Ask yourself: How might I make this journey even more meaningful for myself?

Climbing Your Staircase NOW

Imagine if you started your plan and held yourself accountable daily with a vision of having what you really want in life. Imagine, on a daily basis, embracing activities and attitudes that lead directly to your goal.

Make a commitment to check your accountability regularly and take daily steps towards your goal.

Knowing that a good plan and daily activities to implement your plan would make your life more satisfying, what would you be willing to do now?

What action might you take to remind yourself to be accountable and climb your staircase so that your future is filled with a life you love?

Day 13 Surrender

This session is about surrendering to a power greater than yourself.

A pilot was shot down over Vietnam. While a prisoner of war, he worked on his golf game from the darkness of his tiny cell. Day after day he would visualize playing his favorite course back home. The remarkable part of the story is that upon his release 6 years later, he played that course and shot an incredible 74!

How could he be so detached in the midst of the day-to-day drama of the war in Vietnam? Was he hit in the head? Was he delusional? Perhaps he was purposeful. While he surrendered to his fate, he also surrendered his dreams to the Universe. There were forces that he could not control, and he accepted those while purposefully focusing on how to spend his time.

Once you begin to feel your purpose, set a goal and move in that direction. When you start to move with the flow of your life, all the power of the Universe lines up behind you. The next landing in your staircase seems close and easy to maintain.

But what happens if you make your best plan, put in your very best effort, and things still do not seem to be going your way?

Then, let go - just let go!

This does not mean giving up! It means it is time to surrender and release your plan to the power that is bigger than you.

Collaborate with Powerful Forces

A wonderful person once shared these words of wisdom: "*In my world, nothing goes wrong. I am a collaborative partner in my fate and I let whatever happens be okay. There is something much bigger than my idea of me at work! Just look around.*"

Master's Tip Recognize that there is something bigger than you at work.

There is something that grows your hair, pumps your heart, and circulates your blood. We all co-create with this larger force that some call the highest self, some call Spirit or Divine Intelligence, and others call Universe or God. No matter what you call it, it is there! And for that reason, consider that nothing does go wrong!

Master's Tip In every event there is meaning.

If you absolutely knew that this force would help your plans unfold in the way that would benefit you most, would you be willing to let go of the way you think it "should happen"?

Ponder: Could and would you just let whatever occurs be all right?

Accept What Occurs

Accepting what is occurring in your life is freeing! Releasing what we cannot control is required for peace. This is not to suggest passivity. Play a big game, and go for it! And then accept whatever occurs as you surrender to trusting the Universe.

When you prefer reaching your outcome, rather than being addicted to reaching the outcome ***in a certain way***, you are able to go with the flow of life rather than against it.

Visualize and Meditate

Visualization is important so you remain focused on what you want. When you visualize something regularly, always working towards it, even when your plan isn't working, the **Greater Power** finds a way for your better good to come about.

Meditation is also key. When you connect your mind, body and spirit to something larger, answers are revealed.

Yes, this is a spiritual conversation. You may have invested in this book to learn how to achieve goals. And you may be surprised to now learn that connecting to the larger mind and surrendering is part of the **how**.

Sometimes the **Greater Power** has bigger ideas for us, or different plans, than we can create for ourselves.

Clarify and Surrender

Have you ever achieved a goal and then looked back, thinking: ***"Wow! I can't believe I did that!"***

Perhaps you even thought: ***"If I would have known what I had to go through to get here, I might not have taken that first step!"*** Yet, you knew internally that this was a journey you had to take to live a significant and fulfilling life. Well, your life is calling you toward the next step you must take to make your best life a reality.

Surrendering calls for us to acknowledge the higher power. This power brings us whatever meets our deepest needs and values. If we're not clear on what we want, even if we "think" we are, we probably won't see how the higher power is helping us towards our highest good. Our lack of vision doesn't mean the higher power is not in action. But when you're not sure, the higher power recognizes your uncertainty and won't create for you something that won't work for you, even if you think you want it.

Think from the End

Start by doing everything that is within your control for you to reach your goal. Then, think from the end.

Master's Tip Begin with the end in mind.

Imagine yourself already having the result that is linked to your purpose, and then meditate by clearing your mind and giving it over to the biggest idea in action.

If what you want is in your best interest, meditation makes the connection with a **Greater Power**. Surrender to that power; acknowledge that it knows more than you. Let go, watch, and listen. Things happen - sometimes in a very unexpected way!

Being aligned with the energy of the Universe is definitely part of living your purpose, goal setting, and achievement. Some call it *knowing that everything is perfect as it is* or having complete faith in the Universe.

Faith is believing without seeing. Yet even faith is not proof of exactly what mechanism is at work. Quantum physics has an explanation about the link between intention, desire, and results. Scientists have proven that the observer impacts the results, and so we have double blind tests. But we also have data showing that if the observer desires a certain result, objective test data is likely to support that conclusion.

Is it physics? Is it spirituality? Is it the human will? Does it matter?

We understand that when we focus on a dream and do all we can to work towards it, the Universe moves.

Ponder: Are you willing to live at a higher level of consciousness? Are you willing to be in rapport with that which provides everything?

Remember the commitment poem from Day 6?

Master's Tip "The moment one definitely commits oneself,
then Providence moves too.
So, whatever you can do, or dream you can, begin it.
Boldness has genius, power, and magic in it." - W. H. Murray

Once you are fully committed, and make your very best effort to take every action you can, the Universe moves. Surrender and get out of the way!

You are co-creating with a life force! The Universe is in your corner.

Surrendering

INTEGRATION CHECKLIST

Things you will need

Your journal

A quiet space to think and write

Integration-Related Activity

The goal of this activity is for you to take time to acknowledge the power of the Universe and the force at work in your life. With this knowledge, you can comfortably surrender and live a life you love.

Faith

Faith is believing without seeing, believing in the power of that unknown part of ourselves. Let's explore this with a simple meditation.

Relax and get centered. Take three deep breaths. Tune in and be curious.

- **Who or what grows your hair?**

  Notice how you don't put conscious thought into growing your hair but rather surrender and simply accept that the Universe provides you with hair.

- **Who or what grows your nails?**

  Something makes them grow. Notice how you don't put conscious thought and energy into growing them, they just grow.

- **What determines your health?**

  You go to the gym, you work out with weights, you eat right, and you take the steps that are in your control. Then you accept that something outside of your conscious control looks after your body.

  You set your intention, you take action, and when you have done what you can, you accept that a higher power also works in your favor. You go home and relax, knowing that your body and the infinite wisdom it holds builds more muscle cells, more arteries, more veins, more cartilage and tissue and bone. You don't consider the how - it is all done for you - like magic!

- **How does it happen that a sperm and an egg can produce a baby? Ponder the miracle of birth.**

  Anyone who has children can definitely relate to the miracle of birth.

  How does this union happen? Creating a baby doesn't use conscious thought. Somehow the bit of cell structure, egg and sperm, has all the knowledge it needs to develop into a liver, a heart, a skeletal system, a brain, skin - all the necessary components of a human being.

  There is obviously Higher Power at work that tells that bit of cell structure how to grow. Some people say it is DNA. But if it was just DNA, how is it that some people have the genes of a disease, but never get it? No one seems to know the answer. And if it is just DNA, why won't it grow in a lab tube? There is something more needed - that invisible organizing force of God, or Universal Intelligence, or whatever name you want to use.

That force is at work in your life. When you have done all you can towards the outcome of a project, all that remains is to let go and let the Universe do its thing. So as you consider the power of the Universe, write what comes to mind in response to each of the following questions.

ASK YOURSELF: Just suppose I were to trust that there is something bigger at work in my life than just me. How might surrendering create new dreams for myself?

ASK YOURSELF: In what new ways might I move towards living my best year yet?

Think of a time you really wanted something and it came true only after you were willing to drop your attachment to it.

Ask yourself: Who was I being in this moment? What beliefs were guiding me? How might this approach serve me in the future?

Ask yourself: What do I need to surrender now?

Ask yourself: How might I surrender control of the things I cannot change in the future?

Ask yourself: How might surrendering work to my advantage?

Ask yourself: What am I willing to get go of now?

Let Go Daily

At the end of each day, after you have done your best, while flexibly dancing with the Universe, just let go. Any time a worry comes to you, let the words fade off into the distance. Let any disturbing pictures disappear into the distance as they move further away from you. Bring in a new picture of yourself, relaxed and confident, enjoying having achieved your goal. And then, just let it go.

Surrender NOW

Imagine if you accepted that whatever comes into your life as okay. Imagine embracing even those events that do not seem to fit your plan or your belief about how to reach our goal.

Make a commitment to take action, and then let go and let the Universe or Greater Power take charge.

Knowing that releasing and accepting what is happening makes your life less stressful and brings you closer to your goal, what are you willing to do now?

What action might you take to remind yourself to surrender and go with the flow of life, let it be okay, and then see what you can learn so the future you move into is a life you love?

Day 14 It's Your Time

This session is about the time of your life and how you choose to spend it.

In the song 'Summertime' from George and Ira Gershwin's classic opera Porgy and Bess, Bess sings an ode to the simple and slow-motion summers of the 19th century.

Summer time and the living is easy

Fish are jumpin' and the cotton is high

What an incredible contrast to the speed with which we live this modern life! The modern version of that song should go something like this:

Summertime and the livin' is busy!

Kids are jumpin' and Summer Camp is nigh!

No doubt most of us are filled to the brim with activities - whatever the season. Remember the phrase from Ecclesiastes that the Byrds sang:

"To everything there is a season, and a time to every purpose under the heaven."

In the last few sessions you surfaced your significant value-based offering to the world, set a goal or two, made a plan, and started up the steps of success. If you make your vision your priority on a daily basis and take action to live your best life, you really have some celebrating to do!

In the last session you learned that looking at the staircase is not the same as climbing it. Many people just look at the staircase - they just think about success. But when you actually take steps to have success, you are truly playing a big game!

Celebrate the Kid Within

Here's a secret to staying in the game: There is a kid in each of us! And that kid needs some recognition and celebration. So give yourself a pat on the back, or an internal high five for taking action.

If you never recognize your small successes, or if you talk badly to yourself, or try to motivate yourself with your boot camp voice - ***"Come on, get up, and get moving!"*** - a part of you **will** rebel. And that part will not be motivated or want to support your climb.

Think about it! If you saw your child, best friend, significant other, a parent or grandparent take a step to living their best life, wouldn't you say something nice or treat them in a special way?

PONDER: How does treating myself any differently than I would treat others support me in living my best life?

When you reward yourself with genuine self-care, love, and celebration, you are more likely to continue up the staircase to your success.

- If something works, don't fix it.
- Once you know what works, do more of it.
- If it doesn't work, don't do it again - **Do Something Different!**

Being a jerk to yourself does not work.

MASTER'S TIP Being your own cheerleader when you reach a milestone works!

Let's cater to that kid in you. Add a 'just because' landing point to the staircase of your plan. Set it at some specific date and use it to check on how well you are staying on track. And then reward yourself for progress!

Check Your Progress

So how often should you check? Some people work very well when they structure their time. Others don't. Consider creating these points on a regular basis - daily, weekly, or monthly - whatever best suits you for reviewing your progress and making sure you are on track to your goal.

Set Deadlines

It is time for another secret - one you probably already know.

MASTER'S TIP A plan without deadlines isn't effective, but neither is a plan that's too tightly scheduled.

Most people need some unstructured time to allow for unexpected happenings. If your plan is too tightly structured against the clock and the calendar, you may be setting yourself up for disappointment. After all - life happens and your schedule can get rearranged; so leave some space for unexpected happenings.

Use the Clock and Calendar

The clock and the calendar function as timekeepers. Our plan cannot be effective if we never check to see if we are making our deadlines!

Did you take the Accountability Quiz from Day 12, page 140?

Accountability means checking the clock and the calendar, asking if we did what we planned to do, and did we do it when we said we would.

A sports team knows it has a set period of time to play a game. You determine your goal, your game plan, and define the time you have to play this big game of life and accomplish that goal. The clock and the calendar are the timekeepers that tell you how close you are to meeting the deadline and winning the game.

Determine your Priorities

Speaking of deadlines, have you ever said, ***"I don't have time to do that!"*** If so, consider that what you were really saying was that you gave something else a higher priority.

To get things done, we have to make them a priority. If you want to achieve your goal, you have to make your vision a higher priority than some other things you might normally spend your time doing, such as watching TV. If you keep doing things the way you've always done them, and spending your time doing the same things you've always done, you continue to get the same results.

MASTER'S TIP To achieve your goal, re-prioritize your life and how you spend your time. Do what works in producing the results you want!

Choosing Rewards

Remember the kid inside who needs rewards?

Master's Tip When you meet a deadline or milestone, reward yourself!

Ponder: What is some small reward I can give myself when I achieve a small success?

Perhaps your small reward is renting a movie or having a cup of coffee at a new coffee bar that you've been wanting to try.

Larger successes need larger rewards that recognize the extra effort.

Ponder: What is a larger reward I can give yourself when I achieve a large goal?

Perhaps for you that means a dinner out, a new technology toy, new clothes, jewelry, a hiking trip, a massage, or a trip with a friend. Think of things that you can use as rewards to support yourself as you work towards your goal. Then build these rewards into your plan to help keep yourself motivated!

Like the steps in our staircase, rewards can also take on a staircase effect - a series of small rewards for small successes, leading into a larger reward for achieving a series of small successes. Rewards motivate you and compensate you for the changes you're making in your routine. Perhaps you gave up TV to get your goal accomplished - reward yourself. Without rewards, you may feel deprived, and then sabotage yourself. So keep those rewards coming, every time you meet your schedule!

Add Rest and Recreation Days

Rest and Recreation Days, that many of us call R&R days, are extremely important days for you to be effective, efficient, and live a life you love. These days extend from midnight to midnight with no work-related activities of any kind. These days are free from all business-related activity including business meetings, business-related phone calls, emails, faxes, and projects. They exclude contact with staff or clients unless there is an absolute emergency.

R&R Days support you in coming back to work refreshed, renewed, and ready to take on any new challenging projects that may arise from normal day-to-day life.

PONDER: How would I like to spend an R&R day?

Schedule Your Time Review

In review, remember the key is in scheduling - using the clock and calendar as timekeepers in your game of life.

- Schedule your plan.
- Take action.
- Celebrate yourself - both small successes and larger one.
- Take R&R days.

Using Your Time

INTEGRATION CHECKLIST

Things you will need

Your journal

A quiet space to think and write

Integration-Related Activity

The goal of this activity is for you to learn how effective rewarding yourself can be and how you might reward yourself for your efforts. With this knowledge, you can continue to work through your plan and move forward to achieving your goal.

Celebration Clarification

Please answer each of the following questions by writing whatever comes to mind.

If I were to choose to play the game of rewarding the kid within:

ASK YOURSELF: What will happen if I reward myself?

ASK YOURSELF: What won't happen if I reward myself?

ASK YOURSELF: What will happen if I don't reward myself?

Ask yourself: What won't happen if I don't reward myself?

Ask yourself: What 10 things could I do for myself that rewards my efforts for following through and achieving my mini-goals?

For example, you might want to list a special coffee drink, a foot massage, a ticket for a play, a special dinner, a movie, or buying yourself something special.

-
-
-
-
-
-
-
-
-
-

Ask yourself: If I were to gift myself for achieving my larger goal, with what reward(s) could I honor myself that would create an even greater incentive for me?

Now look at what you wrote.

Ask yourself: How might I be even more generous with myself or make these rewards even more meaningful?

Ask yourself: What structures might I need to put in place to be sure that I reward myself for achieving my mini-goals and to guarantee that I recognize achieving these goals?

Ask yourself: What structures might I need to put in place to guarantee that I reward myself for achieving my larger goal?

Ask yourself: What four vacations might I plan this year that will inspire me to play a big game and support me to live my best year yet? And when will I schedule these?

Ask yourself: As I pursue my goal, what five ways might I show more appreciation for myself through out this journey?

It's Your Time NOW

Make a commitment to develop a rewards system that entices you to keep moving forward.

Imagine creating a terrific plan, an enticing reward system, and also building in days for rest and relaxation as you move towards achieving your goal.

Knowing that rewards and a solid break-through plan would help you achieve your goal, what are you willing to do now? What action might you take to remind yourself to reward yourself and make the kid within reach for the future filled with a life you love?

Part 5: **Start!**

You have built a strong foundation, created a vision, made a powerful choice to go for it, and planned how to reach your goal. Now it's time to get started and put your plan in action.

The next phase of the 30-day program is two days during which you take a good look at any unconscious commitments that may keep you from reaching your goal and then learn to take daily action to reach it.

The architect has a solid foundation, has designed the home, and has decided to build it. Construction is now beginning and it's time to anticipate any possible obstacles to reaching the completion date.

You continue to be the architect of your life, creating the blueprints for success, and learning how to be the construction coordinator - determining what must be completed first and then how to proceed. Now it is time to start! For example, you must have permits before you can start construction and you must have the walls done before the roof is put on.

Journals

Your journal continues to fill up. Your blueprint is becoming better defined so you can reach your goal.

What should be in it now? It's time to take yet another look. Check out your blueprint and make certain that you have completed all the details - done the exercises you might have skipped or put extra effort into ones you might have found challenging. Make sure you are ready for the construction phase of your goal.

2-Day Starting Overview

The first five days of your journey were about building a foundation. The next two were about inspiration and vision, learning to live **your** dream. Then you spent four days learning how to make your decision powerful and compelling, and three days planning your steps of action. It's time now to discover how you can take effective and consistent action.

In **Day 15** you learn to clear your path. This requires that you wake up to unconscious commitments and ways you may sabotage your plan for success.

In **Day 16** you learn the magic of the number three and how to take three steps, however small, every day so you continue to make progress in reaching your destination.

Are you ready?

CHECKLIST

- Be sure you have your journal.
- Set a time aside each day to do your life's work.

Day 15 Clear the Path

This session is about taking stock and clearing anything that may be in the way of reaching your goal.

William Blackstone wanted to make his wife's life easier and had to do it quickly because his family's future depended on it! At the time he had no idea that he would give the entire world an easier, cleaner place in which to live.

Mrs. Blackstone spent hours every day boiling, scrubbing, hanging and folding the family laundry, leaving her little time for romance. At the end of the day, she was tired, exhausted, and grumpy.

Mr. Blackstone knew he must do something to simplify his wife's life so he could have the family of nine that was his dream. That's when he had an epiphany and created the first electric clothes washer!

In Lesson 14 we talked about deadlines and rewards. Consider that even if you are progressing at the speed you want, there could be something stopping you from moving even faster! So it's always good to check for things that slow our progress. And sometimes we have toxic things in our life that prevent us from climbing the stairs to our goals.

Stop, Take Stock

Now is a good time to stop and take stock.

What might be hindering you in your quest to reach your goals and live your best life? Is there anything toxic in your life that could possibly be getting in the way of your living your best life? Is there anything you are tolerating?

Sometimes we get in our own way. Sometimes someone else gets in our way. In fact, as you start to live your best life, you start to change and other people have to deal with you changing! Be aware that your changes may or may not be comfortable for them. And if your changes pull them from their comfort zone, be prepared for some resistance.

Hidden Gains

Have you ever thought that there is a part of you that is committed to keeping you stuck? Sometimes there is a part of ourselves that gains something very valuable from not changing, from not succeeding, from not living our best life. It may even seem that this part of us is doing its best to keep us trapped in our current condition.

MASTER'S TIP We are always committed to something.

Not even a second passes when we are not committed. You might say, ***"Oh yeah - what about when I'm lying around reading romance novels instead of working on my business? I am not committed then."*** However, at that very moment you **are** committed to lying around reading romance novels. And if this is not taking you towards your goals, if this is not an R&R day, then there is a part of you that gains something by doing the exact opposite of what does take you towards your goal. Or this action could mean you are committed to not succeeding in your business or to proving that you're not really an entrepreneur, or you have too much to do and not enough time, or that you're not really smart enough to run your business. Or it could be as outrageous as being committed to financial insecurity because poverty is all you have ever known; and unconsciously you are afraid that money could turn you into a selfish person. Talk about self-sabotage!

Unconscious Commitments

There are infinite possible commitments that may underlie your actions for lying around reading romance novels when your business is suffering. Any commitment that you have not consciously chosen is what we call an unconscious commitment. Some of these commitments support you, others do not. The bottom line is this:

MASTER'S TIP Unconscious commitments are running your life and you are likely not even aware of it.

You must wake up to your sabotaging unconscious commitments and the secondary gains they provide, or you will sabotage yourself over and over without even being aware that you are doing it.

Sabotage can take many forms. Suppose you decided you want to lose weight and you are going to brown bag your lunch and make it healthy. If you happen to forget to buy the groceries you need, that's an example of self-sabotage. Maybe the secondary gain is that you enjoy being able to get out of the office and go shopping with your friend during lunch. Or perhaps you are unconsciously committed to being heavy so that you do not attract men, since your last relationship ended badly. Notice the inner conflict at work in this example - a secondary gain and an unconscious commitment are sabotaging this person. On the surface, perhaps this person is frustrated with his or her choices, yet cannot figure out why he or she makes them.

Discover the Need

Unconscious commitments serve hidden needs. The secret is to discover what these needs are and meet them in a healthy way. If we have a vested interest in having people feel sorry for us, we won't be as motivated to succeed as we could be. The secondary gain might be that we get attention, comfort, or help from our friends. Our friends feel sorry for the "poor you" who keeps trying but just can't make it.

Consider how important it is to start looking for sabotaging secondary gain and unconscious commitments in your life.

One place to find answers is to ask yourself:

PONDER: Is there something I would lose if I achieved my goal?

PONDER: Is there something I am more committed to than having my desired result?

Discover Your Story

Most of us have a story that we are attached to at an unconscious level. However, we can be conscious of this story as well. It usually says something about us, a belief about ourselves that we have trouble letting go of. And if we let go of it to achieve our goal, a part of us believes we won't be the same person. Just as others may resist our changes, there is also some self-resistance to change, and it shows up as a secondary gain.

We resist when we leave our comfort zone because we unconsciously and habitually relate the old way of doing things with security. Resistance comes up because it seems to be easier to keep doing things the old way. The story runs the show!

Master's Tip Everything in your life serves a purpose!

Your unconscious commitments fill a need you have. To stop sabotaging yourself, you must first discover what it is and then find another way to meet these inner needs. Or you can learn to let go of the need - simply look at it, evaluate what it's done for you, and decide if you want to keep it or not. If not, then release it.

Clear the Resistance

Some people feel resistance is about changing the ego. But you already know that resistance is nothing more than an image of yourself to which you've grown accustomed and that is connected to safety.

The tricky part of clearing resistance is that we are accustomed to it so we are no longer attuned to it's sabotage; it has become invisible and unconscious. And we may even complain about or explain how we *can't change.*

When we realize the ego is nothing more than the automatic, unconscious, habitual way we view ourselves, we can choose to view ourselves in a new way. We can build new images of who we are.

Now is the time to focus on how you might be holding yourself back. Then take action towards what you want!

Imagine yourself as someone with the new, unconscious commitment to live your best life in every moment, do what works, and no longer be held back.

Make a Clean Start

Try it! Stand up!

Stand like someone who has a commitment on an unconscious level and has taken action to consistently do what works to live your best life.

Feel the feelings inside of someone who is no longer attached to the old view of you.

Hear yourself saying ***"I choose to release the old me; I'm making a new choice for my life."***

Know that the unconscious commitment of ***"I choose to live my best life in every moment!"*** is the one running the show now.

Letting go of old issues and constraints helps you make a clean start.

Consider the difference between an engine running on clean gas through a clean carburetor and an engine running on dirty gas through a clogged up carburetor.

You choose to hang onto the dirty stuff clogging up your life, or choose to let it go. It's up to you!

Clearing the Path

INTEGRATION CHECKLIST

Things you will need

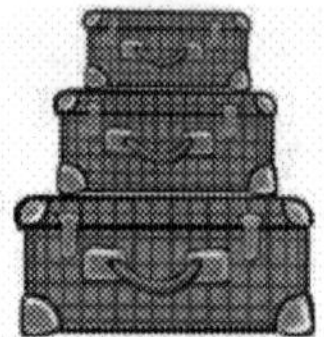

- Three suitcases, bags, or pieces of paper
- A pen for writing
- Some floor space for the suitcases

Integration-Related Activity

The goal of this activity is for you to get through your emotional baggage and recognize what holds you back and what creates resistance for you. With this knowledge, you can let go of your baggage and move faster towards Enlightened Internal Leadership.

IMPORTANT INSTRUCTION **COME WITH AN OPEN MIND.**

Letting Go Exercise

It's time to let go of what is holding you back. Consider that the emotional baggage you have is weighing you down, making it more challenging than it needs to be to get what you want.

There was a famous statue in Penticton, British Columbia, Canada - the baggage handler. It was a life-size statue of a naked man, carrying a suitcase, and surrounded by another 14 suitcases. The suitcases symbolized our emotional baggage. The naked man symbolized that when humans, even when we are stripped of everything else, often still choose to carry our emotional baggage.

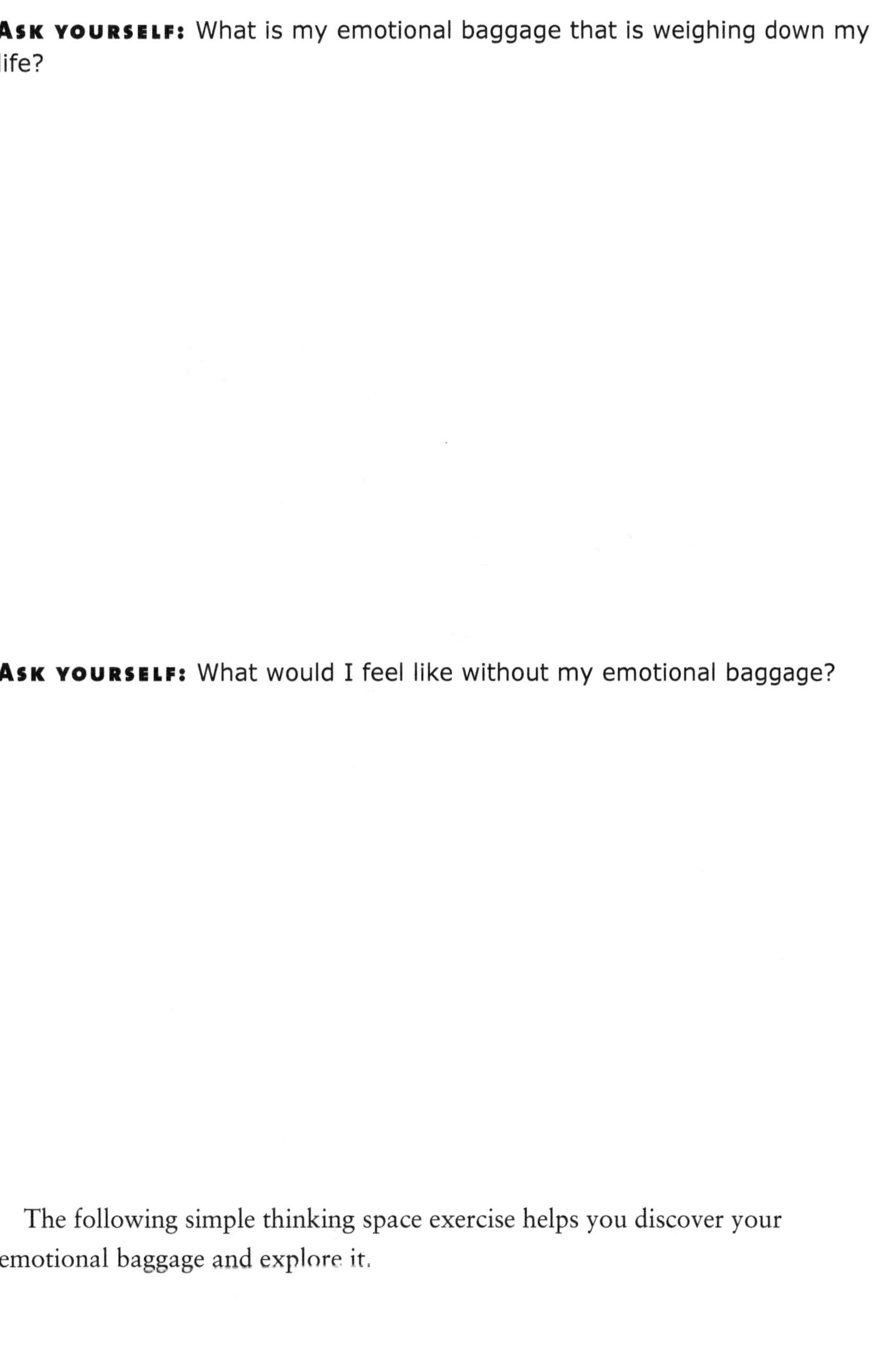

Ask yourself: What is my emotional baggage that is weighing down my life?

Ask yourself: What would I feel like without my emotional baggage?

The following simple thinking space exercise helps you discover your emotional baggage and explore it.

Thinking Space Exercise

1. Stand up and relax.
2. Place three bags or suitcases on the floor.

   If you don't have bags or suitcases, you can use pieces of paper to symbolize your bags.
3. Open your bags up and place a piece of paper inside each of them.
4. Organize your suitcases in a circle on the floor, and stand in the center.

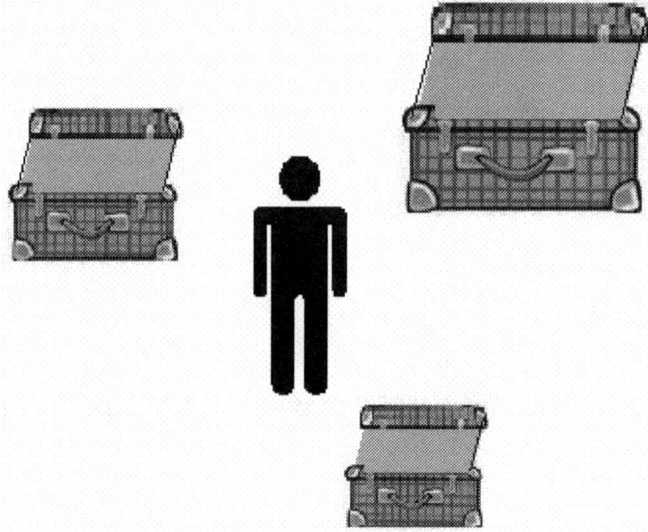

5. Discover your largest obstacle.

   A. Picture right in front of you the biggest thing that is holding you back from reaching your goal. It sometimes helps to close your eyes.

   Hear the sounds, voices, or feelings you have that brings up a memory.

   B. Remove the paper from the largest bag and write a description of the image on it.

   Consider that your beyond-conscious mind works in pictures and metaphors, so take the time to write out a description of what you noticed. Be thorough and write out as many details as you can.

   C. Replace the paper inside the real or imaginary suitcase.

6. Discover your second-largest obstacle.

   A. Picture right in front of you the second biggest thing that is holding you back from reaching your goal. It sometimes helps to close your eyes.

      Notice the sounds, voices, or feelings you have that brings up a memory.

   B. Remove the paper from the second-largest bag and write a description of the image on it.

      Be thorough and write out as many details as you can.

   C. Replace the paper inside the real or imaginary suitcase.

7. Discover your third-largest obstacle.

   A. Picture right in front of you the third biggest thing that is holding you back from reaching your goal. It sometimes helps to close your eyes.

      Notice the sounds, voices, or feelings you have that brings up a memory.

   B. Remove the paper from the third-largest bag and write a description of the image on it.

      Be thorough and write out as many details as you can.

   C. Replace the paper inside the real or imaginary suitcase.

8. Now, physically pick up these suitcases or pick up the paper you wrote on.

   Ask yourself: How does it feel to be holding my three biggest suitcases of emotional baggage?

   Take a few minutes to really feel the weight of the emotional baggage.

9. Put the suitcases down, one at a time, and feel how good it feels to just let stuff go.

   Take a few minutes to savor this feeling.

10. Take your notes from the suitcases, sit down, and spread the three sheets out in front you.

Ask yourself: What are the benefits I get for carrying this bag?

Ask yourself: Are there any other benefits, perhaps to someone else?

Ask yourself: What costs do I pay?

Ask yourself: How would my life improve if I chose to no longer carry this baggage?

Written Activity

Take a few minutes to think this through.

Time to decide

When you're done, it is time to decide. Decisions can be made in an instant.

Ask yourself: Do you want to pack these bags around, or do you want to let them go?

If the answer is to let them go, then burn, shred, or in some way symbolically destroy the paper. Let your beyond-conscious mind know that it's time to let go of this baggage, and that it is okay to let it go. Clearing the old allows the new to come in.

Now stand up and step forward, without the baggage, into your new life.

Clear the Path NOW

Imagine that you let go of your emotional baggage and were no longer carrying the extra weight of thoughts and practices that stop you from reaching your goal.

Make a commitment to work through other emotional baggage you might notice.

Knowing that releasing your emotional baggage makes reaching your goals easier, what are you willing to do now? What action might you take to remind yourself to notice your baggage and release it when it gets in your way so that you can live a life you love?

Day 16 **Make Three the Charm!**

This session is about the significance of the number three and the value of threefold actions.

We all know the story of the person who stumbles across the magic lantern, polishes it and has a Genie materialize from it, offering to grant the owner three wishes.

"You have just been granted three wishes" said the Genie from the magic lantern.

Wouldn't it be fantastic if life **was** that simple? If all we had to do was wish for some thing or some desire to have it materialize before our very eyes.

In fact, bringing miracles into our lives is not much more difficult than that. The power already exists within us. Each of us has a "Genie" within us, called the beyond-conscious mind. It is capable of making all our wishes come true provided that we know how to make full use of it.

There's magic in the number three! And the magic is threefold!

A Three-part Magical Formula

Try this for yourself and see for yourself that it is a magic formula.

1. Perform three actions a day and achieve your dream life.
2. Visualize yourself being successful in three different scenarios.
3. Limiting changes to only three at a time.

Let's take a look at these steps in more detail.

Three-Step Plans

The first magic happens, when everyday - yes, every single day - you take three steps towards achieving your goals. These steps can be small or large, as long as you take three actions every day.

Challenge yourself to create a three-step action plan for each day. Of course, choose the three steps daily that create the greatest gain.

If you decided to improve your health, and going to the gym to exercise is part of your plan, these three steps:

(1) Get out your gym bag,

(2) Pack it, and

(3) Fill your water bottle

will not improve your health - unless you get to the gym!

An action plan with greater gain might be:

(1) Pack your gym bag and prepare your water bottle so you're ready to go to the gym in the morning with no excuses

(2) Walk on the treadmill for at least 30 minutes, and

(3) Stretch for 10 minutes.

Three Steps to Action

What if you find a part of yourself resisting getting into action?

- **First:** Remember that we resist when we leave our comfort zone.

  We unconsciously and habitually relate the old way of doing things with security, so leaving old habits behind and achieving goals takes commitment, focus, and discipline.

- **Second**: Start with three tiny steps.

  Make your steps small enough to enroll your nagging friend **Resistance** to play with you.

- **Third**: Be clear that your three steps lead you to naturally take action.

  For example, if your three steps to take a walk are to (1) get dressed in your running clothes, (2) get out to the street, and then (3) walk a block, you might feel really silly if you decided to turn around and come back home; so you would probably keep going! You might find yourself enjoying the walk enough to keep going for 10 blocks - after all, you've already started! You are already in motion! And, as they say, an object in motion stays in motion.

Be Consistent

The key to succeeding is consistency, to **always** take three steps, **every** day.

Taking three simple steps every day, moves you a step, or three, upwards on your staircase to success. It's a simple, effective rule!

MASTER'S TIP Just do it! Every single day, take three small steps.

When you take action every day you begin to live your life on purpose and get what you want - guaranteed!

MASTER'S TIP A journey of a thousand miles starts with a single step.

Even if you can't see the top of the staircase, every single step you take is moving you towards success.

Achieve Your Dream Life

To live the life of your dreams, simply consider these three steps:

1. Make a wish list of the activities, finances, and lifestyle you will enjoy once you are there.
2. Break down each wish into the steps you need to take to achieve your dream life.
3. Choose and schedule a number of those steps each week, month, or year, remembering to take three actions each day.

Visualize to Make Real

The second magic happens when you can visualize yourself achieving something three times in three different scenarios - the mind thinks it's real! That's right - the mind starts that gravitational pull, pulling your goal towards you. A circuit in the brain, the Reticular Activating System, activates when you see something your mind thinks is important or something it wants.

For example, suppose you're thinking about buying a black Jetta. All of a sudden you start to notice how many black Jettas there are on the highways. Your mind realizes this is important because it is something you want and shows you more of them. Those black Jettas were already on the road, and you didn't notice them until your Reticular Activating System brought them to your attention.

When you imagine yourself achieving your goal at least three times, the Reticular Activating System takes action. From everything going on around you, your mind begins to select the opportunities for you to achieve your goal. The magic is to have visualized your success at least three times. Then the Reticular Activating System takes your goal seriously. You learn more about this system in Day 17, "Reticular Activating System (RAS)" on page 194.

Limit Change to Three

The third magical element of the threefold Magic Formula is knowing what you can handle. Most people can make only three changes in their lives, or have three major projects, or focuses, in life at one time! True, a few people can handle more for small amounts of time, but most of us can only handle three.

When you are goal setting, commit to working on only three different aspects of your goal at a time. If you try to change too many things at one time, your brain and body may feel overloaded. And putting more on your plate than you can handle may set yourself up for frustration or failure.

For example, with a weight loss project, focus on changing three things about your diet. Everyone can handle three changes happening at the same time, as long as they are not too big! So choose the changes that are the difference that makes the difference.

Three Magic Reminders

Remember the threefold magic of the number three.

1. Take three action steps a day.
2. Visualize your success at least three times to set your mind in motion.
3. Limit changes to three at a time to build forward motion and avoid overloading yourself!

Making Three the Charm

INTEGRATION CHECKLIST

Things you will need

Your day-timer, diary, or whatever method you use to track actions you plan to do each day.

A quiet space to think and write

Integration-Related Activity

The goal of this activity is for you to plan three actions you can take each day for a week to jump-start moving toward your goal. With this knowledge, you can continue to develop your daily three-step actions and create a masterful plan to move forward to your goal.

IMPORTANT INSTRUCTION **BE SURE TO HAVE YOUR PLANNER AVAILABLE.**

Three-Step Action Plans

Any big accomplishment can be achieved by taking just three actions a day. When you take three actions, every single day, you quickly see yourself progress to success!

In this exercise you plan three actions you can take each day this week. Of course, we invite you to do this with the state of mind of an Enlightened Internal Leader, while you link what you want to your larger life purpose.

Taking these actions helps you build forward motion. And forward motion supports you to get where you want to go.

MASTER'S TIP Anthony Robbins says: "The most important thing you can do to achieve your goals is to make sure that as soon as you set them, you immediately begin to create momentum."

What is in action tends to stay in action; what is at rest (stopped) tends to stay at rest! Consider that commitment is the ignitor of forward motion. Follow through makes it real.

Coach yourself to say, ***"Of course!"***

If a friend asked, ***"Did you take your three actions today and will you take your three actions tomorrow?"***, you would say with conviction, ***"Of course!"***

Write Your Three-A-Day

Make your commitment to reaching your goal a reality by having the pen meet the paper. It is time to use your dairy, daytimer, weekly planner, or whatever method you use to plan your days. If you do not have anything, try using the weekly planning worksheet available on page 182. In fact, we encourage you to try the method in this worksheet and then create your own version that works even better for you.

First: Consider what you want to accomplish this week - which step on the staircase you want to reach! Perhaps it is to weigh one pound less, have a week where you live from the values of love and contribution, spend five quality hours connecting with your kids, gain two new clients, cook five meals, attend yoga class twice this week, or create a marketing strategy. Whatever your goal is this week, as you consider the outcome:

ASK YOURSELF: What value will I live from this week?

ASK YOURSELF: What will I have?

ASK YOURSELF: What will I have that is evidence of my outcome?

ASK YOURSELF: What will I see, hear, and feel at the end of the week that proves I accomplished my goal?

Second: Keeping in mind your responses to the preceding **Be**, **Do**, **Have** questions, write out all the action steps you could be doing this week to accomplish your goal for the week.

Third: If you achieve what you set out to do, write down how you will reward yourself? Now you can plan and follow through with your reward. The rewards will add wind in your sails!

Complete This Week's Plan

It is time to take your best guess as to which specific days you do each task on your list. So write each task into your day planner or onto your weekly planning worksheet.

Commit

As you write the task in, make a commitment to follow through. By writing this on a certain day you are saying, ***"Of course I choose, I decide, I dare to do this action."*** Remember, sometimes the Universe has a bigger or different idea for you, so do your very best each day and then accept whatever occurs and release your attachment to the outcome.

Take a Day Off

There are seven days in every week, and remember that time to relax and rejuvenate is an important part of staying focused and being effective. Consider taking one day off from your **3-a-Day schedule**, especially if it is an action that is externally-focused, such as writing a book, building a business or finding a job. This day off helps you maintain integrity to the overall commitment to your goal. It is not a day to "fall off the apple cart", such as throwing your new eating plan out of the window. Rather, this day is time to maintain your internal focus while you renew, rejuvenate, and exercise extreme self-care.

Final Review

Now that you have your **3-a-Day schedule** and a plan in place, take one last look at your list. Planning, committing to and then following through with three things maintains your internal focus, and supports greater possibility and movement towards your goal. And don't forget to go with the flow of the Universe. Flexibly adjusting to what the Universe presents is the "difference that makes the difference" in enjoying your journey.

Daily Check-up

We encourage you to check off your accomplishments at the end of each day.

Ask yourself each day: Did I do the things I said I would?

As you ponder this question, consider linking what you learned from the tasks you performed that day. You can decide if you did as well as you could, if you did better than you hoped, and what worked best for you.

Master's Tip Frances Willard said, "The world is wide and I will not waste my life in friction when it could be turned into momentum."

Remember, if you do more of what works, and less of what doesn't work, you achieve your outcome a lot faster and enjoy the process a lot more!

Take three steps daily with an Enlightened Internal Leader state of mind and at the same time accept the sequencing that shows up in the world of form. Consider that there is always more to be revealed.

Make Three the Charm NOW

Imagine if you took three steps each day to work towards a life you love. And imagine embracing even those events and side trips that are not part of your plan.

Knowing that a **3-a-Day plan** would make your life more rewarding, what would you be willing to do now? Would reaching your goal be worth committing to three actions each day - with a day off a week for rejuvenation?

What action might you take to remind yourself to complete your daily tasks, examine your actions, and reflect on what you can learn so the future is filled with a life you love?

The "Three-a-Day" Action Planning Worksheet

For Week of ______________

My goal for this week:

The actions I need to take to achieve it are:

Transfer the actions to the appropriate days on the 7 day calendar below. We encourage you to **take one day off** from activity while you maintain "integrity" to the overall commitment to your goal.

At the end of each day, check in and note if you did what you said you would do. What's the learning in this for you? Then, write what you are grateful for that day.

As Buddha said, *"Let us rise up and be thankful, for if we didn't learn a lot today, at least we learned a little, and if we didn't learn a little, at least we didn't get sick, and if we got sick, at least we didn't die; so, let us all be thankful."* Yes, Buddha had a sense of humor.

Monday's Action Plan ▪ ▪ ▪	What I learned: What I am grateful for:
Tuesday's Action Plan ▪ ▪ ▪	What I learned: What I am grateful for:

Free copy privileges granted by Powerful Choices Coaching

Wednesday's Action Plan ■ ■ ■	What I learned: What I am grateful for:
Thursday's Action Plan ■ ■ ■	What I learned: What I am grateful for:
Friday's Action Plan ■ ■ ■	What I learned: What I am grateful for:
Saturday's Action Plan ■ ■ ■	What I learned: What I am grateful for:
Sunday's Action Plan ■ ■ ■	What I learned: What I am grateful for:

Part 6: **Continued Success**

You have built a strong foundation, created a vision, made a powerful choice to go for it, and planned how to reach your goal. You started your plan in action and have found some challenges.

The next phase of the 30-day program is five days during which you take steps toward your continued success. You learn some specific things you can do to help you to continue on your successful journey towards achieving your goal.

The architect has a solid foundation, has designed the home and begun construction, flexibly anticipating possible obstacles to reaching the completion date. It's time now for the architect to get support in overcoming any obstacles that come up and then to take action towards building forward motion to reach the completion date.

As you continue to be the architect of your life, creating the internal and external blueprints for success, we share with you the Enlightened Internal Leadership secrets of seeking help and using all your resources to keep your forward motion going. As the construction coordinator, building your best life, you may need to become more resourceful during trying times or seek expert help in finding solutions to unique problems. These next lessons provide tips on finding these solutions and the right people.

Journals

Your journal continues to fill up. Your blueprint is becoming complete and you are taking actions to reach your goal.

What should be in it now? It's time to take yet another look at the journal. Check out your blueprint and make certain that you have completed all the details - done the exercises you might have skipped or put extra effort into ones you might have found challenging or exciting.

Review your plan and tweak it since you now have more information about how the plan is working.

And take a look at where you may need to seek help or support to keep the project on schedule.

5-Day Continued Success Overview

The first five days of your journey were about building a foundation. The next two were about inspiration and vision, learning to live **your** dream. Then you spent four days learning how to make your decision powerful and compelling. The next three days you planned, and then you spent two days getting started. It's time now to make certain that you will continue to make progress.

In **Day 17** you learn about your brain - actually about your four brains - and how to keep your brain functioning most effectively and efficiently. Since each of the brains has something unique to offer, the better the connections between all four brains, the more access we have to our own creativity and resources.

In **Day 18** we invite you to stay totally focused on what you want, learning from the results you have thus far, and refocusing after setbacks, and rewarding your progress. We also invite you to look at how you can make an even deeper commitment to reaching your destination.

In **Day 19** you learn about the value of support - whether it be in the form of a coach or a friend. No one gets a gold medal at the Olympics without a coach. If you go it alone, you may not fail, but you probably get less success than you deserve. So we invite you to seek support.

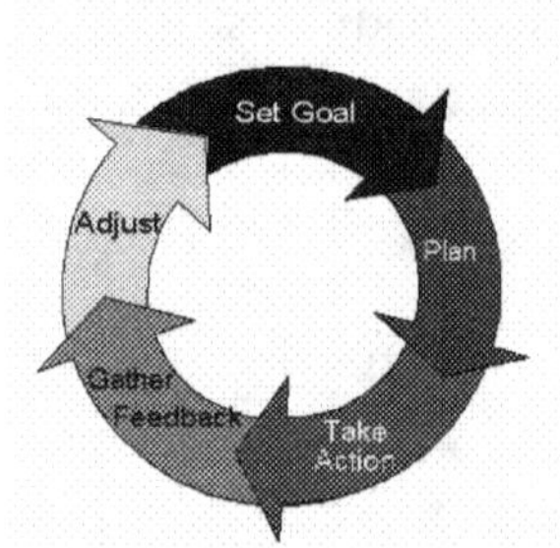

Day 20 is about the cycle of progress. In this cycle, you begin with clarity on exactly what you want. You set a goal and proceed to set up your plans. Then, based on the information you have at the time, you start taking action. As you collect feedback, you make adjustments and reset your goals to be more specific, modify your plan and so on.

In **Day 21** you learn to review your progress and keep the big picture in mind. As you build Enlightened Internal Leadership with each of the actions you take, you build Enlightened Internal Leadership with the overall goal. And with forward motion and Enlightened Internal Leadership, you become capable of more actions and further progress.

As you continue to step up your staircase, notice how wonderful the view is from the landing you have already reached. And notice that the end is in sight.

Are you ready?

CHECKLIST

- Be sure you have your journal.
- Set a time aside each day to do your life's work.

Day 17 Use Your Brains

This session is about identifying specific regions of your brain, what they do, and how to best use your brain to support you in living a life you love. This topic is quite complex and what you hear about today is only a small portion of the amazing information about the brain. If you want to learn more in-depth information, the source we highly recommend is the work of Dr. Marilyn Atkinson of Erickson College International, www.erickson.edu.

A Story

A Brief Tale

Blind Men and the Elephant

-John Godfrey Saxe

It was six men of Indostan, to learning much inclined,
who went to see the elephant (Though all of them were blind),
that each by observation, might satisfy his mind.

The first approached the elephant, and, happening to fall,
against his broad and sturdy side, at once began to bawl:
"God bless me! but the elephant, is nothing but a wall!"

The second feeling of the tusk, cried: "Ho! what have we here,
so very round and smooth and sharp? To me tis mighty clear,
this wonder of an elephant, is very like a spear!"

The third approached the animal, and, happening to take,
the squirming trunk within his hands,
"I see," quoth he, the elephant is very like a snake!"

The fourth reached out his eager hand, and felt about the knee:
"What most this wondrous beast is like, is mighty plain," quoth he;
"Tis clear enough the elephant is very like a tree."

The fifth, who chanced to touch the ear, Said; "E'en the blindest man
can tell what this resembles most; Deny the fact who can,
This marvel of an elephant, is very like a fan!"

The sixth no sooner had begun, about the beast to grope,
than, seizing on the swinging tail, that fell within his scope,
"I see," quoth he, "the elephant is very like a rope!"

And so these men of Indostan, disputed loud and long,
each in his own opinion, exceeding stiff and strong,
Though each was partly in the right, and all were in the wrong!

So, oft in theological wars, the disputants, I ween,
tread on in utter ignorance, of what each other mean,
and prate about the elephant, not one of them has seen!

This parable demonstrates that people tend to understand only a tiny portion of reality and then extrapolate beliefs from that portion, each claiming only his version is the correct one. This approach is how the mind works.

Your Multiple Brains

Did you know that inside your head you have four different brains - the brain stem, the limbic system, and the neocortex with right and left hemispheres? Using your whole brain effectively, including your Reticular Activating System and amygdala, is important to living your best life and achieving your goals!

Brain Stem

The first brain is one all reptiles have - a primitive brain called the **brain stem** or the **reptilian brain**. In humans this brain is a tiny enlargement of the brain stem at the top of the spinal column. Its main function is to keep us safe, looking after our survival. So the reptilian brain becomes active when we're really stressed and responds automatically. For example, when you are scared, the flight, fight, or freeze syndrome kicks in.

Limbic System

It's been around for 50-million years. This tribal brain looks after the survival of the family. The emotional brain has an **either/or** quality, so a person operating only from the emotional brain thinks in terms of black and white, good or bad, yes or no, right or wrong - with no room for compromise!

The second brain, called the **limbic system** or **mammal brain**, is small and wraps around the top of the brain stem. Even though it is younger than the brain stem, it is significantly more advanced.

This brain has five important qualities.

- First, all mammals have this brain and it focuses on taking care of the family system.
- Second, the limbic system engages in dichotomous thinking.

  A person operating only from this part of his or her brain thinks in terms of black and white, good or bad, yes or no, right or wrong - with no room for compromise! Ever been in this state of mind? If so, your limbic system was running the show.
- Third, this brain is conscious only of the immediate present moment.

  Although this brain has "past memory," it cannot conceive of the future. It only considers what is going on right **now**.
- Fourth, the mammal brain loves routine and does not like change.

  Remember our friend resistance? Resistance hangs out in the mammal brain that has a strong desire to maintain long term habitual patterns - doing the same thing over and over again. And remember that resistance happens when we leave our comfort zone because we unconsciously and habitually relate the old way of doing things with comfort and security.
- Fifth, this brain communicates with tone. For example, have you noticed that dogs have different barks that tell you how they feel? You can usually tell from the growl if a dog is playing or if he means business! And if he means business, he means business right now! Right?

  Speaking of negative emotions, have you ever noticed how some people just seem to look for everything that is wrong, or scary, or unhappy about the world? These are people who have an area of their limbic system, called the amygdala, stimulated the wrong way!

The Amygdala

The amygdala is a small, almond shaped gland, located on both sides of the head between the top of the ear and the outer edge of the eye, inside your brain. The amygdala is part of the limbic system that decides if incoming sensory information is a threat or a pleasant event.

If something is perceived as a threat, the brain stem, or reptile brain becomes even more active, and may take over control of your brain!

Daniel Goldman, author of the book called *Emotional Intelligence*, describes this "take over control of your brain" as an "amygdala hijacking".

Someone caught in the throws of road rage, for instance, is experiencing an amygdala hijacking. They no longer have access to rational thought. Ever experienced this or seen this in action? It is pretty intense.

Now, once calm, the person may be regretful and ashamed of their behavior, but at the moment of the amygdala hijacking, they had no control! Their amygdala was totally 'clicked backwards'. Yep, clicked backward!

Amygdala Clicked Backward?

It is hard to stay positive if your amygdala is clicked backwards. Why? Because when the back half of the amygdala is stimulated over and over, it causes us to be fearful and stressed. And, in this state, we see all the reasons why something won't work.

Studies show that Vietnam veterans who suffer from Post Traumatic Stress Disorder have the back half of their amygdala highly overactive. These people tend to interpret many normal events of life as a threat, and may experience flashbacks. For instance, the sound of a car backfiring may be interpreted as the sound of enemy weapons, with the brain stem taking over the brain and sending signals to get down and take cover!

With your amygdala 'clicked backwards', you don't have access to most of your brain power, and are limited to fight-or-flight, aggression or fear, and basic survival skills.

Amygdala Front Half

Conversely, when the front half of the amygdala is stimulated, we tend to interpret events as positive. This interpretation keeps the brain stem quiet, and uninvolved in your thinking process, so the rest of your brain can find ways for everyone involved in a situation to win.

According to T.D. Lingo and Neil Slade, researchers at the Dormant Brain Research and Development Laboratory, when your amygdala is properly clicked forward, you experience a lasting sense of wellbeing.

Your Choice

What would you rather have, your amygdala clicked backward or forward?

Research by Lingo and Slade showed dramatic increases in creativity and intelligence by learning how to ensure your amygdala is clicked forward, as measured on some well known scales of creativity and intelligence.

So how do you 'click' your amygdala forward? Easy - through imaginary self-stimulation! Just find a quiet and private area. Imagine holding a feather in your hand. Now imagine the amygdala as a small, almond shaped gland lying horizontally between your ear and the outer edge of your eye. Now, in your imagination, gently 'tickle' the end of the amygdala closest to your eye with the feather.

Click! Keep it up for 30 seconds or more, and repeat often.

According to Neil Slade, "Most people feel a slight sensation when they first click: a tingling in the forehead; a giggly light feeling; a cessation of internal noise; an automatic smile. A few see lights and hear sounds. Some feel a wave of euphoria. Others sense sudden calm."

PONDER: What did you feel? Did this exercise click for you?

Clicking your amygdala forward on a regular basis, over a period of a few weeks, can help turn down excess brain stem activity, and increase the availability of the big brain resources. As a bonus, some people report a 'brain orgasm', a feeling of intense pleasure, from amygdala clicking when carried out on a regular basis over a few weeks.

Now that you are feeling really good, let's consider something quite important.

Reptile and Mammal Teamwork

The mammal brain and brain stem work very powerfully together. As a team, these two brains have a lot of pull in times of challenge. Their combined power might take you off course from what you really want, especially if you have you amygdala clicked backward!

For example, have you ever had a great vision for your life that you feel totally committed to, such as to be healthy and slim? Perhaps, when you get a little stressed out, you sabotage yourself by choosing to eat chips, drink beer, and sit on the couch rather than go to the gym? This is the power of your emotional brain - you forget about the future vision, and do what seems to give you the most pleasure in the moment **now**!

Neocortex - Left and Right Brains

If you stay focused on your future - being healthy and slim - you are using your other two brains, commonly referred to as the left brain and the right brain, and housed in your cerebral cortex.

These brains occupy the majority of the brain cavity, and allow us to imagine and plan our future. However, they are only about 2-million-years old. They are not fully integrated with the reptilian and mammal brains, since they have had relatively little time to evolve and develop together.

Future Visioning Capacity

The neocortex houses your future visioning capacity in the frontal lobes, and is much more resilient than your mammal brain. For example, close your eyes and notice that you can play a movie of yourself in Tahiti, at the top of the mountain, or having a conversation with Gandhi.

Using these right and left brains of the neocortex gives access to infinite creativity and possibility!

Two Hemispheres Cooperating

As we said earlier, the neocortex has two hemispheres - our left brain and right brain. Because neither one can work exclusively without the other, they must cooperate. Our left brain tends to be better with numbers and logic. Our right brain tends to be better at visualization. Both evolved to see possibilities. The neocortex is very creative and likes situations where everybody wins. Together the left and right brains excel at planning, visualizing scenarios, and determining how realistic our plans might be.

Reticular Activating System (RAS)

Your Reticular Activating System (RAS) helps you make sense of all the sensory input you receive.

Our senses bring in so much information that we can't pay attention to all of it and stay sane! By necessity, we learn filtering habits. We pay little attention to routine activities, and we learn to delete or ignore much of the incoming information. The job of our Reticular Activating System is to select what's important or meaningful for us.

The RAS is the attention center of the brain. It connects to the spinal column, receiving information directly from your nervous system. This part of the brain connects your inner world of thoughts, images, and emotions, with the outer world of sensory input. Because the RAS activates the neocortex, some people call it the **seat of motivation**.

The RAS also acts as a sentry. As we said earlier, we develop filtering habits. Have you ever been in a crowded room with a babble of conversation, and picked out the sound of your name from all that noise? This is your RAS picking out what's important or meaningful for you. Hearing your name is pretty meaningful! It could mean a reward, or a threat, or anything! Because your name addresses you, specifically, your RAS sorted through all the incoming auditory information and brought the sound of a voice speaking your name to your attention.

Ever bought a new car and then noticed how many of those cars were on the road? That was your RAS. It assumes, because you chose that car, that this kind of a car must be important to you; so, of the thousands of cars on the road, now your RAS brings your attention to all the cars just like the one you just bought.

Your RAS takes its cue from what you focus on, consciously or unconsciously. If you focus on how hard it is to get ahead, your RAS acts in complete agreement and brings you examples of it being hard to get ahead. If you focus on finding ways to get what you want from life, that's what your RAS brings to your attention. By making a conscious choice to continually focus on what you want, your RAS receives its instructions and brings opportunities to your attention.

Whole Brain Integration

With your four brains, your RAS, and your amygdala, you can make conscious choices to best use your brainpower - the better the connections, the more access we have to our own creativity and resources. The whole brain together created mind.

The great geniuses of the past integrated all four of their brains to accomplish magnificent things. Einstein wrote the theory of relativity after imagining what it would be like to be riding on a beam of light. Look what he accomplished when he combined visualization and math! By putting all of his brains to work, he made massive contributions to the world.

Did you know Einstein was considered a dunce as a schoolchild? If he can achieve greatness, you and I can too. When we have all four brains working together, we can accomplish what might seem to be miracles.

If we visualize failure, then we become fearful, the brain stem becomes active, and we no longer see win-win situations. Further, the mammal brain kicks in - we start seeing things in black and white, win or lose. We lose access to the left and right hemispheres of the cerebral cortex and lose our ability to see possibility and to plan effectively.

If we visualize success, we feel confident enough to cooperate with others to help them achieve their goals **and** help ourselves achieve our own goals. That's one of the secrets of success. When we look for win-win situations, we feel great about ourselves and others feel great about us.

Activate Your Whole Mind

One way to effectively activate all four brains is to look at your plans from the viewpoint of each brain. Try it now! Think about your plan, or perhaps a single aspect of it.

Reptilian Brain Involvement

The brain stem is concerned about your survival.

PONDER: Is there any danger in my plan?

PONDER: Is there a point where I might feel really scared?

PONDER: And if so, have I planned for that point?

Reticular Activating System (RAS)

The RAS wants to stop sensory overload, therefore it needs to know what it can delete or ignore.

PONDER: What are the most important or meaningful things to pay attention to?

PONDER: What routine do I need to develop to build momentum?

Emotional Brain Involvement

Take a moment to click your amygdala forward and remember that the mammal brain wants to know how your plan affects your family or the group you live and work with. It cares about the moment now and finding habitual patterns that work well.

PONDER: How do the changes I'm making affect the group or my family?

PONDER: Will my family or my group's reaction affect my plans?

PONDER: How might I enjoy the moment now as I go through the process?

PONDER: What positive habitual patterns can support me in finding a groove?

PONDER: How can I be emotionally aware and tuned into my body throughout the journey?

Left and Right Brain Involvement

Now involve the left and right brains. The neocortex wants to know about logic and creativity.

PONDER: Is my plan logical?

PONDER: Is my plan realistic?

PONDER: Is it creative?

PONDER: Have I expanded my mind to look for all possibilities?

PONDER: Is there more than one way to get to the same goal?

By consciously working with all your brains, you can build a better plan and have fewer setbacks as you progress. People sense when you're using both your right and left hemispheres. They can tell if you're looking for a win-win situation. Being out for yourself only scares people off - and perhaps the ones you scare off are the very people you need to help you!

People who sell houses say it is all about Location, Location, Location. Well, for your success - it is all about practice, practice, practice!

Practice using all four brains together. As you consider new adventures, manage the parts that might scare you, and then look at how people can help you move forward as you let yourself think "out-of-the-box" and open your mind to the infinite possibilities waiting to help you succeed.

Using your Brains

INTEGRATION CHECKLIST

Things you will need

Your journal
A quiet space to think and write

Integration-Related Activity

The goal of this activity is for you to understand your brain better so you can effectively use its full potential. With this knowledge, you can create a masterful plan on how to move forward to Enlightened Internal Leadership.

Balancing the Four Brains

We went into detail about the four brains of man and each of their functions. Let's now look at the brain, the organ of the mind and the cerebra-spinal system of nerves that puts us in conscious communication with every part of our body. This system of nerves responds to every sensation of light, heat, odor, sound, and taste.

A Balanced Mind

When your mind is balanced and thinks correctly, when it understands the truth, when the thoughts sent through the cerebro-spinal nervous system to the body are constructive, positive or focusing on what you want, then the sensations in the body are pleasant and harmonious.

A Balancing Brain Exercise

Let's begin by balancing the four brains of your mind.

If possible, stand up. You are going to learn an exercise called **cross-crawling** that you can do at anytime to balance the right and left hemispheres of your brain.

- Please stand erect looking forward.
- Lift your **right** knee up and touch it with your **left** hand, and then put your leg down.
- Pick up your **left** knee and touch it with your **right** hand.

Repeat this process over and over, doing it **at least 30 times.**

- Now begin to create a horizontal figure-8 pattern with your eyes.

  It may feel odd and you may feel like you look completely ridiculous, but just keep doing it - **at least 30 times.**
- When you're done, pause and take a deep nourishing breath in and out.

Brain Integration Visualization

Remain standing.

- Imagine a red ball. See the red ball in your mind.
- Add the number **4** to the side of the ball.
- Now imagine the ball bouncing, four times, and then expanding into a larger purple ball.
- Turn the purple ball and paint a flower on the side.
- Turn the ball some more until the number **4** shows up again.
- In your mind, bounce the ball, four times, and start to feel the feeling of safety, of being safe to play and have fun.
- Now imagine your friends arriving, and feel the joy of all of you playing with the ball, hearing the ball as it gently bounces each time, and hearing your friends talk and laugh.
- Keep turning the ball, and each time it bounces, erase the old picture of the flower and paint a new one.
- Change the number **4** to a **5** and bounce the ball five times in your mind. Each time the ball bounces erase the flower and see a new one. You are still feeling safe, playing with your friends, hearing them laughing and talking.
- Keep turning the ball - and see the numbers **6, 7, 8, 9, 10.**

Finally, express deep thanks, love, and gratitude for all of your four brains as well as your higher self or your deeper knowledge system that is connected to the larger mind - the **morphogenetic mind**.

Focus your attention and give gratitude to your whole mind, your deeper knowledge system and the unifying field that extends beyond the mind with as much passion as you can muster. No need to express exactly what you are thankful for, just express thanks. It may help to think of your four brains as a person or entity that you're thanking.

Take a deep breath and show even more gratitude.

Ask yourself: How do I feel?

You are now in conscious communication with every part of the body.

Do you understand what we did with the visualization? We engaged the right with the image and color, then the left with the number, then both with the four bounces, then we went back to the right for the flower, and showed the left brain the number again. Then we brought in the feeling of safety and play to connect to the brain stem; and then brought in your friends and the feeling of joy to connect to your emotional brain; and finally, added hearing, which more deeply connected you to the limbic system.

Mind and Goal Connection

Now that the mind is balanced and thinking correctly, let's consider your goal. Since the brain stem is concerned about your survival:

Ask yourself: What danger might show up on this journey?

Ask yourself: How might I best deal with this?

Ask yourself: At what point might I feel really scared?

Ask yourself: How might I best deal with this?

Now get the mammal brain involved. This brain wants to know how your plan affects your family or the group you live and work with.

Some of these questions may help.

Ask yourself: How might the changes I'm making affect my family, friends, colleagues, community, or anyone else relevant in my life?

Ask yourself: How will I best deal with this?

Ask yourself: How will my family, friends or communities reactions to my changes impact my plans?

Ask yourself: How will I best deal with this?

Ask yourself: How can I be emotionally aware and tuned into my body throughout the journey?

Ask yourself: How might I enjoy the moment now as I go through the process?

Ask yourself: What positive habitual patterns can support me in finding a groove?

Ask yourself: What old habitual patterns might I need to transform in order to maintain my groove through time?

Now let's involve the left and right brains.

The neocortex wants to know about logic and creativity.

Ask yourself: On a scale from 0 to 10, how creative is my plan?

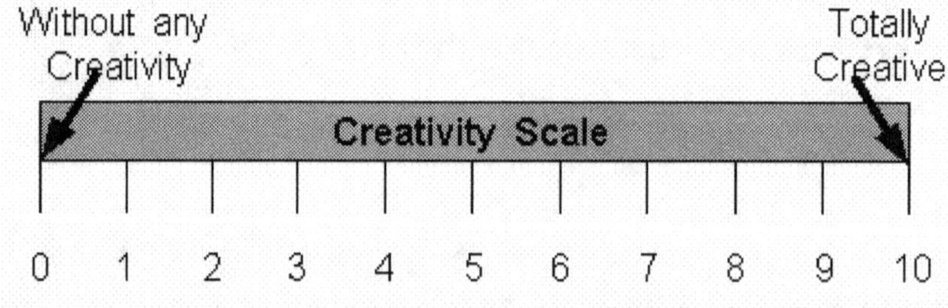

Ask yourself: On a scale from 0 to 10, how logical is my plan?

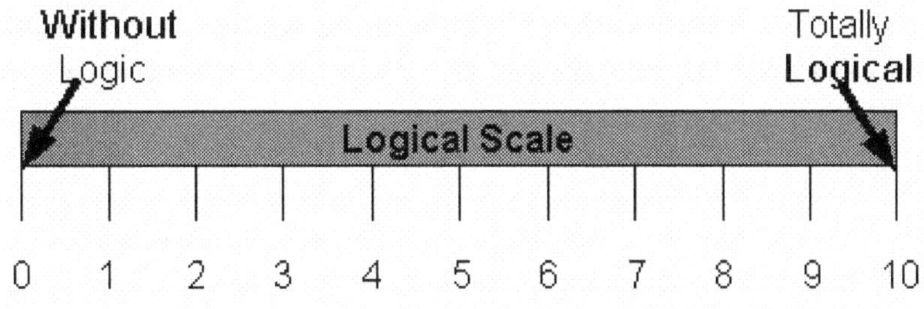

Ask yourself: On a scale from 0 to 10, how realistic is my plan?

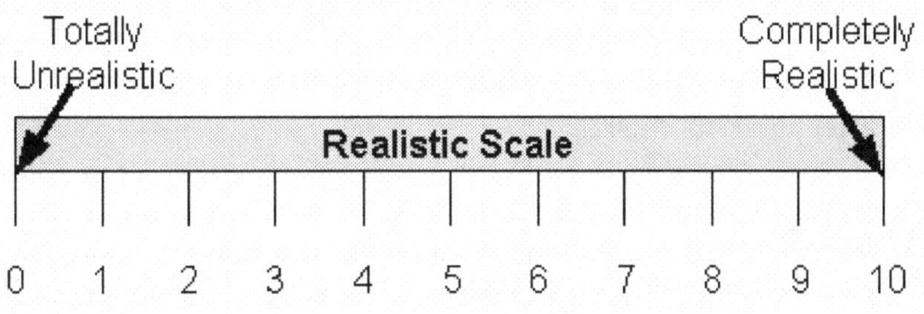

Ask yourself: How might I move each of these numbers up one notch so my plan is more creative, logical and realistic?

Ask yourself: What might be some other ways to achieve this goal?

Ask yourself: How might I expand my mind to look for all the possibilities on how to achieve this goal?

Just suppose you could access the Infinite Intelligence mind - the One Mind.

Ask yourself: How might Infinite Intelligence advise me on making my plan even more satisfying, rewarding and aligned with my larger purpose?

By consciously working with all your brains, you can build a better plan and have fewer setbacks as you achieve your goal.

Master's Tip Be grateful for all aspects of your mind and use your whole mind to make powerful choice after powerful choice.

Use Your Brains NOW

Imagine if you used all four brains consistently and were accessing the **One Mind** throughout your day.

Knowing that using all four brains helps you build a better plan and have fewer setbacks, what would you be willing to do now to more consistently be of **One Mind**?

What action might you take to remind yourself to engage the full power of your whole brain daily so you can more easily reach a future filled with a life you love?

Day 18 Stay Totally Focused

This session is about staying totally focused on your goal.

Did you see the movie ***Pollyanna***?

We use the word "Pollyanna" for people who are always looking on the bright side of dark situations in life. In the movie, Pollyanna was so chipper she was annoying to the people around her. Yet, when the chips were down for Pollyanna, those same people were so inspired by what she had taught them about "accentuating the positive and eliminating the negative" that they did everything in their power to support her.

As you learned in the last lesson, how you use your mind is very important. Unfortunately your brain does not come with a user manual, nor were very many people taught how to use it effectively in school. So, for many of us, running our brain "on all cylinders" is a total mystery.

Imagine Success

Have you ever noticed that when you don't keep your vision in mind and imagine yourself being successful, doubts about your own abilities creep in? You might hear yourself say, ***"Maybe I can't do this. Maybe I'm not smart enough. People are going to find out that I am not really confident and tell other people not to work with me."***

If you listen to and believe the voice of your inner saboteur, the next thing you know, you might actually envision yourself failing! This unconscious negative programming can convince you that there is nothing you can do about failing.

In cartoons they often have a bubble over the character's head that tells you what they're thinking. Visualizing failure rather than visualizing your success is like sticking a knife into your bubble - deflating your dream of living your best life. POP! OUCH! It hurts, doesn't it?

Create Your Destiny

MASTER'S TIP You create your own destiny!

What you think about all day long is what you get! If you consciously or unconsciously think you will fail, chances are you will. We go where our thoughts go. If you see failure in your mind's eye, you produce failure. So consciously keep imagining success. See it in your mind's eye. Be totally focused on your success.

MASTER'S TIP You are what you think about all day long. - Wayne Dyer

In general our society tends to look for what's wrong, not what's right. Most individuals learn to do problem analysis and problem solving in life. It becomes easy to focus on what didn't go well, and completely ignore what did. Problem analysis may be deeply ingrained in our thinking, but it is not the best way to get what we want. Thinking about what you really want in a situation is far more useful than analyzing what might go wrong. So focus on getting the desired outcome, rather than dwelling on the difficulties or setbacks in the situation.

See the Silver Lining

You learned earlier the importance of celebrating successes - even small ones. But often we disregard our successes. Of course, sometimes we have a setback or two. If this happens, let it be okay and focus on what you can learn from it. Remember that every dark cloud has a silver lining.

MASTER'S TIP Avoid asking failure-based questions.

Do not focus on what went wrong.

When you ask questions, such as: ***"What's wrong? Whose fault is it? Why did this happen? Why can't I solve this problem? How could this limit me?"***, you frame the situation as a problem or a failure. This approach will throw you into a downward spiral or unresourceful behavior - guaranteed!

I bet you can think of a time in your life when you made a mistake and learned a lot from it. Perhaps when you were learning to drive you turned the wheel really fast and noticed that the technique was not an effective way to stay on the road. Whatever your example is, you know you can learn from what you might otherwise call mistakes.

Master's Tip Milton Erickson used to say to his children: "Be sure to make lots of mistakes today."

Milton Erickson's genius knew that the way to Enlightened Internal Leadership is through being okay with making mistakes and learning from them.

Learn from Setbacks

In your life journey, you can also learn from setbacks by asking yourself questions that support learning and resourcefulness! For example, you might ask:

What do I really want?

What is possible here?

What have I learned from my results thus far?

How might this challenge have happened?

How might this challenge have been maintained?

What could I have done differently that might have worked better?

How might I solve this problem?

How is this an opportunity?

Once you discover what you can learn, reframe the setback as an opportunity!

Reframe

What is a reframe? Our **frame of reference** determines the meaning we give to a situation. And this meaning has a powerful effect on later decisions and actions. A familiar example of framing is seeing the proverbial glass as 'half empty' or 'half full'. The difference that makes the difference is the ability to **reframe** the situation in a productive way.

When we reframe, we repackage our thoughts and actively choose a resourceful way to look at each situation. If your goal is to start a new business, and your sales aren't what you forecast, what do you need to do? What options do you have to rectify matters and learn from the feedback? Focus your mind on what is possible, not on what has not worked so far. If you allow thoughts of failure to creep in, then your mind focuses on failure. Rather, focus on how you can change things, visualize yourself being successful, and let your mind help you succeed.

Reminder Whatever you focus on, you get more of.

See each setback as an opportunity to get more focused, more aligned, more determined, more committed to do what you need to do to take another three actions today to move towards your goal.

Master's Tip Your greatest success usually comes after you've experienced your greatest failure. - Napoleon Hill

A positive reframe powerfully refocuses your mind. Once you have done this, be prepared, open, and ready for the Universe to reveal a bigger plan to you. Listen, watch, and feel as your life speaks to you.

Ponder: How might this deepen your commitment to your goal?

Reward Reframing

Refocusing after a setback is a valuable step towards your goal, so reward yourself. Reframing the setback into an opportunity is a reward in itself because you immediately start to feel better. Consider being even more generous with yourself and double your rewards. Reward getting refocused with a reframe, and then reward yourself for taking three steps, that very day, to get back on track! Perhaps ask how you can reward yourself with something that leads into a bigger reward as you accomplish more and more! You may even want to hold a "Reframing or Refocusing Party" to provide wind beneath your wings as you soar to the next level. To make the party more meaningful, check in with yourself before the party.

Ponder: How committed am I, on a scale of 0 to 10 to deepen my commitment?

Deepening your commitment can be done by reviewing the value behind your goal, the **compelling reason why** you are doing what you are doing. Then party!

Deepening Commitment

Try deepening your commitment right now. First, focus on your goal. Then picture the end result that you are after. And finally,

Ponder: Why am I doing this?

Ponder: Why is this important to me?

Ponder: Why else?

Ponder: Why else?

That conversation with yourself should be energizing enough to keep you focused on what you want!

Now watch the magnetic pull of the Universe help move your goal towards you.

Staying Totally Focused

INTEGRATION CHECKLIST

Things you will need

Your journal

A quiet space to think and write

A current challenge you are having

Integration-Related Activity

The goal of this activity is for you to experience two forms of questioning. With this knowledge, you can create a masterful plan for staying totally focused.

IMPORTANT INSTRUCTION **ANSWER THE QUESTIONS WITHOUT CENSORING YOURSELF**

Quality of Life

Consider that the questions that you ask yourself, that you ask your mind, determines the quality of your life. In this exercise you try two different sets of questioning formats. Notice how you feel as you answer these questions.

Problem Analysis Questioning Format

Before you begin, write down a current challenge you are having. It can be associated with your goal or something else.

No matter what comes up for you, please answer the question and just notice how you feel in your body.

Using your current challenge, answer the following questions:

Ask yourself: What's wrong?

Ask yourself: What is not possible here?

Ask yourself: Whose fault is it?

Ask yourself: Who is to blame?

Ask yourself: Why did this happen?

Ask yourself: Why can't I solve this problem?

Ask yourself: How badly have I failed?

Ask yourself: How could that limit me?

Stand up and shake out your body.

Get a clean sheet of paper.

Using the same challenge, answer the following questions:

Questioning Format 2

Ask yourself: What do I want?

Ask yourself: What is possible here?

Ask yourself: What have I learned from the results I have gotten so far?

Ask yourself: How can I learn from the results I have gotten?

Ask yourself: How might this challenge have happened?

Ask yourself: How might this challenge have been maintained?

Ask yourself: How might I solve this problem?

Ask yourself: How can I get from where I am to where I want to be?

Ask yourself: How is this an opportunity?

Failure-Focused Questioning Format

Notice in the Questioning Format 1, which we call **failure** questions, you focused on the negative, on what you don't want, and were likely creating negative images in your mind.

This questioning format possibly had you feeling bad. Right? Yet, how often do you consciously or unconsciously ask these questions? Probably a lot, if you are like most people - which is why you feel bad.

Most of us have been taught to do a lot of problem analysis and problem solving in life. So often in life we think that if we figure out **why** something is the way it is, we can get to the root cause and feel better.

While problem analysis is deeply ingrained in our thinking, it is not the best approach to getting what we want.

Desired Outcome Questioning Format

The second questioning format is far more useful because the focus is on getting the desired outcome, rather than dwelling on the difficulties or setbacks in the situation.

Generally speaking, **how** questions are more useful than **why** questions in problem solving because they uncover the structure of the problem. **Why** questions tend to only illicit reasons or justifications without changing anything. We all know that everything is explainable and justifiable with hindsight.

Why questions are useful for eliciting values - ***Why is this important?*** - but they are not useful when eliciting solutions.

If you were to integrate three questions that you could ask yourself, especially in the moments that you are spinning out of control, questions that would serve you to feel better and get back on purpose, what might they be?

Some empowering, resourceful questions that we have shared so far are:

- What do I really want?
- What is possible here?
- What do I want that is within my control?
- What is my true intention?
- How might I get what I want?
- How would I know if I actually got what I wanted?
- How does this choice align with my purpose?
- How is this an opportunity?
- How can I get what I want while supporting others to get what they want?
- Will this choice move me towards a future I love or keep me stuck in the past?
- Will this choice add to my life energy or take away from it?
- Does this choice empower me or disempower me?
- Am I standing in my power by making this choice?
- What unreasonable request might I make of myself right now?

Your Three Questions

Ask yourself: What are the three best questions for me to integrate on an unconscious level?

-
-
-

Ask yourself: How will I integrate these so they are available to me when I most need them?

Now consider posting your questions around the house, in your daytimer or journal, on a card you carry in your wallet or purse, or on a vision board. Also consider asking a friend to support you by asking them when you are complaining or focusing on what you don't want.

Give Your Ego a Bone

One fun way to stay focused is to give your ego a bone. How?

Every time your ego brings up an objection to your plan, throw it a bone to gnaw on.

For example, if your ego says to you, ***"That would be selfish to achieve that goal. Who do you think you are?"***, you promptly say right back to your ego, ***"You know, you're right. Who <u>do</u> I think that I am? You're right, it might be selfish. And you know what? I'm going to do it and have it anyhow!"***

Notice that with this approach, your ego can no longer argue – you've agreed with it. It will go away and gnaw on its bone, comfortably knowing that it's right. Whether you're selfish or not is not the point, nor is it important to ask who you are. All we are doing is getting the ego out of the way so you can progress towards what you want.

Stay Totally Focused NOW

Imagine if, in every moment, you remained totally focused on your outcome and, when life's challenges presented themselves, you were able to ask yourself effective questions and stay on track.

Make a commitment to create the best three questions possible to support you in staying totally focused on reaching your goal.

What action might you take to remind yourself to stay totally focused, asking your questions and addressing your ego objections, so you can have a future filled with a life you love?

Day 19 **Get Support**

Don't do it alone!

This session is about getting support and help from others on your journey to your goal.

There is a great quote by an unknown author:
"The journey to finding your true self takes a commitment to keep going no matter what. Keep going despite your feelings. Keep taking action despite your fears. Keep focusing on your journey, the process, and get the support you need. If you do, the results will take care of themselves."

Almost everyone does better with encouragement, backing and support.

Remember the song *I'll get by with a little help from my friends*?

Or how about the saying *No man is an island*?

In the Bible, Matthew 7:7 says, "Ask and it will be given to you, knock and the door will be opened to you."

We all reach our goals faster with strong support.

A Story

A Brief Tale

Count On Me
by Whitney Houston and Cici Winans

Count on me through thick and thin
A friendship that will never end
When you are weak, I will be strong
Helping you to carry on

Call on me, I will be there
Don't be afraid
Please believe me when I say
Count on me

I can see it's hurting you
I can feel your pain
It's hard to see the sunshine through the rain
I know sometimes it seems as if
It's never gonna end
But you'll get through it
Just don't give in cuz you can

Are you getting the support you need? And are you being the support others need?

Get a Little Help

When support is just a phone call or knock away, many people do not knock or make the call. Are you one of these people? Perhaps you think it is better to do it on your own, or maybe you fear being seen as needy, incompetent, or silly. A lot of us fear hearing someone say **no** and experiencing rejection. Have you ever felt this way?

Consider that when we take on these fears, we get in our own way because we have already rejected ourself by failing to give others a chance! Everyday we hear about people who receive incredible gifts - just because they had the courage to ask.

NOTE You are on day 19 of a journey that you choose powerfully to take. And this session recommends ways to get support. Because we at Powerful Choices Coaching value the support of each other and use coaching for internal support, we encourage entering into a coaching relationship in this session. Later in this journey you learn more about additional methods of support.

Fear of Rejection

Let's talk about that fear of rejection. We often try to get the support we need from friends and family. There are some reasons why this sometimes fails.

- Your friends and family don't always know how to support you.
- Your friends and family sometimes have their own agenda, often unconscious; and this agenda might interfere with offering you support in the manner you need.

Have you ever had an experience where you weren't quite sure of yourself, perhaps when you were doing something you felt was a real stretch for you? If someone comes along and gives you the gift of confidence by saying, "Yeah, go for it! You're really good at that! I know you can do it! How can I support you?", how would you feel then? More confident? More able to do it?

Get a Coach

In 2002, we worked for the Olympic Organizing Committee and it was an amazing experience. One striking realization was that no athlete makes it to the Olympics without a coach - **no one**!

Peak performers do not reach their potential on their own. They seek support, accountability, and encouragement to be the best they can be. So why would you try to live your best life without the support you need to be your best?

Master's Tip If you think you can, you can - it's that simple.

This is where support can be extremely helpful. Suppose you told someone your dream and they snorted in disgust. You'd probably feel hurt, right? Or maybe you'd be angry or feel that you didn't measure up to their standards. This, of course, is anti-support! It drags you down.

While some people rebel against this reaction just to prove the anti-supporter wrong, rebellion is not the best way to be motivated. What if, instead of proving someone wrong, you could get the support you need to be your best on all levels?

Personal and professional development coaches are trained to do just that - to support you to do what it takes to be your best, and to ask the questions that help you focus on exactly what you want and how to get it. And with no conscious or unconscious agenda, a coach can be totally focused on you and what you want.

A Coach's Support

Consider that a coach might be a valuable investment in yourself because your coach has no agenda other than your success. When you succeed, your coach succeeds.

Think how helpful regular support times, either with a friend or with a skilled coach could be. You can stay focused on your success. Each month, week, or in some cases each day, you get to **re-mission** and recommit to living your best life and reaching your goals.

Is life easier when you have someone to bounce ideas off of, celebrate your successes, and help you plan? Think about what any Olympic Gold metal athlete would say about getting the support you need!

Choosing Support

Choosing the right support person means choosing someone who understands you and supports your goals, someone you trust, and who keeps your conversations confidential. You may be saying, ***"I have the perfect friend for this!"***

Consider that professional athletes select profession coaches for a reason! Professional coaches, whether in sports or in life, understand the process of goal achievement and know how to build skills and confidence. They know how to help you see where to adjust to make the most of your efforts so you stay on track towards your goal.

A coach can be your vision keeper. Have you ever been deep in the trenches - so wrapped up in the **doing** that you don't take time to look up and see the big picture, the destination?

Getting support means having someone who can help you see the big picture. A coach reflects your issues back to you, so you can see, hear, and feel them. And a coach asks you great questions to provide clarification, inside-out transformation, and motivation to keep you moving towards living your best life.

Your life-work support person must also understand how the mind works. Remember the whole-brain conversation? You want someone to support you in asking questions that develop your whole mind muscle and point you towards more progress. The more progress you make, the more you build self-esteem and confidence. You also see more clearly the areas that still need work as you progress towards being an Olympic Gold medalist in living your best life!

Phone Support

Just like you chat with your friends by phone, you can do great phone-work with a coach. You don't have to meet in person, so you are not limited to a coach in your geographic area.

When we try to reach our goals on our own, it can be hard to stay motivated. Talking to a supportive person on a regular basis often is the difference between success and failure.

If you go it alone, you may not fail, but you might get less success than you deserve. Something about the human soul cries out for support. Coaches fill that need. They keep you focused, help you feel good about yourself and your progress, help you see where to make adjustments on your journey, and ultimately, help you succeed.

Getting Support

INTEGRATION CHECKLIST

Things you will need

Your journal

A quiet space to think and write

Integration-Related Activity

The goal of this activity is for you to determine your most effective support system. With this knowledge, you can create an Enlightened Internal Leadership plan on how to create your most effective support system to reach your goals.

Effective Support Systems

Having an effective support system is extremely important in reaching your goals. Without support you might accomplish the goals, but it is much harder. It is interesting to start the conversation by checking in with yourself. Be open, honest and direct with yourself.

ASK YOURSELF: Am I someone that radiates positive energy and creates energy in others, or do I come to the conversation taking energy or zapping the life energy from others?

ASK YOURSELF: How much and how often do I add wind to people's sails by being optimistic, supportive and encouraging in all relationships in all situations?

Ask yourself: How much and how often do you steal the wind from people's sails?

Ask yourself: On a scale from 0 to 10, how nourishing, empowering am I for others?

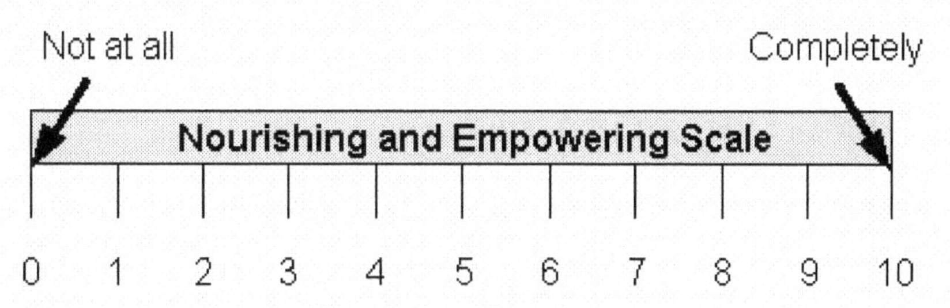

Ask yourself: If I were to be more of the type of person I want to attract into my life and moved my number up one notch, what might I do differently now?

Ask yourself: On a scale from 0 to 10, how nourishing and empowering am I for myself?

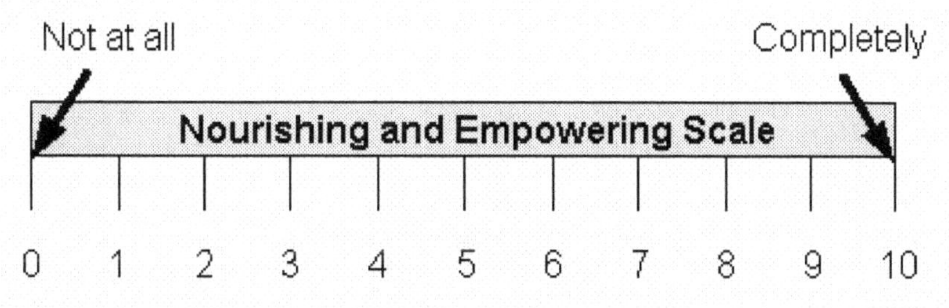

Consider how you talk to yourself, the tone you use to motivate yourself. Of course it is always an inside-out journey.

Ask yourself: If I were to be the type of person for myself that I want to attract into my life and moved my number up one notch, what might I do differently now?

Ask yourself: When will I start to do these things?

Take a moment and think of your support system.

Ask yourself: On a scale from 0 to 10, how satisfied am I with my existing support system?

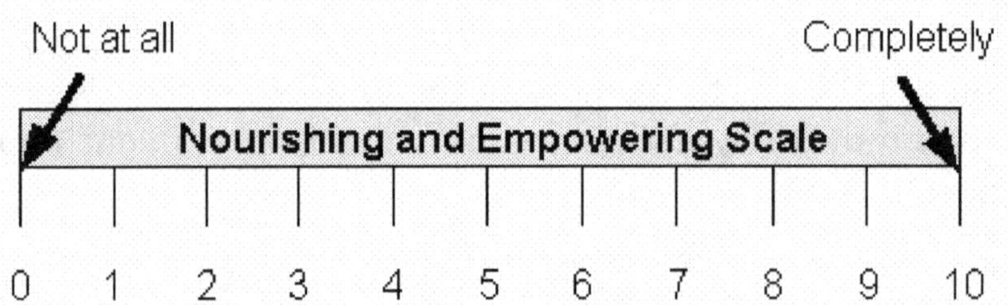

If your supporters act in ways that steal your life energy - they are negative, disempowering, and discouraging. Some people may just be present - neither encouraging or discouraging – just present. However, we all are seeking people who are completely nurturing, who challenge us to play a bigger game and to be more than we currently are - all the while loving us just as we are.

Ask yourself: What would having an even more effective support system do for me?

Ask yourself: Who would it allow me to be?

Ask yourself: Why is this important?

Ask yourself: If I were to design the most perfect supportive relationship, what type of person or community would I look for?

Ask yourself: How do I want this person or community to support me? Encourage me? Challenge me? Hold me accountable to what I say?

Ask yourself: What are the questions that I need to ask the person or the community so I am clear that I will have the most supportive system possible for me?

Ask yourself: What would be my specific request of them?

Ask yourself: How might I find this person or this community that is perfect for me? Where might they be located?

Ask yourself: What actions might I take to connect with them?

Ask yourself: When will I do this?

Ask yourself: What is the benefit of following through with this commitment to myself?

Ask yourself: What is the cost of not following through with this commitment to myself?

Get Support NOW

Imagine if you started right now building the support system that would help you reach your goals with ease and support you to live a fabulous life!

Knowing that getting support helps make your life less stressful and more powerful, what would you be willing to do now? What action might you take to create the best support system ever so that your future is filled with a life you love?

Day 20 **Ride Your Cycle**

This session is about the cycle of progress that you follow as you live life.

"There is no such thing as failure, only results! Consider that failure is just a way of describing a result you did not want. These results can be used as feedback, helpful corrections, and a splendid opportunity to learn something new." - Author Unknown

As Steve Covey says: "Effective people are not problem-minded; they're opportunity-minded. They feed opportunities and starve problems."

You no doubt realize by now that there is a cycle of progress that everyone follows as they work towards living their best life and achieving their goals.

Start the Cycle

In this cycle, you begin with clarity on exactly what you want. You set a goal and proceed to set up your plans. Then, based on the information you have at the time, you start taking action.

Every day you take the three actions that produce the greatest gain and decrease the gap between where you are and where you want to be. Day after day, you commit and follow through with those three actions. You have already started doing this!

The next phase in the cycle is to gather feedback so you can gauge how well you're doing and whether your plan is working the way you wanted it to.

Remember the staircase and those landings where you can stop and take stock? At each landing, you can gather feedback to clarify if you're making the progress you want. But how can you tell if it is quality feedback? The results you get or don't get are useful information.

Quality Feedback

Consider that the quality of the feedback depends on what you measure, how you measure it, and how accurately and precisely you take the measurement. You could consider defining in advance what evidence would prove you are on track. However, when you are focused on what you want, all observations and results are helpful to direct and redirect your effort.

A fun way to think about observations that might seem like failures is simply to see them as short term results you did not want. Or see them as a solution to a problem you didn't have or were not solving.

To illustrate feedback, let's look at a simple road trip example. Suppose you plan to drive from New York to California, and you see a sign that says "Alaska, 2300 miles". This is probably a sign you're going the wrong way. And monitoring where you are at anytime provides feedback to ponder. In this case, the signpost is the feedback. The Alaska sign would make you wonder, right? Of course, you can get to California via Alaska, but it's the long way around - the 'scenic tour' approach to your destination.

ALASKA
2300 Miles

Make Adjustments

When you have quality feedback that does not support you in your journey to where you want to go, it's time to adjust. Adjusting is the next step in the cycle of progress. When the sign post says **Alaska** and you're heading for southern California, it is time to get out your map.

Your plan, with each little step, is your map of how to get to your goal. Check your map. Are you on track? Are you headed for California by way of Alaska? If so, it is adjustment time - time to start to head south instead of north!

The bottom line is this:

Master's Tip The sooner you gather feedback, the sooner you know if you have to make adjustments to get what you want.

Cycle and Recycle

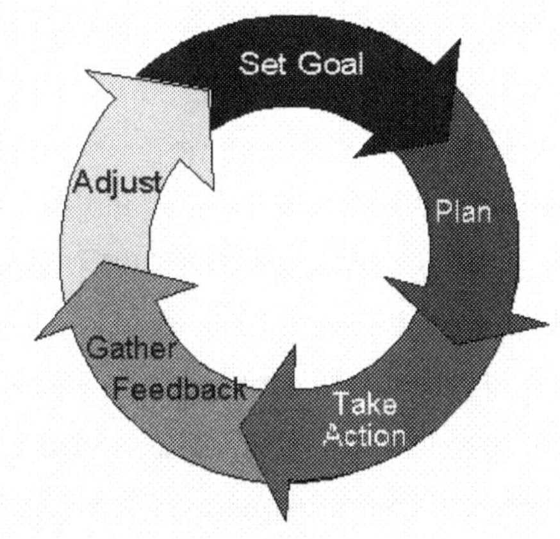

It's all part of the cycle:
(1) set a goal
(2) make a plan
(3) take action
(4) collect feedback, and
(5) make adjustments according to the feedback you got.

Once you have checked for feedback and made adjustments, you are ready to start the cycle over again, this time deepening your commitment to your goal and clarifying your plans to be even more effective.

Keep in mind that setbacks are just feedback that something isn't working quite right for you. Consequently, your plan and your mind must be flexible. If something isn't working for you, you do have a choice - you can map a different route and change how you are getting to your goal.

Adjust and Align

Some people, as they get closer to their goal, adjust the goal to make it even more in alignment with what they want or with all other areas of their life. This alignment is part of the cycle of progress. We set our goals and make our plans, based on the information we have at the time.

As you progress closer to your goal, you have more information, so you can make clearer choices. Sometimes you may change the plan, sometimes you may adjust the goal itself.

For example, suppose your goal is to have a dream house on the ocean in California. Perhaps along the way, you realize that you get a heat rash easily or you don't like the California traffic. You might say to yourself, "Hmmmm, I am not sure California is for me, but I sure enjoyed the coast of Oregon when I traveled through it." Then you realize that the California dream home was not what you really wanted at all. Living on the ocean was the important part of the goal. With this new information about what is most important to you, you can adjust. And your new goal becomes a dream house on the beautiful coast of

Oregon, where you don't get heat rash and there is less traffic. The effort you put into a dream house in California is not wasted. You can still use those skills and what you learned about ocean-front living when you move to Oregon.

When you adjust your goal based on feedback, it's just part of the cycle. Every stop for feedback and each adjustment is our chance to clarify what we really want, and to make new plans to get it. Clarity is your friend, and it comes from continually restarting the cycle of progress.

The Universe speaks to you in amazing ways - as a whisper, a message, a lesson, a challenge, or a crisis. Continuously monitor the information you are getting from the Universe. Pay attention and be flexible. Listen to the whispers, messages, and lessons; and adjust before you run into major challenges.

Riding the Cycle

INTEGRATION CHECKLIST

Things you will need

Your journal

A quiet space to think and write

Integration-Related Activity

The goal of this activity is for you to determine if you are where you want to be in the cycle of progress. You also examine how closely you are tuned in to the small voice inside of you that provides feedback about how aligned you are with your results. With this knowledge, you can adjust your plan to avoid major challenges as you move forward to Enlightened Internal Leadership.

Integration Space Exercise

Think of your goal.

ASK YOURSELF: What am I measuring that lets me know I am on track?

ASK YOURSELF: How am I measuring this?

ASK YOURSELF: What are the logical points for me to gather feedback?

How effectively are you tuned in to the still small voice inside yourself, the whispers happening in the outer world, as well as the obvious tangible results you are getting? Remember, if what you are doing is not working, it is time to recognize this and do something different!

It is essential for you to have some way to know you are on track, because only you can know if what you are doing is working in the way you want it to.

Evaluate Your Progress

The following questions can help you decide if you are where you want to be, or if you need to do some adjusting.

As you answer these questions, the key is to listen to the feedback without allowing shame or blame if you are not on track. Your responses are merely information from which you can learn.

WRITTEN ACTIVITY PLEASE WRITE DOWN YOUR ANSWERS IN YOUR JOURNAL.

ASK YOURSELF: Am I where I thought I would be by this date?

We call this **gross feedback**, not meaning that it is gross, but rather that the feedback is general and allows a **clock and calendar connection** check.

ASK YOURSELF: Is there a match between my projected dates and my achievement right now?

ASK YOURSELF: Have I achieved what I wanted by this date?

Perhaps you are ahead of your schedule! Maybe you are a bit behind. Again, this is just information. Whatever your situation, even if you are not exactly where you want to be, you have likely achieved a small part of your goal.

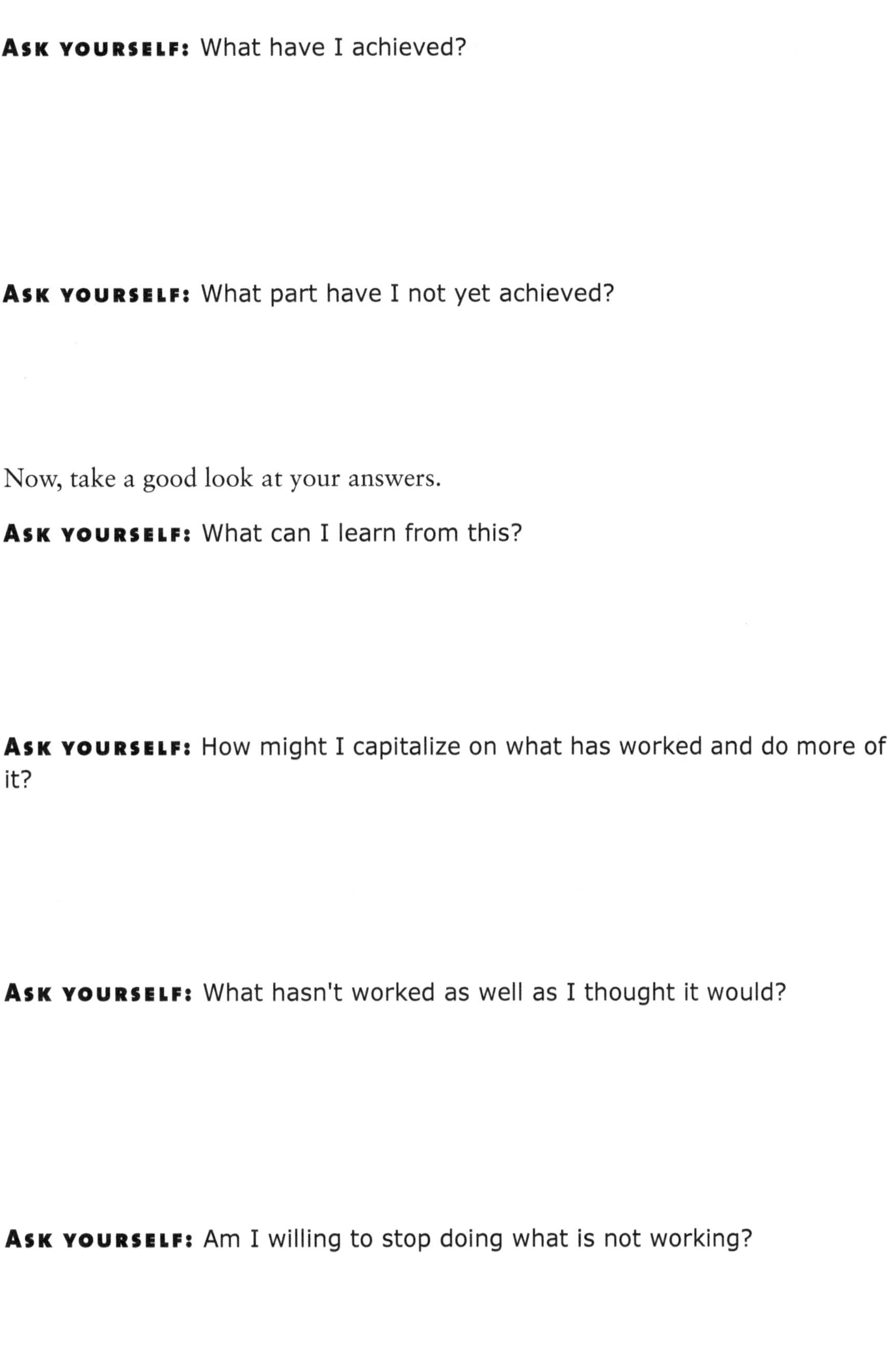

Ask yourself: What have I achieved?

Ask yourself: What part have I not yet achieved?

Now, take a good look at your answers.

Ask yourself: What can I learn from this?

Ask yourself: How might I capitalize on what has worked and do more of it?

Ask yourself: What hasn't worked as well as I thought it would?

Ask yourself: Am I willing to stop doing what is not working?

Ask yourself: What might I do differently now that will work better?

If you are having trouble answering or possibly thinking: "***I don't know.***", then just pretend that you do know. Act as if the answer is easy and obvious to access, and try again.

Ask yourself: What might I do differently that might work better?

Ask yourself: What needs to be done right now?

Ask yourself: What adjustments can I imagine myself making that support me in making the journey more fun and more effectively getting what I want?

Ask yourself: What might be the best way to make these changes?

Moving Through the Cycle

Your answers are all feedback. It is impossible to know where you're going if you don't stop to see where you are and if you are on your way to where you want to go!

Consider asking yourself these questions on a regular basis so you can continue to look at your results, and constantly improve how you get those results. And remember, do more of what works and less of what doesn't work.

Looking Beyond

Let's take a moment to look beyond your immediate goal to your whole life. We invite you to have an open and honest conversation with your highest-self or deeper knowledge system.

Tune in for a moment.

Become aware of your whole life.

Listen.

CONSIDER: Consider that your life is inviting you to look into something important that will support you in playing a bigger and more effective game.

ASK YOURSELF: What opportunity might I miss?

ASK YOURSELF: Where is there the beginning of a challenge that I can solve before it grows into a problem?

Ask yourself: What is the next step my life is inviting me to take?

Ask yourself: What might the still small voice within or the whispers outside of me be telling me?

Answer: The still small voice within and the whispering outside of me is saying…

Suppose you were to listen and take action on the advice you received.

Ask yourself: What might my next step be?

Ask yourself: When might I take it?

We have done some incredible work on getting feedback from the results of your immediate goal and your life in general. Be awake to the Universe. Your life is speaking to you **right now**!

Ride Your Cycle NOW

Imagine if you regularly examined all phases of the cycle of progress and listened to your small voice within that guides you.

Knowing that consistent feedback, accepted as information, helps you reach your goal sooner, what would you be willing to do now?

What action might you take to remind yourself to regularly examine your progress, and then adjust and align so that you can efficiently reach a future that is filled with a life you love?

Day 21 **Stay in Motion**

This session is about building forward motion on your journey to your goal.

The truth of the matter is that there's nothing you can't accomplish if:
(1) You clearly decide what it is that you're absolutely committed to achieving,
(2) You're willing to take massive action,
(3) You notice what's working or not, and
(4) You continue to change your approach until you achieve what you want, using whatever life gives you along the way.

- Anthony Robbins

Wow! You've been on your journey for twenty-one days now, and built some momentum! Let's keep that momentum going, or even expand it by asking some really important questions.

If you have been taking three actions a day, you have definitely made progress.

Build Habits

Do you realize that it takes 21 days of consistent action to build a new habit of success? And this is Day 21! So today is a perfect day to look at where you've been and how you've moved toward your goal.

PONDER: Where was I twenty-one days ago?

PONDER: How many actions have I taken since I began this journey?

Momentum builds internally when we realize how far we've moved and how much we've accomplished. Think of what your life would be like if you hadn't set this goal and were not taking any action. You probably wouldn't have made any changes at all, and your life would still be the same, right?

Let's continue building momentum, taking your daily three actions today, and even adding a fourth, if you can, as a sign of how deeply committed you are to your goal.

Ponder: How am I doing with evaluating and adjusting with the feedback I am getting?

Ponder: Am I close to meeting the deadline I set for myself today? Perhaps surpassed it?

If so, great! Keep doing what you've been doing. If not, what adjustments might you make? What worked for you?

Notice What Works

Notice the three things that worked best to support you as you took action towards your goal. Do more of that!

Notice what is not working - and don't do that again! It is time to make an adjustment and do something different. Sometimes progress is a matter of trial and error - taking your best guess, and then adjusting according to your feedback.

Build Mastery

Know what works for you and consider how you can build on it so it works even better.

Ponder: Are there some actions that are now so easy they are now habits?

If so, you have mastered that action, so add in another action to continue building new habits and momentum.

Ponder: What else might I do to add even more momentum?

Have other ideas occurred to you that might move you to your goal even faster? Take a look at each of your actions and your plan. You know more now than you did when you started, so you have better information on which to build a plan and take action.

Monitor Progress

Let's try reflecting on where you were and review your plan.

Ponder: How am I doing?

Ponder: Am I making the progress I wanted?

Ponder: What might I do to make the progress I desire?

Now is the time to adjust and make some corrections to your course.

Ponder: Is there any improvement I might make?

Ponder: How can I adjust what I have been doing so that I get the results I want?

Ponder: What hasn't worked as well as I thought it would?

Ponder: Is there a way I can replace some actions with different actions that I know work?

The answers to these questions are your adjustments.

When you monitor your progress, you know right away if you need to build more momentum.

Momentum eventually takes on a life of it's own. As you build mastery with each of the actions you take, you build Enlightened Internal Leadership with the overall goal. And as you build forward motion and Enlightened Internal Leadership, you become capable of more actions and progress.

As we build skills, taking action, step-by-step, each small action or skill we learn multiplies over time.

Here's to playing the Enlightened Internal Leadership game!

Invest Early

Investment advisers tell their clients that the dollars invested early in life multiple significantly to add to the retirement portfolio. This phenomenon is also true of investments we make in ourselves to support living a life we love. We are investing in our growth and evolution bank account.

Master's Tip The small actions we take now multiple significantly over time - leading to huge rewards and returns of happiness in the future.

Take a moment now and think about the cumulative effect on your life of having achieved your goal. See yourself twenty years from now, looking back, and saying, ***"It all started when I decided to live my best life. I set the goal, built the plan, took the action, and over the years, here I am. Look what I gained!"***

Ask yourself the right questions now while focusing on achieving your goal. Build the momentum and stay in motion!

Embrace this law of physics as your ally:

Master's Tip An object in motion tends to stay in motion! And a person on their path to a life they love, building momentum and taking action, tends to stay on the path and live their dream life.

Staying in Motion

INTEGRATION CHECKLIST

Things you will need

Your journal

A quiet space to think and write

Integration-Related Activity

The goal of these activities is for you to learn how to build and maintain forward motion. With this knowledge, you can create a masterful plan on how to move forward to being the Enlightened Internal Leader of your life.

★ **IMPORTANT INSTRUCTION** **KNOW YOUR GOALS.**

Building Momentum Exercise

As you have heard many times before: an object in motion tends to stay in motion! We build momentum when we stay in motion - when we keep going in the face of any obstacle or roadblock.

Sometimes it can be challenging to visualize the big goal being achieved when you are in the phase of high **Intensity**. Your concentration may drift to the things that are not turning out exactly the way you planned with your goal. If this happens, you can still get into action by visualizing your three-steps-a-day.

Long Term Achievement

In addition to each day, we can also visualize our goals being achieved each week, month, or year.

MASTER'S TIP Our big successes are built from a series of small successes.

It is easier to get yourself in motion if the steps you have to take are doable and do not look too daunting.

Visualization Plus Action

In this exercise we combine visualization with our three actions.

WRITTEN ACTIVITY WRITE THE THREE IMMEDIATE ACTIONS YOU NEED TO TAKE TO ACCOMPLISH YOUR LONG TERM GOAL.

-

-

-

The first part of the exercise reminds you of the power of visualization and how it works in achieving your goal. The second part makes it relevant to your goal.

The Power of the Mind

Are you ready to play a game?

1. Stand up and face forwards.

   Reach one arm out to the side, parallel with the ground. Keeping your hips facing forward, turn from the waist and bring your arm and head as far around to the right (or left) as you can comfortably turn.

   Make a note of how far you have turned by noting visually where your fingers are pointing.

   Repeat three times, to establish just how far you can comfortably turn.

2. Close your eyes, and imagine yourself turning, without actually moving.

   See yourself turning further than you have been. Repeat three times.

3. Once again reach one arm out to the side, parallel with the ground. With your eyes closed, turn as far as you comfortably can.

4. Holding the position, open your eyes and note how much further you have turned, just by visualizing how much further you can turn!

Relevance to Goal

MASTER'S TIP Visualizing yourself doing something enhances your performance.

1. Choose one of the immediate actions you listed that you need to perform to accomplish your goal.

   Make a picture - bright, close up, life-size of yourself accomplishing the immediate goal.
   When the picture is clear, step into the **you** that is in the picture, and feel how it feels to be doing that action.
   Feel how good it feels to have the satisfaction of knowing you have started to achieve your goals.
   Enjoy that feeling.
   Notice that how you are thinking makes doing this task easy.
   Step out and look at yourself again in bright technicolor.

ASK YOURSELF: What am I thinking that makes this so easy?

2. Choose another of the immediate actions you listed that you need to perform to accomplish your goal.

   Make a picture - bright, close up, life-size of yourself accomplishing the immediate goal.
   When the picture is clear, step into the you that is in the picture, and feel how it feels to be doing that action.
   Feel how good it feels to have the satisfaction of knowing you have started to achieve your goals.
   Enjoy that feeling.
   Notice that how you are thinking makes doing this task easy.
   Step out and look at yourself again in bright technicolor.

ASK YOURSELF: What am I thinking that makes this so easy?

3. Choose the third immediate action you listed that you need to perform to accomplish your goal.

   Make a picture - bright, close up, life-size of yourself accomplishing the immediate goal.
   When the picture is clear, step into the you that is in the picture, and feel how it feels to be doing that action.
   Feel how good it feels to have the satisfaction of knowing you have started to achieve your goals.
   Enjoy that feeling.
   Notice that how you are thinking makes doing this task easy.
   Step out and look at yourself again in bright technicolor.

Ask yourself: What am I thinking that makes this so easy?

4. Form a picture of the benefits you will have from accomplishing your long term goal.

   See yourself enjoying the results and benefits of achieving your goal, of completing the job you have set out to do.

   Make this picture bright, close up, and life-size.
   Make sure the picture is placed right in front of you.
   Move it so close to you that with just one step, you can step right into the picture and physically become that you in your mind.
   Step into the picture now, and really enjoy being there, accomplishing the actions that take you towards your goals.

   Step out and see yourself and notice how motivated you are.

5. Now go into the world and take the first action!
   First in mind, then in reality. And **you must take action.**
   Keep reviewing the pictures every time you need inspiration to add wind to your sails.

Doesn't that feel good? Okay, let's take massive action and use the pictures to keep your momentum flowing!

Build Forward Motion NOW

Imagine if you visualized all the steps to reach your goal daily, so each step became easy to accomplish.

Knowing that visualizing and then taking action helps you reach your goal more efficiently, what would you be willing to do now?

What action might you take to remind yourself to regularly visualize and then take action so that you can efficiently reach a future that is filled with a life you love?

Part 7: **Satisfaction Check**

You have built a strong foundation, created a vision, made a powerful choice to go for it, and planned how to reach your goal. You started your plan in action, found some challenges, and learned some techniques for continuing your success.

The next phase of the 30-day program is seven days during which you learn a variety of ways to check your satisfaction and correct your course when you are drifting away from achieving your goal.

The architect has a solid foundation, has designed the home, begun construction, anticipated possible obstacles to reaching the completion date, sought support in overcoming obstacles, and is taking action towards building momentum to reach the completion date. It's time now to look at the level of satisfaction with the progress and with the successes thus far.

As you continue to be the architect of your life, creating the blueprints for success, seeking help and using all your resources to keep your momentum going, it is useful to stay on your path, avoid obstacles and surround yourself with people who help you succeed. As the construction coordinator, it is useful to collaborate with others who know your challenges and strengths, and to seek feedback on how to succeed in the most efficient and effective manner possible.

Journals

Your journal continues to fill up. Your blueprint is complete and you are taking actions to reach your goal. You have momentum and can see the structure being built on the strong foundation.

What should be in your journal now? Check out your blueprint and make certain that you have completed all the details - done the exercises you might have skipped and put extra effort into ones you might have found challenging.

Review your plan, and tweak it as you receive feedback and more information. Make certain that you get the support you need and stay focused on what you want.

7-Day Satisfaction Check Overview

The first five days of your journey were about building a foundation. The next two were about inspiration and vision, learning to live **your** dream. Then you spent four days learning how to make your decision powerful and compelling. The next three days you planned, and then you spent two days getting started and five days continuing your successful journey. It's time now to check your level of satisfaction and find other successful people whom you can ask for input and collaborate with to reach your destination powerfully.

In **Day 22** you learn to acknowledge the thoughts, feelings or inner voices that appear to want to sabotage your progress. By listening to these voices and seeing the messages as wise, we can take actions to resolve the issues that are arising, keeping us safe and moving us forward on our path to success.

In **Day 23** we invite you to witness the emotional undercurrents of your life that inform your thoughts and eventually create your destiny. Then you can make the tiny shifts necessary to support yourself to live your best life.

In **Day 24** you learn about the impact of the people with whom you spend your time. Do you spend time with people who steal your life energy or do you spend time with people who give your life energy, people who radiate optimism, support, encouragement and whom you love to be around? The implications are huge and we provide some tips on how to develop win/win situations with successful, positive people.

Day 25 is about the staying on course. Consider committing to constant and ever-ending improvement, looking at each new step with a beginner's mind, so you can live your life on purpose by asking yourself: "Am I moving in the right direction?"

In **Day 26** we encourage you to recognize that, despite what happens in our physical environment, we are totally free inside our heads. And the ultimate freedom is to choose how you think and respond to poor circumstances and negative people around you.

Day 27 is about Mastermind groups - small groups of people supporting each other on their life path. Focusing on the success of others is a sure way to improve the success of your own life. What you give comes back to you tenfold!

In **Day 28** you learn to ask for feedback. Feedback is simply information, the guidance system on the airplane to your goals. New information helps you make the corrections that support you in reaching your goal. So we provide some tips on how to ask for feedback and how to accept it openly.

As you continue to step up your staircase, notice how wonderful the view is from the landing you have already reached. And notice your level of satisfaction now that the end is in sight.

Are you ready?

CHECKLIST

- Be sure you have your journal.
- Set a time aside each day to do your life's work.

Day 22 Befriend Your Gremlins

This session is about making friends with what appears to be our sabotaging feelings and self-talk.

The Drill Sergeant's attention to detail was incredible. From sun up to sun down he made sure Collins and anyone within earshot knew, with utmost clarity and in the most colorful language, how much work Collins had to do to be worthy of his uniform. Everyday the Drill Sergeant made absolutely certain that Collins' rack, weapon, running, shooting, and maneuvering were top notch. Collins couldn't tell if the Sergeant couldn't stand him personally, knew something about his family, or if his apparent sadism was generally directed toward people of 'his kind'.

For Collins, every day of camp was full of challenges and opportunities. When he first arrived, the Drill Sergeant made him cower. Later he made him think. And eventually, with all of the personal attention, Collins was well regarded in his training class. In fact, on graduation day, he was given special recognition for his efforts.

But it wasn't until January of 1944, lying in a ditch with a dozen Panzer main battle tanks rumbling by, that Collins realized the true gift of his wise Drill Sergeant. He could access the voice of his mentor, and this voice guided his thoughts and actions. Collins stepped up to his potential that day and was awarded the Medal of Valor.

We all have thoughts, feelings, or inner voices that appear to want to sabotage our progress. Some people hear a drill sergeant voice in your mind that says, ***"You'll never make it!"*** Do you?

Many people feel inspired and powerful as they take action, but every once in a while they have thoughts that seem to be trying to stop their progress! Can you relate to this?

These voices might say things like, ***"You're not good enough! You're not smart enough! No one will take you seriously because you are so young, old, black, white, short, tall, thin, heavy, and so on."*** And for some people, these inner voices seem so intense, they aren't sure they can overcome them.

Wise Elder Gremlins

Consider the possibility that these voices are not to be overcome, but rather to be embraced and aligned. This may sound a bit crazy, but consider that these are the **wise elder gremlins** in your life.

Have you heard of gremlins? Remember the movie? Well, we use gremlins as a light term for the group of feelings or thoughts that tend to stop us from moving forward and getting what we actually want in life.

If you let them, these gremlin voices can cause a lot of damage, because they are linked to our friend Resistance that is located in our emotional brain. Do you remember resistance - our friend who likes to do that same thing over and over, and only knows the moment now? If you let these gremlins take over, you may never achieve what you want.

As you are aware, we resist any time we leave our comfort zone because we unconsciously and habitually relate the old way of doing things with security. Your gremlin voices are also trying to keep you safe and maintain the status quo. Yet these voices have something important to offer you.

Remember we said they were wise elder gremlins? They are **wise** because they ask you to look at something else in your life. They try to help you by supporting you to see a new perspective; to look from a new angle. Gremlins aren't really malicious, though it may seem that way. They just want you to listen.

Listen Differently

Listen to what? That negative self talk?

Actually, your negative self talk is a part of you that isn't aligned with what you're trying to do. Part of you feels threatened, uncomfortable, and concerned. The gremlin voice is trying to alert you, saying, ***"Stop! You have not thought this all the way through. What about me?"***

That part of you usually has an issue or a concern that you did not address in your goal and your plan.

The wise elder gremlin has been with you for a while and wants you to take a look at an issue in your life that has been holding you back - perhaps for a long time without you even being aware of it. Isn't it great that this part of you is pointing this out so clearly?

Ponder: Should I just ask it what it wants?

Sure! Tune into this part of you that has a concern and ask:

- "What's your positive purpose?"

  Or
- "What do you want for me that is positive?"

If you wait quietly, you will receive an answer that guides you to look at something you need to resolve to be successful.

Inner Alignment Example

Let's pretend your answer was **safety**. Then, ask that part of you again:

"If you felt completely safe, what do you want through safety that is more important to you?"

Now pretend the part said, ***"I want to be happy and not disappointed."***

Then, ask the question again:

"If you were happy and not disappointed, what do you want through this that is more important?"

Pretend the part said, ***"I want you to get what you want and have fun and peace of mind while you do it."***

By now you probably understand this process. You may have to ask the question a few more times to go even deeper, but the point here is that **every part of you**, all the gremlins, are focused on what's good for you! They may seem to have nasty ways that are out to sabotage you, but their true purpose is to get your attention so you look at the big picture and consider all the factors involved. As **wise elders** they're really trying to help you - even if the talk seems negative.

Gremlin Value Example

Perhaps your gremlin is having you doubt that your actions are worthwhile or could be successful. Let's look at another slightly difference question you could ask the wise elder gremlin.

Try asking your gremlin:

"What would it mean if they were worthwhile or if they did work?"

Then wait for an answer.

Suppose the answer was ***"I'd be uncomfortable if it worked. I wouldn't know how to respond, or what to do."***

The gremlin gave you a tip so you can prepare now for what you need to do when your progress towards your goal ***does*** work. Knowing this, you can start preparing.

What do you need to do in order to feel comfortable with actually achieving your goal? If you're not certain, you can ask the gremlin what it needs. It may need reassurance that you have considered its concern. It may be warning you that you have a deeper issue that needs to be resolved. Sometimes we actually have **competing parts** - that is, part of us wants comfort and security, and another part of us wants adventure!

When we hear our gremlins, a skilled coach can benefit you by helping you determine the values behind each of the desires, and by guiding you to find ways of meeting competing values.

MASTER'S TIP Know this: If you ignore your gremlins, they keep talking to you and you continue to be torn, frustrated, and possibly taken off track from your goal. And, you miss out on living your best life.

Honor Gremlin Wisdom

Just as we often ask a wise elder for advice or help, make use of the wise elder gremlins. They are here to help, even though it may seem otherwise. And when we align all the parts of us with what we want, we're unstoppable!

Picture a race horse racing out through the gate. With every fiber of its being, the horse wants to run. That's what we can be like when we resolve the issues the gremlins bring forward. And without knowing these issues, we are likely to get into trouble down the road. We don't want to be the race horse with a nail in our shoe, nor do we want to slip as we charge through the gate to our goal. So appreciate the message the gremlin brings.

Listen and honor the wisdom of your inner gremlins. The key is to find out their positive intention and then actively work to meet their needs and resolve the issues.

Partner with Your Gremlin

Let's review the steps:

1. Listen to what the gremlins are trying to tell you.
2. Ask for their positive purpose.
   "What do you want for me that is positive?"
3. Consider the value of what the gremlin is offering and appropriately meet the needs the gremlin addresses.
4. Review your plan and build the new actions into it.

The wise elder gremlins want you to be your best, and have the best. They are true friends and partners in you living your best life, your most significant offering. Embrace them and be grateful.

Befriending your Gremlins

Things you will need

Your journal

A quiet space to think and write

Integration-Related Activity

The goal of this activity is for you to learn effectively how to befriend your gremlins. With this knowledge, you can anticipate roadblocks in your plan and more efficiently move forward to Enlightened Internal Leadership of your life.

Befriending Gremlin Exercises

Since this exercise is very powerful and deals with our inner dialog and feelings, it may take a little more time than some of the other integration activities. Consider revisiting this exercise and notice that you can experience it on a deeper level each time.

As you know, a gremlin is a feeling or inner dialogue that seems to sabotage our goals by wanting to maintain the status quo.

Today's exercise is an inner process on how to turn a gremlin into a wise elder and inner ally in your life.

Gremlin Challenge

The following questioning format was developed by Byron Katie.

WRITTEN ACTIVITY WRITE DOWN AN INNER DIALOGUE THAT IS GOING ON IN YOUR LIFE - AN INNER CONVERSATION OF WHY YOU CAN'T DO SOMETHING.

Think of anything. It may or may not be related to your goal.

My inner conversation:

ASK YOURSELF: Is it true?

ASK YOURSELF: Am I absolutely certain it is true?

ASK YOURSELF: What might I lapse into when I think that thought?

ASK YOURSELF: Who am I now without that thought?

Reflect on these four previous questions for a few moments.

ASK YOURSELF: How might these questions be of value to me?

Ask yourself: When might I use them?

Wise Elder Gremlins

In today's session we invited you to consider that your inner voices or feelings are actually *wise elder gremlins*. This next exercise helps you work with your inner gremlins. Once you've learned how to connect with your wise elder gremlins, they turn into inner allies and are no longer enemies.

Important Instruction **Allow at least 15 minutes for this exercise.**

If you don't have time right now to complete this exercise, you might want to come back to it when you have time to complete it.

Let's concentrate on showing you how to get in touch with the gremlins. If this seems a little "woo-woo," just enter into a spirit of play and dive in!

Go Within: Please find a quiet spot where you can sit or lie down comfortably.

Relax your mind and body, and let the thoughts of your significant success come. Act as if having these thoughts are easy. Tune inward, and notice any part of yourself that seems to be taking you off track from your goal.

Ask yourself: What part of me is creating feelings or inner dialogue that seem to make the journey to my goal a challenge?

Again, just invite the part of you that seems to be taking you off track to come forward right now. You'll know when it does. You may feel a certain feeling in a part of you, or it may be a quiet voice in your head. The gremlins can take on many formats. Just notice where you find it in your body.

Once you've felt the gremlin come forward, notice how it typically behaves.

Ask yourself: What feelings does it bring up or what does it typically say to me?

Ask your gremlin: What is your positive purpose?

Ask your gremlin: What do you want for me that is positive?

Then, wait for an answer. The answer may be a feeling, or it may be a voice. Listen for the answer.

Gremlin Answer: What does it say? Write it down.

Repeat it out loud.

Thank the part for its positive intention.

Once you have your answer, quietly:

Ask your gremlin: If you had this, if you had what you wanted completely and fully, what do you want through this that is more important to you?

Listen for the answer.

GREMLIN ANSWER: What does it say? Write it down.

Repeat it out loud.

Thank the part for its positive intention.

Once you have your new answer, ask again:

ASK YOUR GREMLIN: Okay, if you had that, what you wanted, fully and completely, what do you want through this that is more important?

Listen for the answer.

GREMLIN ANSWER: What does it say? Repeat it out loud.

Thank the part for its positive intention.

CONSIDER: You may have to ask the question a few more times to go even deeper.

Once you have the gremlin's attention:

DECLARE: I know what your ultimate intention is for me. Thank you!

ASK YOUR GREMLIN: What do you need in order to feel good about supporting my goal?

Listen for the answer.

GREMLIN ANSWER: What does it say? Write it down.

Repeat it out loud.

Once you know what that part needs, visualize it. See a picture of it in your mind and then notice it start to turn into a color.

Notice yourself in a field - a big beautiful field that is filled with the color that represents what this part of you needs.

Just notice that there is a boundless supply of what this part needs.

Notice yourself breathing in this color and giving this part exactly what it needs now.

Notice it filling you - in through your nose, filling your lungs, going into the core of your body, down your legs into your feet, then into your chest, arms hands and up into your face, head and brains.

Notice every cell of your body receiving exactly what this part of you needs to align with your goal.

Let it flow until that part has everything it needs to feel totally safe and totally ready to work to support you in working towards your goal.

Ask yourself: What feeling does this part of me have now?

Notice how the feeling has transformed. I'll bet it is pretty happy now, isn't it?

Now invite the gremlin to consider bringing this feeling back into the **now** and simply have it, integrated fully and completely.

The gremlin may want to carry the feeling back or not. You may need to brainstorm with the gremlin to find new ways of achieving your goal that also account for the concern of the gremlin.

Master's Tip Our gremlins have our best interests at heart, and their concerns are real.

Through this simple exercise you recognize that every part of you - all inner feelings or dialogue that may seem to be destructive - are truly trying to do something positive for you. Every thought and feeling you have focuses on what's good for you - whether it seems that way or not! Your gremlins may seem to have nasty ways that are out to sabotage you, but they are merely trying to get your attention so you look at the big picture and consider all the factors involved.

You may need a coach to get the most from this exercise. If so, go to www.powerfulchoices.net to contact a member of our team who will support you in fully integrating this work and getting the most from these sessions. To learn this process so you can do it for yourself and others, consider the course offerings available at www.erickson.edu.

Befriend Your Gremlins NOW

Imagine if you befriended all your inner gremlins and realized they are wise elders who can act as powerful mentors for you.

Knowing that listening carefully to your gremlins helps you reach your goal with great joy and total fulfillment, what are you be willing to do now?

What action might you take to remind yourself to check in regularly with your gremlins and then take action so that you can efficiently reach a future that is filled with a life you love?

Day 23 **Watch for Undercurrents**

This session is about paying attention to the emotional background noise happening in your mind.

During the 1920's the 'little tramp' Charlie Chaplin inspired a whole generation of film makers with his ability to tell a moving story without uttering a single word! Audiences identified with Chaplin because his emotional life was apparent to anyone who watched. Chaplin's great gift to silent movie-goers was his absolute transparency.

An apt title for a silent movie about life on this little planet might be: "A River Runs Through Us". Each of us, in our own unique way, are moving and changing rivers of emotional experience. The truest gift we can give ourselves is to learn to acknowledge the depth of our emotional life and how it impacts our progress toward living a life we love.

Humans have a continual stream of emotions - some subtle and others quite obvious. This emotional 'background' runs constantly, often just outside our conscious awareness. It is like brain scribble in the back of our mind that we rarely realize is happening.

Dark-Cloud Days

Have you ever had a day that just didn't feel quite right - things seemed to go wrong from the time you got out of bed till the end of the day? Consider that your emotional background for that day was probably rather negative. Perhaps you felt too stretched and not quite able to cope. Or maybe someone said something to you the night before that annoyed you, and you had not yet released it. The point is, the little things that normally wouldn't bother you feel larger than usual and a dark-cloud energy seems to persist throughout the day.

If we have "dark-cloud days" over and over again, we might start to think, consciously or unconsciously, that the world isn't a friendly place. We might start to be cynical and resigned about life, or depressed and angry. A hopeless and helpless feeling may overtake us and we may believe we are alone in digging ourselves out of a deep pit of despair. Have you ever felt this way for a day or a series of days?

How we think about the world colors our relationship with it. After a number of "dark-cloud" days, we start to expect negative things to happen. Our "emotional background" stream may have an undercurrent of hopelessness, despair, apathy, or 'why me' - all of which lead to having more of what we are focusing on - hopelessness, despair, apathy, or 'why me.'

MASTER'S TIP Energy flows where your attention goes.

Adopt Positive Attitudes

Successful, happy, peaceful people who are living their best life have regular undercurrents of ambition that carry the tone: ***"I'm going to get this done!", "This has value!", "I have value!", "I am able!", "This challenge is fun!", "I will succeed!"*** And in spite of life's setbacks, these people keep their positive attitude. They remain cheerful and optimistic - especially when times are tough.

The people who find achieving their goals difficult, who are not successful, happy, and peaceful, and who are definitely not living their best life, often have an emotional background stream with an undercurrent ranging from a slight feeling of ***"I'm not good enough!"*** to full blown ***"I'm not worthy!"*** or ***"My life isn't worth living!'"***

Unfortunately, these negative emotional undercurrents are epidemic in our society. TV ads imply that if our hair were shinier, if our teeth a little more brilliant, or if our bodies were perfectly defined, then we would attract gorgeous guys and gals; or if we drink this brand of beer, we could have great parties on the beach!

Because most of us don't have the life depicted on TV or in the movies, we may tend to feel inadequate and let down. We weren't invited to the party happening all around us where the beautiful, smart, rich, and talented people are connecting, laughing, and having fun.

If you had a childhood of criticism and complaints that created dysfunctional belief systems, you might be feeling inadequate even if you do have shiny hair, brilliant teeth, and a beautifully defined body. Depression is prevalent in our society, and more people than ever before feel they are unworthy, unsatisfied, and alone.

Chronic Dark-Clouds

Think about how an undercurrent of feeling unworthy might be working against you. For some people, the lack of invitation is a challenge that drives them: ***"Oh yeah, I'll find a way to get to the party some how!"*** Or, ***"I'll show you, I'll create my own party down the beach and throw rocks at you guys."***

For others, it sabotages them. ***"I'll never be good enough to get invited to the party. And even if I did get invited, everyone there would know that I didn't belong."***

There are a million variations on the theme - all based on the major dazes in which human beings tend to find themselves. To name a few:

- No one likes me - I will always be alone!
- I have no direction - I don't know what I want!
- My life has no meaning!
- Poverty is my destiny!

Physiology to the Rescue

No matter what the dark cloud, there is one easy way to deal with these undercurrents of unworthiness - and it's in your physiology.

Our emotions and our physiology are deeply intertwined. People report that they feel the sense of hopelessness, despair, unworthiness, or some other negative emotion as a particular feeling in their body. After all, it's our body that feels!

Have you ever noticed that when you are feeling bad, you hold your body a certain way? You are more likely to sit, possibly slumped over, looking down and feeling crappy, right?

Contrast that with how you hold your body when you're feeling like Superman or Superwoman. Totally different, right? You possibly are looking up, breathing deeply, or holding a stance that is unique to you.

How about when you're feeling creative? Different again, right?

How about when you are feeling connected to another person?

How about when you're feeling driven or in task completion mode?

The differences may be subtle, but we have a way of reflecting different feelings uniquely in our physiology.

Emotional Undercurrent Inventory

Let's do an inventory of how you feel right now.

PONDER: What undercurrent of emotion am I feeling?

PONDER: When I think about my life ahead, how does it feel?

Does it feel inspiring? Empowering? Freeing? Optimistic? Peaceful? Enlivening? Natural? Or does it feel uncomfortable? Discouraging? Exhausting? Stressful? Overwhelming? Lonely? Uninteresting? What "self talk" do you use when you consider how you feel about your future?

When you first get out of bed in the morning, do you leap out of bed with eager anticipation? Or do you drag yourself out, saying, "Oh God, another day!" in tones of despair? These are clues to your emotional undercurrents.

Change the Undercurrents

Once you've established your emotional undercurrent for the day, it tends to stick with you unless one of two things occur:

- A hugely impactful event happens that changes your life, or
- You choose to deliberately change your emotional state.

Most people are not even aware of the emotional undercurrents that form their thoughts.

MASTER'S TIP Your thoughts become your focus; your focus becomes your attitude; your attitude becomes your words; your words become your actions; your actions become your habits; your habits become your character; and your character becomes your destiny!
- Author Unknown

Once you're aware of the relationship between your thoughts, your feelings, and your physiology, it's easy to change the undercurrent, and your thoughts.

Take note, right now, of how you're sitting or standing. Notice any negative feelings that are awake in your body right now. Tune in and notice if you feel any lumps of apprehension, confusion, tenderness, disconnectedness, unsettledness, fatigue, pain, sadness, tenseness, vulnerability, yearning, frustration, annoyance. Or perhaps you have positive feelings such as confidence, engagement, inspiration, excitement, hopefulness, joy, peace, or renewal.

Practice Physiology Change

Now that you've taken an honest inventory of how you feel, stand or sit as if you are enormously proud of yourself or something you have just accomplished in your life. Can you still feel that feeling of hardness, lumps of despair, or parts of you that don't feel inspired?

If you do, stand or sit even prouder. Try taking a deep breath, open your eyes up and open your chest. Change your physiology until you no longer feel any undercurrents of despair, hopelessness, unworthiness, or any other emotional undercurrent that might hold you back.

Once you've changed your physiology, you won't be able to think negative thoughts without letting your physiology fall back into your old posture.

Try it! Try to get depressed, sad, or frustrated. You might have even experienced a bit of a laugh about trying to go to that negative state. It is impossible unless you go back to your previous physiology.

Anytime you have a negative thought, **immediately** change your physiology. Go outside and throw a ball. Exercise. Stand up straight and proud, take a deep breath and **feel** the difference it makes to your emotions and your ability to support yourself.

As you witness the emotional undercurrents of your life that inform your thoughts and eventually create your destiny, make the tiny shifts necessary to support yourself to live your best life. Anything less would be self-sabotage!

Watching for Undercurrents

INTEGRATION CHECKLIST

Things you will need

Your journal

A quiet space to think and write

Integration-Related Activity

The goal of this activity is for you to notice your own undercurrents of emotion, becoming more conscious of them. With this knowledge, you can set powerful, positive days in motion to accomplish your plan for moving forward to Enlightened Internal Leadership.

Identifying Habitual Thoughts Exercise

Have you ever noticed that it can be challenging to identify your habitual thoughts? Most of them happen on an unconscious level. As you learned, checking your physiology is one way to become more conscious of your habitual thoughts. However there are certainly other effective ways as well!

CONSIDER: The undercurrent of emotion that you feel in each moment is your current mindset. When your mindset is positive, you will think lots of empowering thoughts. When it's negative, you sabotage yourself by putting your attention on the negative. And remember, energy flows where your attention goes.

MASTER'S TIP Starting with a positive mindset can set a very positive and empowering day in motion. The quality of your life is the quality of the state in which you put yourself.

Ask yourself: What is the emotional undercurrent I am experiencing right now?

Ask yourself: How does this benefit me?

Ask yourself: How does this not benefit me?

Morning Watch

You do this exercise first thing in the morning. It tells you, very effectively, if you are starting the day with a positive or a negative mindset.

Important Instruction **Prepare for this exercise the night before. Set out a pad of paper and a pencil on the table.**

Written Activity **When you first get up in the morning, write down every single thought that goes through your head - every last one, no matter how small.**

Leave a few lines between each new thought.

Some people, especially people who talk to themselves inside their heads, find this exercise easy. Others find they don't have a lot of access to their thoughts. Other people have certain feelings or images in their mind.

Note Write whatever comes to mind.

Head Talk

Here's an example of someone who talks to themselves inside their head:

Oh, morning again.

Oh, my body aches.

Where's the coffee?

How come I always have to make the coffee?

Why does Lani insist on sleeping late?

Oh, it's grey outside today.

I wonder if John will have that presentation ready for me at work? I bet he doesn't - he's never on time. Always screwing me up. Oh well, I'll work around it, like I always do.

Hey it's Martha's birthday today, maybe I should grab a cake on my way in to work. No, better not, I'd just eat it and I'm trying to lose weight. I should have picked up a card for her. Now she'll think I don't care. Better get the cake after all and a card.

And so on and on go the thoughts!

Image Talk

Some people see images, a steady stream of images. If this is your approach, write down a brief description of what you're seeing. Here's an example:

A cup of coffee, steaming. Me having to make it.

Picture of Lani sleeping.

Grey skies.

A picture of John at work. A picture of him not having the presentation ready. A picture of myself being screwed. A picture of myself working around it, doing the stuff he should have done.

A picture of Martha. A picture of a birthday cake, then of myself carrying it into work. A picture of myself eating it - eating all of it. A picture of myself gaining weight. A picture of a card, Martha being hurt, a picture of a cake and her reading a card with a smile.

Feeling Talk

Some people just have feelings, with little awareness of the thoughts that trigger those feelings. They just feel tired, grumpy, excited, annoyed, or whatever.

If you feel a certain way, stop and listen for the voice in your head, just notice what you were thinking or focusing on that started that feeling. When you identify it, write it down.

Recreate Thoughts

After you write down your original thought, get up and start getting ready for your day. After a while - before you leave to work, the gym, or whatever you do first thing in the morning - take five minutes to look at your original thoughts.

Now it is time to use the lines you left between your thoughts.

Create a replacement thought that will best support focusing your mind by putting your attention on what you want. Use the space after the thought to write in a more positive thought.

Examples

Original thought: *I wonder if John will have that presentation ready for me at work? I bet he doesn't - he's never on time. Always screwing me up. Oh well, I'll work around it, like I always do.*

Replacement thought: *I wonder if John will have that presentation ready for me at work? If he doesn't how can I make the best of it? And how can I make sure he's on time the next time?*

Original thought: *I always get screwed by John. He's never on time.*

Replacement thought: *John usually isn't on time. That doesn't mean he's screwing me. That might mean he's just too busy.*

This exercise has two benefits:

- You get to actually capture your thoughts and see the mindset you have and how it impacts your day.
- You have the opportunity to correct it! You get to define your mindset, rather than it defining you. Talk about self empowerment!

Although we recommend this exercise for first thing in the morning, you can do it at any time of day.

CONSIDER: An effective time to do this exercise is when you are feeling down about your goal and your chances of success. Try it now.

ASK YOURSELF: What is one thought I am having now that is currently not benefiting me?

ASK YOURSELF: What would be the replacement thought that would be of greatest benefit to me?

ASK YOURSELF: Who might I ask to support me in directing my thoughts effectively?

You are in charge of running your mind. You are responsible for holding your focus in a manner that works to create a life you love. Often we are distracted by life's events, strong feeling, or other possibilities. Also consider inviting your support system to assist you to redirect your energy to the mindset that serves you in reaching your goal.

Watch For Undercurrents NOW

Imagine if you were so aware of your thoughts that you consistently were able to be in charge of your mind and correct negative thoughts quickly.

Knowing that a positive mindset empowers you, what would you be willing to do now?

What action might you take to remind yourself to be consciously aware of your thoughts and to take action to rewrite the negative ones so you can reframe and efficiently reach a future that is filled with a life you love?

Day 24 Find Successful People

This session is about finding successful people with whom you can connect and who support you in reaching your goal.

Mary was in her second year of undergraduate work earning a degree in Music Performance. She was doing well academically, but because she was self-conscious, she suffered terribly whenever she was required to sing in recital. As a 6-foot tall, 57-year-old African American woman, she was something of an unconventional student - yet that really wasn't the source of her angst. What worried her most was how she carried herself on stage.

A young woman named Jennifer had become Mary's unwitting role model. At nearly a third Mary's age, Jennifer had the qualities that Mary deeply admired. She had the kind of poise that only a seasoned and experienced performer could bring to the stage. She was calm under pressure and always well rehearsed. Mary wanted all those qualities for herself. So one afternoon, after what she considered a not-so-successful sophomore recital, Mary approached Jennifer for help.

The two became inseparable. Despite their differences, they created a bond of sisterhood founded completely in their common love of music. At the next recital, Mary stood back stage waiting to go on and looking for her friend. Jennifer had not yet arrived, and Mary worried and prayed that her friend was alright. But she was running out of time and had to prepare.

Mary closed her eyes and projected an image of Jennifer singing in her imagination. Then she superimposed an image of herself doing what Jennifer did naturally and easily. She heard the first notes introducing her song and walked out on stage and into the lights. She took her position in the crook of the grand and began to sing - the way Jennifer would have done it.

Master's Tip "You are the average of the 5 people you spend the most time with." - Jim Rohn

Do you know people that radiate optimism, support, and encouragement, and whom you love to be around? Do you spend time with people who give your life energy? Or do you have people who you spend time with who steal your life energy, who create stress and disorder in your life just by connecting to them?

Energy Enhancement

Consider that one way to accelerate your progress towards your goal is to surround yourself with people who know what works - positive, successful people who are living their best life! And consider that negative people are toxic. They discourage you from moving ahead. Remember that you get what you want by doing more of what works.

Master's Tip "Success Leaves Clues!" - Anthony Robbins

Suppose every single day we had to re-invent the wheel before we could get in our car and drive it away. How slow would progress be? By using success secrets from successful people, you avoid having to reinvent your own personal wheels.

Choose Proven Strategies

Suppose your goal was to clean a wall. Given the choice of one of fifty different substances that might clean the wall, or a substance that you know cleans the wall, which would you use? If you are in an investigative mood, you might work your way through the fifty possible solutions to see if you could find one that works. But most people would choose the one they already know works well. After all, why bother wasting time and energy testing out fifty substances, when you already know how to get the wall clean? Use the proven performer, the proven formula, get the wall clean, and you're done.

This example demonstrates the value of having a relationship with positive, successful people who are already living their best life. People who are already successful in the way you want success can act as a model, a mentor, and an inspiration to you. They are the proven performers with proven formulas. They can support you in taking the shortest path and making the right choices to get what you want and live your best life.

Seeing is Believing

Our minds can only visualize what we believe can happen. Successful people show us that it is possible to be successful. That knowledge inspires us and makes our success real in our minds. If we hang out with people who have not succeeded, we don't see what success looks like, so it is much harder to visualize our own success. And, as you know, visualizing your success is an important step to getting it.

If you don't have someone around who has successfully achieved a goal similar to yours, read biographies of people who have! Or check out the Internet for stories of people who accomplished what you're working on or something similar. As you get inspired, you start to believe success is possible. And from your reading, you can discover tips on what successful people do that might be just what you need to do or know to reach your goals and live your best life.

Modeling and Mentoring

To increase your success in getting the support you want, let's take some tips from proven approaches - modeling and mentoring.

Imitating the practices of successful people is **modeling**. You find out how someone else built success in the area you are working on, and then adopt similar techniques and strategies yourself. And modeling can include learning to think the same way a successful person thinks.

Would you be flattered if someone asked you the secrets to your success? Of course! So if you know someone who succeeded at your goal, ask them for help and advice.

What do you have to lose by asking? Perhaps there is a gremlin conversation about you feeling rejected. Just realize that your gremlin wants to keep you safe and then consider that your safety is not really at risk. Suppose you ask someone to mentor you and they say no. Remember that they were not your mentor before you asked, and since they said no, they are not your mentor after you asked. You have spent your entire life so far not working with this mentor, so your life didn't get any worse, it stayed exactly the same! And you know how to handle it!

Sometimes the best way to learn is to work with someone successful, and absorb everything they do, say, and feel. Lots of people learn a great deal by working - often for free - for someone who is successful.

Create Win-Win Situations

One tip to help you get support is to be clear that the relationship is a win-win situation. Most win-win situations involve both parties giving **and** receiving. While someone may be pleased to offer some advice, perhaps you could also do something for them or someone they care about. Without a reciprocal relationship, sooner or later the well of advice runs dry.

Another way to work with someone successful is through a **mentoring** relationship. Mentoring works well when there are intangible skills to be learned. A mentor meets with you on a regular basis, you discuss the situations you are in, and the mentor helps you clarify and decide on the best action to take. And sometimes, during the process of mentoring, you might find yourself modeling the skills of the mentor, and practicing those skills.

Tips For Support Requests

Once you are clear that a supportive relationship can be a win-win situation, there are a few techniques you can use to ask for support.

- Ask with positive expectations - expect a **yes**.
- Assume that the relationship will happen - never assume otherwise. That is, assume you will work with the person and that they will meet with you regularly.
- Ask the person directly. Do not ask their spouse, secretary, friend, or child.
- Be clear and specific about what you want and what you are asking of them.

  Tell the person why you want them in your life, what skills you want to gain from them, and what things you want to be able to do after working together.

  Be specific about the amount of time you are requesting. And, of course, relate what the win is for them.

- If they say **no**, ask again, at some later date, with even more conviction about the benefits to both of you. Or ask someone with similar skills. Do not give up.

  When we ask people to participate in the fulfillment of our goals, some people initially say no because they are too busy and have other commitments. This is not a reflection on you. They may say yes on a different day, when they know you better or trust you more, when their schedule has lightened, or when circumstances have changed.

  Have you noticed that children keep asking for what they want over and over again without hesitation? This is the attitude that works. Consider adopting it.

- If the relationship does not work out or you keep getting a **no**, it is time to seek help from someone else. There are 6 billion people on the planet. You will find the perfect mentor for you.

We started this session with Jim Rohn's quote: "You are the average of the 5 people you spend the most time with."

Think of the five people with whom you currently spend your time.

PONDER: Are these win-win relationships?

PONDER: Are you modeling or mentoring or neither?

PONDER: Are you giving their lives energy and getting energy from them as well?

Later in the exercise we ask you to write down the names of all the people you know, or have heard of, who have been successful in a goal similar to yours. Then you determine if it's possible to have a relationship with any or all of these people. If a relationship is not possible, you decide what you can do that will let you model as many skills as you can. Alternative activities may include reading, attending seminars, or other methods of study, perhaps even reading what these people have written.

For those people you could have a relationship with, you will determine what would be a win-win situation for you both. First you define what you want from the relationship. Then you determine what you have to give. Decide on an approach - how will you approach this person? Also decide which person you would most like to have a relationship with.

Be prepared for a few '**No**'s. Not everyone is open to new relationships, and it has nothing to do with you. Some people are already too busy, or are already mentoring others, or perhaps had a mentoring relationship that went sour. Keep going down your list and asking - sooner or later you'll find a mentor or model.

MASTER'S TIP Keep in mind that mentors are masterful in their area yet humans. Do not expect them to be enlightened gurus at all times in all situations.

And even if every last person you asked said **no**, you still have the instructional resources available to you. Look for what has worked for successful people, and do more of that. If nothing else, you'll get a glimpse into their world, so you'll know that achieving your goal is possible!

Finding Successful People

INTEGRATION CHECKLIST

Things you will need

Your journal

A quiet space to think and write

Integration-Related Activity

The goal of this activity is for you to discover your best method to build relationships with successful people. With this knowledge, you can create a support system that supports you to move forward to Enlightened Internal Leadership on all levels.

Building Relationships Exercise

ASK YOURSELF: Who are all the people I already know, or don't know but have heard of, who have been successful in a goal similar to mine?

WRITTEN ACTIVITY MAKE A LIST OF EVERYONE YOU CAN THINK OF WHO IS SUCCESSFUL IN A SIMILAR GOAL TO YOURS.

ASK YOURSELF: In what way might I connect or form a relationship with some or all of these people?

Some examples would be mentoring, modeling, socializing, working, or reading, attending seminars, or other methods of study.

Ask yourself: For those I feel I might be able to connect or build a relationship with, how might I create a win-win situation for us both?

Ask yourself: Who are the top three people I would most like to have a relationship with?

- ❒
- ❒
- ❒

Ask yourself: How might I approach these people?

If this seems challenging mentally, emotionally, or spiritually, for whatever reason, just suppose it was extremely easy and you knew that this person would be thrilled to have a win/win connection with you. Then...

Ask yourself: How might I approach them?

CONSIDER: On a scale from 0 to 10, how committed are you to following through with this?

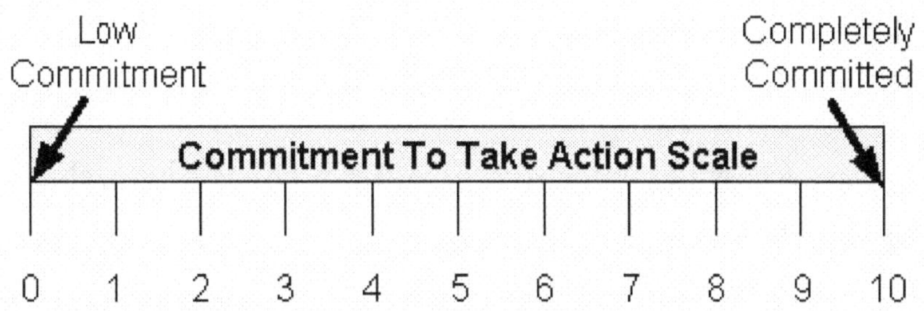

ASK YOURSELF: What is the benefit of following through with this?

ASK YOURSELF: What is the cost of not following through with this?

ASK YOURSELF: When might you do this?

The power of building relationships with successful people is astounding.

CONSIDER: Building these relationships is worth your while. At one point in time, each of these people were likely where you are now. Consider acting with courageous conviction and creating win/win relationships with these people now.

Find Successful People NOW

Imagine if you took steps to build relationships with successful people and modeled the genius to reach your goal, so each step was likely to succeed rather than being a game of "trial-and-error."

Knowing that building relationships creates success for you and help you reach your goal more efficiently, what would you be willing to do now?

What action might you take to remind yourself to take action towards building relationships with successful people so that you can efficiently reach a future that is filled with a life you love?

Day 25 **Stay on Course**

Follow your map!

This session is about staying on course, even though your path may wander from the most direct route.

Florence Chadwick committed to being the first woman to swim the channel between Catalina Island and the California mainland. Her first attempt wasn't going well. The water was freezing cold, her chase team was fending off hungry sharks and jelly fish, and the salt water she was swallowing was making her sick. Worst of all, there was a dense fog preventing her from seeing the mainland, so she was struggling to stay on course. Millions watched on television as she climbed out of the water ending her first record attempt.

Two months passed before she made her second attempt. However, something was dramatically different this time - a difference within Florence's mind. The same dangers lurked in the quiet cold depths and the fog was just as thick, but this time she was prepared for the dangers and obstacles. On her first attempt, the main reason she stopped her swim was lack of clarity as to why she was doing it. She had no vision - no compelling reason why it was important. On her second attempt, Florence was living her values and vision and preparing for the worst, but expecting the best. She remained on course and won the record for crossing the Catalina Channel.

Whether it be a roadmap, an aerial map, a nautical map, or an *internal* map, maps help keep us on course.

Constantly Correct The Course

When most people think of flying in an airplane, they think of flying straight to their destination. What is interesting about flying is that nothing could be further from the truth.

Did you know that airplanes are off course almost every second they are in the air? From the time the wheels lift off the runway, the plane is buffeted by winds and weather. Every second, the atmospheric pressures are forcing the plane - which is considerably less powerful than they are - to move. So how does the plane ever get to it's destination? By making constant course corrections - some small, others huge. And the result of all the corrections is the plane arriving at it's destination.

Let's take a closer look at how this works. Let's say a plane takes off and heads for Seattle. As soon as it gets into the air a side wind pushes it a few degrees off course. The pilot corrects, and in fact, has to over-correct, as the wind is still pushing the plane off course.

Then let's say, the wind dies down, and the plane is now going too far in the other direction! The pilot corrects again. The winds buffet the plane again, and the pilot corrects the course once again, and over and over.

For most of the trip, the plane is headed in the wrong direction! But each time the pilot corrects, the plane gets back on course, making it's zigzag way across the sky towards Seattle. Isn't this amazing?

Right now you are moving towards your goals that are aligned with you living your best life. And, like the pilot, you must also make corrections to stay on course. Seldom is it a smooth trip to your goal. We may want it to be smooth, but when we realize that there is something bigger than ourselves at work, we can keep taking action while doing the dance with the Universe. And just as the pilot flies the plane, you can pilot your own life!

Evaluate Your Course

Let’s change images. Do you remember your staircase to success? The landings are great places to stop and evaluate your course. Sometimes you find you've taken a wrong turn and bumped your head on the railing. Perhaps you discover that a new tool exists to help you be more effective, or a new person shows up in your life to mentor you and share something you never considered.

Expect course corrections.

When you choose your goals and make your plans, avoid being totally attached to the plan that is further out in time. You never know what winds of change or possibility the Universe might conjure up! While it is important to plan what to do now, next week, next month, throughout the year, it is equally important to be flexible and know there **will** be course corrections to your plans.

You can't foresee every variable in the future! And the Universe might put something exciting - possibly even a better idea - in your path. So be open to possibility while tracking toward your outcome.

Know Your Destination

One very important thing about course corrections is to always know where you are heading. The end point - your destination - is always the measuring stick.

PONDER: Have I moved closer to or farther away from what I want?

If you've moved closer - great! Celebrate yourself, then ask yourself questions to see if you could move even faster or easier towards your goal - towards living your best life.

If the goal appears further away, ask correction questions that will help you evaluate where you are and whether you need a course correction.

Staying on Course

INTEGRATION CHECKLIST

Things you will need

Your journal

A quiet space to think and write

Approximately 10 feet of floor space

Integration-Related Activity

The goal of this activity is for you to consider your course and end with a powerful visualization. With this knowledge, you can create a masterful plan on how to move forward to Enlightened Internal Leadership.

TAKE AS MUCH TIME AS YOU NEED TO PONDER EACH QUESTION CAREFULLY.

Destination Check Exercise

Let's start with some questions to help you clarify your course.

Take the time needed to ponder them fully, even if you don't write down complete answers right now.

ASK YOURSELF: On a scale from 0 to 10, how close am I to where I want to be?

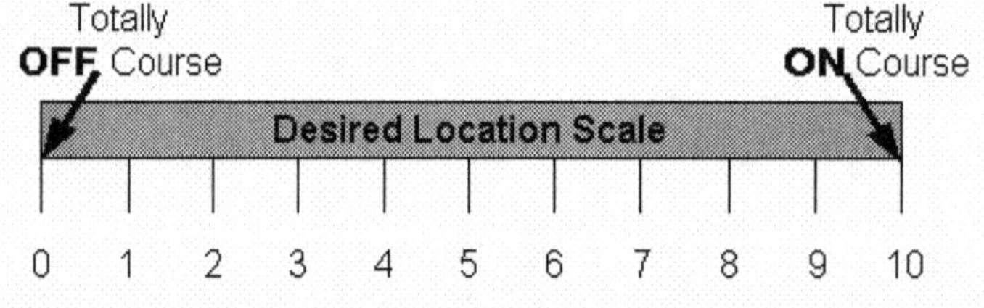

ASK YOURSELF: Since I started, have I moved closer to my destination or further away from it?

If you have moved closer, let's evaluate how much closer.

Ask yourself: On a scale from 0 to 10, where am I on the destination scale?

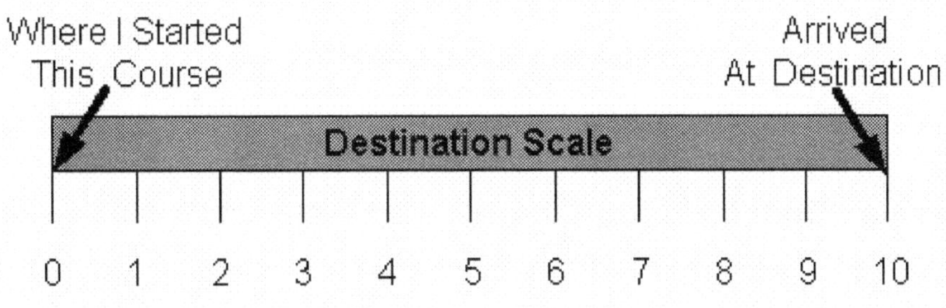

If you have moved at all, even .05 of a step, thank yourself for taking action and moving in the direction that closes the gap between where you are and where you want to be.

Ask yourself: As I consider the information I have received, what has worked well for me so far?

Ask yourself: What hasn't worked well for me so far?

Ask yourself: With all the information I currently have from this program and all the feedback I received along the way, how can I now make the best use of my time and effort to move towards my goal?

Ask yourself: What piece of knowledge do I need that would make this easier?

Ask yourself: How can I get that knowledge? Who might I ask? Where might I go?

Ask yourself: On a scale from 0 to 10, how well is my plan working?

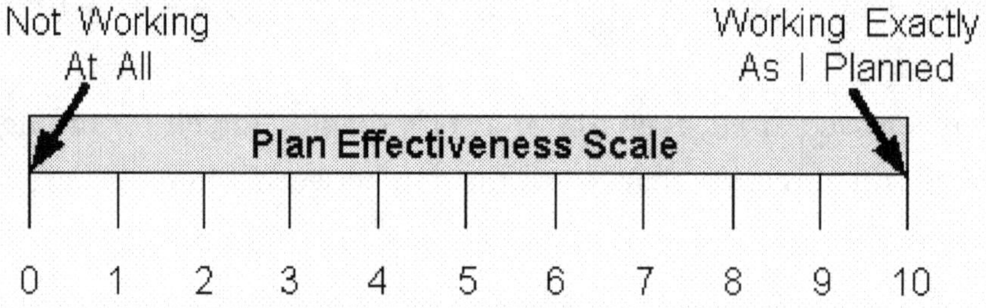

If your plan effectiveness score is lower than a 10:

Ask yourself: What might you do differently to move yourself up one notch to have your plan work even better for you?

Ask yourself: What would be best to stop doing?

Ask yourself: What would be best to start doing?

Ask yourself: What would be best to keep doing?

Ask yourself: What one unreasonable request can I make of myself or someone else that will support me in being more effective in getting what I want?

Ask yourself: When might I take action on this request?

The Magnetic Attraction

Using 10 square-feet of floor as a framework for thinking, design a space that signifies your future. It is useful to organize this space as a line that signifies time:

- One side of the line is where you are now
- The other side of the line is where you want to be

Visualize an important goal on your course.

Begin to make it a large, attractive image.

Notice how it is beginning to move toward you. It is like a magnetic pull in how deeply it is attracted to you, and how natural the attraction is. Notice that you are irresistible to your goal - it wants you.

Notice that gradually it moves closer and closer to you. And you are more and more clear that you will achieve it.

As the visualization moves towards you, notice it becomes both brighter and more interesting, and it also becomes something you can try on as a feeling.

Imagine it becoming very close. Try it on.

Ponder: How do you feel from the inside?

Now once again see yourself having achieved your goal and feel the magnetic pull. Notice how naturally attractive you are to the vision that inspires your life.

Notice yourself living your life on purpose and being absolutely certain that you are moving in the right direction.

Stay on Course NOW

Imagine if you were so aware of your destination and attuned to its magnetic pull that you were consistently able to adjust and stay on course.

Knowing that staying on course empowers you to reach your destination, what would you be willing to do now?

What action might you take to remind yourself to be consciously aware of your diversions from your course and to take action to stay on course so you can efficiently reach a future that is filled with a life you love?

Day 26 **Build Nurturing Relationships**

This session is about surrounding yourself with people who bring energy to your life and avoiding those who do not.

Sally was telling me for the hundredth time how having started a business with her brother Kelly was one of the worst choices she ever made. Kelly is a nice enough guy. He's hardworking, honest and a supportive father. His one flaw: he is extremely negative. He brings the whole family down. After a five minute conversation with him, you feel like you've been hit by a bus. He has the knack of sapping your energy with his negativity.

What's interesting is Kelly's life. He owned a number of businesses, none of them successful. And his venture with Sally is not going well either. He constantly gets sick. He's been married twice and is ready to tie the knot (or not!) again.

Kelly blames his woes on everyone and everything except himself. And, needless to say, he is definitely affected by the company he keeps. He has a couple of very negative friends, whom he loves being around because they commiserate with each other. As the saying goes 'misery loves company'.

Kelly avoids any personal development. As a matter of fact, if you bring that up with him, he hisses at the idea because he is convinced that he doesn't need it.

Sally says she is tired of being around him and asked me what she should do. Hmmmm.....

In Session 24 we talked about two broad groups of people in this world - those who are poisonous to you, who steal your life energy and those who nurture, support and empower you, who give you life energy.

Avoid Poisonous People

Have you ever dreamed about doing something, expressed that dream to someone, and had them express their disbelief? ***"Who are you kidding? You'll never do that! The last time you tried that it was a total failure! Who do you think you are - some "uptown" girl who is really going to make it? How can you do that? You don't know anything about that!"***

People who steal our energy and excitement are also typically jealous and resentful of others who succeed at a higher level than they do. Our success threatens their comfort level. But, even if we recognize their motives or their limited world view, their comments often leave us wondering: ***"Am I making a mistake? Can I really do this? Who am I kidding? Maybe I am incapable of doing this!"***

Supportive and nurturing people act in a totally different manner. They might say, ***"Wow, great idea! Why is this important to you?"*** And when they know why it is important they might ask, "How can I help you achieve what you want?"

Actually, we are all natural nurturers. But some people have absorbed poisonous emotions for so long and been hurt so many times that they have become poisonous. Consider that these people are dream killers.

Free Yourself

If you let them, dream killers can bring your enthusiasm to a screeching halt. However, you can choose whether or not this happens. Though it may not feel like it, you get to choose the emotions you feel when confronted with a poisonous person. The ultimate freedom is to choose how you think and respond to poor circumstances and negative people around you.

Victor Frankl, a medical doctor, wrote *Man's Search for Meaning*. Imprisoned in a Nazi death camp, he noted that some prisoners still found meaning in life despite their horrible circumstances. These amazing people would save their bits of food for those who were even worse off and they expressed hope that they would be free someday.

Frankl realized that, despite what happens in our physical environment, we are totally free inside our heads. The only person who can imprison us is ourselves. If we allow dream killers to destroy our hope, our joy, our visualizations, then we allow them to imprison us inside our own heads - which, of course, we actually are doing to ourselves.

Nelson Mandela was imprisoned for many years, yet he survived and became a great voice in the world. And if we use these survivors as examples, we know that we, too, can survive dream killers and still become great human beings and live the life we love!

Think about Mother Teresa, an excellent example of a nurturing person, always expressing her love for everyone. Would you have felt privileged to know her? Despite the despair of the streets where she worked, the overwhelming poverty and disease, she maintained in her mind the greatness of those around her, and became an inspiration to millions.

Consciously Choose Your Responses

We choose, consciously or unconsciously, the response we make to life. When we encounter a person who acts like a dream killer, we can let them kill our dreams. Or we can choose to keep our dreams alive and find a way to see them flourish - a choice that is the way to greatness.

Would Nelson Mandela be the man he is today if he allowed his prison guards to destroy his dream of freeing South Africa from racial suppression? Would South Africans have made the progress they have towards a true democracy and freedom from racial suppression?

The choice is yours. When you feel a twinge of negative emotion related to what someone says to you, stop yourself immediately and ask, ***"Does this emotion empower or disempower me?"*** If it supports you in living a life you love, keep it. If it doesn't, you have an important choice to make.

- Determine if you feel this type of emotion often when you are around this person. Are they poisoning you slowly with negative attitudes or is this an isolated case?
- Ask yourself if you might address this situation with the person. How will your relationship be affected if you simply tell them that their comments are sapping your enthusiasm and confidence?
- Recognize they can choose whether or not to change. And you can choose either to avoid this poisonous person or to find freedom of mind inside yourself.

It might be difficult to let go of a long-term relationship, especially when you may see secondary gains from staying. Yet, do not let negative people destroy your dreams.

Change Anyway

When we transform, others have to change how they see us and relate to us. And sometimes this is the death of the relationship. Change anyway!

People are often unreasonable, illogical, and self-centered;
Forgive them anyway.

If you are kind, people may accuse you of selfish, ulterior motives;
Be kind anyway.

If you are successful, you will win some false friends and some true enemies;
Succeed anyway.

If you are honest and frank, people may cheat you;
Be honest and frank anyway.

What you spend years building, someone could destroy overnight;
Build anyway.

The good you do today, people will often forget tomorrow;
Do good anyway.

Give the world the best you have, and it may never be enough;
Give the world the best you've got anyway.

You see, in the final analysis, it is between you and God;
It was never between you and them anyway.

- Mother Teresa

If you stay the same person who is not living your best life, a part of you, possibly the best part of you, dies. In the long run, you are better off without poisonous people around you, just as you are better off if the water you drink does not contain poisonous chemicals!

While poisonous people make it much harder to progress towards your goal, this seldom happens with supportive people. And it is your job to remove the negative influence of poisonous people and surround yourself with supportive, nurturing people.

Decide today what you can do to help remove yourself from the influence of poisonous people or to negate their influence. The first step is to be aware of negative emotions from the moment they start. Perhaps you can remind yourself that your goal is not their goal, and you'll be the one enjoying the benefits of succeeding.

Reward Nurturing People

Now think what you can do, right now, to start adding more nurturing people into your life. How might you reward those nurturing people for their help and their belief in you? Rewards can take the form of a hug, an email, a phone call, or simply saying "Thanks for believing in me." And consider that the more you reward people, the more they'll nurture, support, empower you, and bring energy to your life.

In Day 25 you learned the value of win-win relationships. Think of ways you can become a more nurturing and empowering friend yourself. When we support others, they tend to support us.

Master's Tip If you want love, give love. If you want money, give money.
Deepak Chopra

The same applies to the Universe. If you want support, give support!

Avoiding Poisonous People

INTEGRATION CHECKLIST

Things you will need

Your journal

A quiet space to think and write

Integration-Related Activity

The goal of this activity is for you to evaluate the relationships in which you spend the most time. With this knowledge, you can make educated choices that help you powerfully move forward to Enlightened Internal Leadership.

Evaluating Relationships Exercise

Today we invite you to honestly evaluate the people around you. Being someone who takes 100% responsibility for your life, you can choose with whom to spend your time. And from this perspective it is very important to evaluate who supports you and who doesn't. Even if a poisonous person is a close family member, you can choose to limit the time you spend with them, or you can learn techniques to deal with toxic people so you don't absorb their poison.

Levels of Sensitivity

Keep in mind that people are seldom deliberately toxic. Yes, there are a few who are simply, for lack of a better word, obnoxious. However, most people are in so much pain that their only way of coping is to lash out and hurt others. Quite a few don't realize they are doing it or if they do know they are doing it, they may not realize how their words and actions hurt others. They may think they are being funny. Also, people vary widely in their degree of sensitivity, so what hurts one person may "slide off the back" of another.

You can definitely learn to lessen the effect of poisonous people, which we will investigate in a moment. First, let's start by determining who you choose to spend time with.

WRITTEN ACTIVITY LIST ALL THE PEOPLE WITH WHOM YOU SPEND TIME.

As you list the people, group them into these four groups:

- People with whom you work
- People in your home life
- Friends
- Family members outside of your home.

Make a list of everyone you spend significant amounts of time with, or who has significant influence over you. The two may or may not go together. For example, you may spend a lot of time at work, but care little for the opinions of those with whom you work. On the other hand, you might live far from your parents, but a few words from them has the power to make you cry, be humbled, or very proud of your accomplishments.

People with whom I work	**People in my home life**
Friends	**Family members outside my home**

This is just a start on your list. Feel free to add to it as you think of more people in the different groups.

Rate Your Relationships

First, let's evaluate the energy we feel from these people.

- If the person steals your life energy, meaning they are someone who is consistently bringing you down, put a frowning face beside their name.

- If the person is someone who consistently supports you, someone that adds to your life energy, put a smiley face beside their name.

- And if the person is outstandingly supportive and gives wind to your sails, put a smile and a star beside their name.

Now, it is time to count.

- How many frowns do you have?
- How many smiley faces do you have?
- How many stars?

We all need a star in our lives. If you don't have a star, the exercise in Day 27 shows you how you can find a group of stars to support you.

Rate Your Support

Looking at the distribution of smiles, frowns, and stars, and knowing that who you are is defined by the five people with whom you spend the most time:

Ask yourself: On a scale from 0 to 10, how satisfied am I with quality of people and support I have in my life?

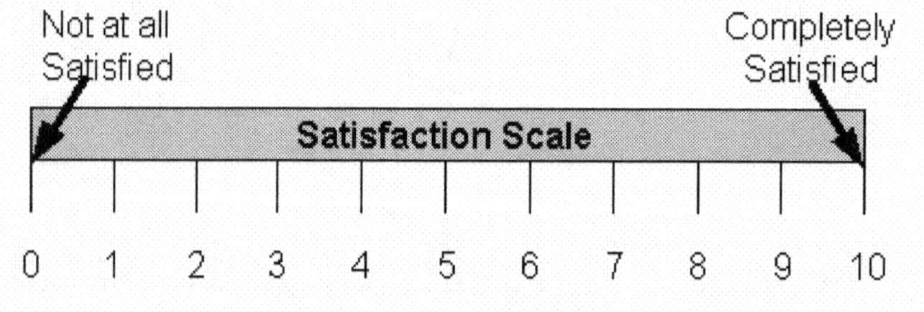

If you rated yourself a 10 - things couldn't be better.

However, if you are less than a 10:

Ask yourself: What might I do to improve my level of satisfaction by one number? By two numbers?

Relationship Reality

Ideally, everyone you spend significant amounts of time with would be a smiley face, or a smiley face with a star. However, sometimes it doesn't always work out that way.

Consider: The occasional grump in our lives might be there to show us how very different people can be. And some people whom we think are grumpy may simply be people who show us where we need to improve. In some way, they might be a mirror to something that we don't like about ourselves. While we are not going to discuss this in detail today, consider pondering these possibilities.

Learning from Relationships

Take another look at the people who you put frowns next to. These are people to consider carefully.

Ask yourself: What might these people be pointing out to me that may need to be fixed or considered in my life?

Ask yourself: Is there a genuine poisonous quality to me when I am around them?

Ask yourself: What do I do inside of myself to create this?

Look at each person on your list. Cautiously consider anyone who brings you down.

Ask yourself: Is there some great learning in this relationship that I am hiding out from?

Ask yourself: Is there something I need to heal within myself to deal with this person?

Ask yourself: Does this person really bring value into my life or am I better off without them in my life?

There can be ramifications to cutting people out of your life. Sometimes it needs to be done, yet sometimes we just can't do it. Have you ever been in a situation like this? Maybe that poisonous person for you is your parent, your child, your spouse, or your boss! While it is possible to turn our back on family, and in some extreme cases, advisable, we're going to assume here that it isn't that bad. For today, we're going to look at some ways to reduce the poison that toxic people spread, while keeping them in your life.

Reducing Poison

Begin by always monitoring your internal state with people.

As soon as you notice that you are feeling bad - stop and think:

Ask yourself: What set that off?

Ask yourself: What am I putting my attention on?

Ask yourself: Am I focused on what I want or on what I don't want? Am I moving away from something or towards something?

Ask yourself: What did I do inside of myself that created this feeling?

It was a thought that **you** thought that created the feeling. You may have created it yourself or it might have been a thought you had in response to someone else. What **you** choose to think is always up to you. Another person cannot tell you what to think or make you feel a certain way.

Let's suppose someone has said something or maybe you've just thought it yourself. For example: ***"I can <u>never</u> get anywhere."*** Then you start to feel bad.

How can you handle this?

Try this approach:

Ask yourself: Is it true that I can never get anywhere?

Ask yourself: Am I absolutely certain it is true?

Consider always questioning the thoughts and words that start bad feelings.

Ask yourself: Is it really true that I have never gotten anywhere? Really?

Master's Tip Your thoughts and your feelings are totally within your control.

Challenge Global Thoughts

In the example, notice the huge globalization in the thought, 'You will **never** get **anywhere**.'

This statement is simply not true, unless you are still lying in the cradle you were placed in when you were born.

Using words like **never** and **always** severely sabotage you because this type of thinking leads to a hopeless, helpless state of depression. For this reason, consider staying away from global thoughts that include **You never** or **I never** do **anything**, **anywhere**, **anytime**, or **any place**. Challenge those kinds of thoughts by placing extreme emphasis on the globalization words.

For example is, "*I will never get anywhere?*"

Challenge this by asking: **Never? Anywhere? Really?**"

Always is another globalization. ***"You always do that!"***

Unless you do the same thing over and over, and **never** do anything else, it's simply not true that you **always** do that. Again, challenge the thought with the extreme emphasis on the globalization, and you and others can see that it's just not a true statement! For example, use this challenge: ***"I* always *do this,* really*?"***

Limit Exposure to Poison

If you have poisonous people in your life, chances are that they think and speak with globalizations! Remember to challenge their statements. Avoid accepting these globalizations and learn to:

Ask yourself: Is what they are saying true?

Ask yourself: Am I absolutely certain this is true?

Ask yourself: What is the possible learning in what they are saying; that is, what is their positive intention?

Of course it won't be true because what's true is that you have accomplished a great deal in your life and there is nothing that you **always do** or **never do**. And, of course, these statements also do not apply to anyone else.

Consider that taking on someone else's dramatic global language and projection as if it is true does serious - very serious - disservice to your mind and heart, and ultimately to your results in life.

Master's Tip You do not need to react or respond with spite when you hear toxic things. Ask to let them go - just release them to the Universe, and look for the opportunity to learn.

And, of course. consider limiting your exposure to all the toxic people on your list. If you must be around them, watch for the use of the globalization language, either in what they say, or in what you think when you're around them.

Avoid Poisonous People NOW

Imagine if you surrounded yourself only with people who brought great energy into your life.

Knowing that avoiding toxic people and building nurturing relationships makes your life more productive and less stressful, what would you be willing to do now?

What action might you take to remind yourself to build nurturing relationships and releasing toxic thoughts so the future is filled with a life you love?

Day 27 **Help Others Succeed**

This session is about building reciprocal relationships, creating a balance of give and take - helping others succeed as you live your best life.

It was such a small town. Each woman watched as the fortunes of others rose on government grain subsidies and fell on farm auctions and factory closings. So when Maxine called Carnell to say she wanted to start an investment club, they both had a good chuckle before they got down to business. It was the spring of 1983 when sixteen women joined together in the basement of the First Lutheran Church to do something about the ups and downs of their finances.

With an average age of 63.5, the women agreed that $100 and a firm commitment to "learning and earning" should be enough to do something. Their profits grew to a portfolio worth well over $90,000, and, at one point an average return of 23 percent. The Beardstown Ladies' Investment Club was outperforming mutual funds and professional money managers 3 to 1.

"We invest with our hearts, our eyes and our stomachs. We buy stocks from companies whose products we know and use. We add our own life experience to the analysis we do on a company before making decisions," Carnell says.

And Maxine proclaims, "We're using the gifts God gave us, and we want to share what we learn."

Together with their collective wisdom and good sense they unveiled the secret recipe for investment success. It's amazing what can happen when people get together to learn and earn.

Avoiding poisonous people and building relationships with nurturing people is a great start. And yet, consider that this approach is not enough.

MASTER'S TIP Martin Rutte put it perfectly when he said, "You have to do it yourself, but you don't have to do it alone."

To go further in life, faster, a Mastermind Group is extremely important.

Mastermind Groups

Mastermind groups are alliances of people who work together to support each other. Each member tunes in and watches for whatever might help the other members. A mastermind group is one of the most powerful tools that successful people use. In fact, successful people reference Mastermind groups as the one thing they credit as having helped them live their best life.

"For where two or three are gathered together, in my name, there am I in the midst of them." - Matthew 18:20

MASTER'S TIP While you must always do the work of becoming the best you, a great group of people can help harness the spiritual energy to support your success.

As we said in Session 26, when you help others succeed, they will naturally want to help you succeed! Mastermind Groups give you and others the opportunity to openly and frankly discuss goals and the best way to achieve them. And discussing how to achieve someone else's goal often gives you great insight into your own journey!

Napoleon Hill discusses the mastermind alliance in his book *Think and Grow Rich*. Hill's belief is that bringing together a dedicated group of achievement-oriented individuals dramatically improves each member's success. He states, "***A mastermind alliance is built of two or more minds working actively together in perfect harmony toward a common definite object.***"

Build Your Group

Henry Ford, an assembly line expert, had a mastermind group that included Thomas Edison (inventor), Harvey Firestone (corporate management genius) and other diverse talents that supported the group in hearing many different perspectives.

You can build your own Mastermind Group. Consider starting with just two or three members, although groups often have six to seven members. Ideally, you select people who are already where you want to be in your life or at least one level above where you consider yourself. Also, think about asking people who you perceive can introduce you to a network of people you normally wouldn't have access to.

Each member brings to the table different viewpoints, an ability to share, personally and professionally, and the desire to support the others as they work towards their goals. If you want to add more members, make sure all of the original members agree on the new members.

You might be thinking "I just want to lose weight' or my goal's too small to have a bunch of people together. Not so! Bringing together a group of people to support each other is a time-tested concept. Look at the success of Weight Watchers™.

So start now and ask people who will provide wind in your sails to join your group. The truth is, most people are not part of a mastermind group. And you never know if they are interested unless you ask.

Mastermind Group Guidelines

Once you have your group, there are a few tips that provide momentum and consistency.

- **Group setup guidelines.**

  Make sure you have some guidelines for your group, so everyone knows:

  - How often you meet.
  - How long the meetings are.
  - What to expect and contribute.

- **Select members who trust each other or with whom you can build a trusting relationship.**

  - The issue of trust is key. Members cannot bring their best experience, or bring their own issues to the table is they don't trust the other members.
  - Select members who share similar values.

    If you have members with widely diverse values, what each brings to the table typically doesn't work for other members. The ideal mastermind group brings together people from different professional arenas without having too wide a spectrum. When a great gap exists among members, sharing advice and experience may have little relevance, though this does depend on your topic.

- **Group meetings**

  When conducting a Mastermind Meeting, have some rules that make supporting each other easy. Your rules can be simple, such as:

  - No put downs are allowed.
  - All comments must be supportive.
  - Matters discussed within Mastermind Groups are kept confidential, so all members feel free to speak their mind.
  - When a member speaks, the rest of the group should listen and brainstorm solutions.

- **Meeting format**

  Developing a format for your meeting is also important. Two effective beginning steps are:

  - Begin your meeting by asking for spiritual guidance - request that the group be filled and surrounded by powerful spiritual energy.
  - Spend some time catching up - sharing the new and good news with a quick update, so all members know how each other is doing.
  - Have the meeting.

    This part of the meeting varies widely from group-to-group. Some groups have meetings that are short, so only one member brings an issue each meeting. Some groups take turns to bring an issue to the table. Other groups hold longer meetings, so each member can bring an issue forward at each meeting and spend 10 minutes on it. Other groups decide ahead of time on a topic for the meeting, and each member prepares for the meeting by bringing a resource with enough copies for all members.

- Close the meeting powerfully.

  Near the end of the meeting, consider having each member commit to stretching themselves and declare their goal aloud.

  Finally, finish the meeting with gratitude, such as a prayer or meditation expressing gratitude and seeking courage to be accountable to your word.

Mastermind Group Benefits

Two major benefits of a mastermind group are the growth of commitment and increased accountability.

Once you form bonds within your group, you want to keep your commitments to keep the respect of the group members. Formal, verbal commitments ensure that each member is continually moving forward - the true benefit of the mastermind group. Consider briefly discussing weekly progress at the beginning of each meeting to increase accountability.

Begin Now

Some very famous people used Mastermind Groups. Ben Franklin highly valued his group, which he called a **Junto**. Tom Peter uses the term **Skunk Works** when talking about Mastermind Groups.

No matter which group term you use, a group of people working together, thinking and sharing ideas for each other's benefit is powerful. The group helps you find possibilities and solutions that you might not consider on your own. And the group also provides positive support and encouragement for you to reach your goals.

While it takes commitment on every member's part to show up and participate fully, being a part of a Mastermind group can make all the difference between success and failure, especially if you do not already have supportive people in your life.

Focusing on the success of others is a sure way to improve the success of your own life. What you give comes back to you tenfold!

Helping Others Succeed

INTEGRATION CHECKLIST

Things you will need

Your journal

A quiet space to think and write

Integration-Related Activity

The goal of this activity is for you to determine how to build a Mastermind Group for yourself. With this knowledge, you can create the best Mastermind Group possible to help you continue to move forward to Enlightened Internal Leadership.

Building a Mastermind Group

Let's talk about how to build a Mastermind Group for yourself. These groups not only bring support into your life, they help you build a sense of purpose. They keep the fire within burning bright in you and in the group members through time.

The most successful people in the world were or are part of a Mastermind win-win alliance. These alliances are one method to ensure you receive the support of a group, no matter what life circumstances may present themselves. Plus, you have the opportunity to contribute to others success. What could be more fulfilling than that?

First steps

Ask yourself: If I were to gather a group of people together to best support me in my current goal, what would be the mission or main objective for the group?

Ask yourself: How many members would I like to have in my mastermind group?

Two - a mastermind partnership? Three members? Four? Five? Six? More?

Your answer about the size of the group is an instinctive answer - one that designates a group size with which you feel most comfortable. This size may not be practical, depending on the skills and abilities you want to include in the group, but for now, let's assume it is. There are a lot of multi-talented people in the world.

Ask yourself: What are the values I would like the people in the group to exhibit?

If you're starting a business-focused group, it may not be useful to have someone in the group who believes that most small businesses fail, or to include someone who is known for unethical business practices. Include in your group the people who share your visions and values.

Ask yourself: What skills and abilities would be perfect to have in a group with my focus?

The focus is your goal. For instance, if your focus is to start a small business, you might want to have someone with financial knowledge, perhaps of the banking industry. This person could be an accountant. Perhaps you want someone who has marketing skills to offer, or production management. Perhaps your group would benefit from having someone who understands franchising or branding. And, for effectiveness, you want to have at least one person, if not more, who is currently running a highly successful small business in the way you would like.

Master's Tip You want to surround yourself with people that are successful in the way you want to be successful.

You may not be able to get exactly the skills you want in your group. For example, you may not find a banker who wants to be part of a group that is focused on developing small business. However, you might! There could be a lot of bankers who would like to start their own small business and would be a good fit, skill-wise, for your group. Or you may find a banker, who doesn't want to be part of the group, but who is willing to act as a support person or mentor to the group.

Now that you have an idea about the people in your group, let's talk a bit about trust.

Ask yourself: How will I build trust amongst the group members?

If the members don't trust each other enough to offer the best knowledge they have, and to be consistently supportive, there's not much point in having the group. The group is not merely about the exchange of knowledge; it is about supporting each other through thick and thin, hard times and good, and always focused on the goal.

Now for some logistical planning.

Ask yourself: How often do I think the group might need to meet?

Ask yourself: Where should we meet?

Ask yourself: How long should the meetings be?

These are logistical questions that often determine who can be a part of the group and who can't. Some people can commit to a morning a week, others can only commit to an hour.

You might consider meeting by conference call, if you need to. For some groups this is quite effective. However, most groups prefer to meet in person. Often a phone group meets at least once a year, in person, for a weekend brainstorming retreat.

Begin To Build

Now it's time to build your list of prospective members.

WRITTEN ACTIVITY WRITE A LIST OF 12-15 PEOPLE THAT YOU WOULD LIKE TO BE PART OF A MASTERMIND ALLIANCE WITH YOU.

▪	▪	▪
▪	▪	▪
▪	▪	▪
▪	▪	▪
▪	▪	▪

Now that you have a list, go back and prioritize the names. Rank the people on the list in order of preference. Consider carefully the skills, abilities, personality, values, and availability of potential members. You might find it useful to create a screening process and develop a set of criteria.

Before you finish your ranking, consider if any potential group member could possibly have some toxic energy. If so, don't take them into the group! That person with poisonous energy can destroy what the rest of you are building.

Now develop your recruitment plan, using the sample if you wish.

ASK YOURSELF: What will I say to these people when I call?

Sample Recruitment Conversation

Here is a sample of something you might say.

Hi, Debbie. My name is Renee Choice. We met one time at the Chamber networking meeting. I am not sure if you remember, but I am a coach and trainer with a new product called the Making Powerful Choices 30-Day Audio Program. My team and I have also launched a book along with some other great products.

Debbie, I am curious - if you had an exceptional group of people with whom you could brainstorm ideas and find solutions, would this be of value to you? This is what I am starting to create. I have just recently learned about the power of a Mastermind Group and though I am just starting out, I have some very powerful feedback from a number of people that starting a Mastermind Group helps everyone in the group learn new ideas through points of view that we probably haven't thought of before, while gaining access to new resources. And this alliance will help all of us become better than we currently are.

I really want you to be in this group. I believe that you would get a lot of value out of it. Are you currently part of a mastermind alliance? If not, can I put you down on my list and then forward you more information once I talk with other people?

Jake Hanson has agreed to be involved. Do you know him? Although I am open to feedback, I see this group connecting on a monthly basis to brainstorm ideas and find solutions around each others' challenges. The first time we will meet in person, and the following sessions will be over the telephone.

Create Practice Scenarios

Before you begin your calls, create three to five sentences around what you might say when you call someone to join your group. Then get started!

Ask yourself: When might I call these people?

When a Mastermind Group is put together effectively, these groups are often so powerful that members form deep bonds, and stay together for years. So, please choose carefully. You may have to ask a number of people to sit down and discuss the idea with you before deciding. The actual discussion with them about the concept of a Mastermind Group typically tells you a lot about what they will be like as a group member.

To be highly effective and get the most from the session, some groups hire a facilitator to help the group stay on track. This can be useful with groups of 5 or more, and is seldom needed with groups of 2 or 3 members.

Professionally trained coaches make great facilitators for Mastermind Groups. You might want to consider using a Powerful Choices Coach to facilitate your group. Our coaches could help you form a Mastermind Group that supports your deepest dreams. Check us out at www.powerfulchoices.net.

Helping Others Succeed NOW

Imagine if you were in a Mastermind Group in which each member totally shared your enthusiasm for your goal and consistently helped you adjust and stay on course.

Knowing that a Mastermind Group is one of the single most effective ways to reach your goal, what would you be willing to do now?

What action might you take to remind yourself to begin to recruit and establish your Mastermind group so you can efficiently reach a future that is filled with a life you love?

Day 28 **Ask For Feedback**

This session is about learning to ask for feedback.

Eight seconds can be a very long time when you are strapped to the back of an irritated bull. Nobody understood that better than Tom "Shorty" Russell. After 14 years in the saddle, Shorty was the grizzliest veteran on the circuit with literally hundreds of rides to his credit. At one time or another, he had broken nearly every bone in his body - some of them twice.

Although a champion in many people's eyes, Shorty was having the most challenging year of his life. After a tough ride Shorty would say to himself, "Man, I just ain't as good as I used to be. I must be all washed up."

For the last ride of the competition, Shorty drew Black Magic. Not a single cowboy and no one in the crowd would wish this terrible beast on anyone - least of all good old Shorty Russell. The bull had a rap sheet worse than any criminal's. Black Magic had kicked, spun, and gored so many cowboys that they all joked that the bull should have faced the electric chair and rightly ended up on their dinner plates a long time ago. But the promoters thought differently.

When Shorty arrived at the chute to ride Black Magic, the guys said he joked as he always had, but unlike before, he asked them questions about the bull he was riding and what they thought would be the best way to ride him. They, of course, gave him the best feedback they could.

Checking his rawhide rope, Shorty's eyes focused like a laser on every step of getting situated on the broad back of the heaving bull. When the gate crashed open, Shorty's world was instantly quiet. Everyone watched with stunned awe as the veteran dueled with his dangerous foe. Shorty's hips swiveled gracefully with every twist and turn the murderous bull made.

A Story

A Brief Tale

The cowboy's arm was like a ship's rudder, sensing the changing direction of the waves, guiding him steadily through a rough and dangerous sea.

And then, the 8 seconds were up. The clowns rushed in and Shorty fell to the ground. His season was over. Tom 'Shorty' Russell could hear the crowd go wild and he knew that it was acting on the expert feedback he had received that made the season finish strong.

That evening he confided in his best friend, "Ya know, Bob, I never would have approached my ride with Black Magic in the way I did if I hadn't listened to the boys in the chute. I wonder what I would have been able to do if I would have started asking for feedback sooner? Hmmm...."

As you know by now, not every step on route to your goal will produce the results you are looking for. In fact, some approaches that you thought would work may land you flat on your back - like Shorty Russell. However, every time you take a step, you get feedback about whether or not it was the right thing to do! Every step you take speaks to you in some way by giving you data, advice, help, suggestions, directions, criticism, and possibly even a reason to celebrate. Consider that asking for expert feedback is the quickest and easiest way to adjust your road map to success.

By now you probably know this Master's Tip by heart.

Master's Tip Consider these three central rules to a fulfilling life.

- **If something works, don't fix it.**
- **Once you know what works, do more of it.**
- **If it doesn't work, don't do it again - Do Something Different!**

In Day 25 we discussed that a necessary part of getting to where you want to go is checking to make sure that you are on the right track and, if you are not, adjusting. We also talked about checking the road signs - if you're heading for California, and the sign says Alaska, you had better check your map!

Consider that all actions are really experiments. We take our very best guess on the best action to take with the information we have at the time, take the action and then sit back and wait. Your road map is the plan you developed to achieve your goal. This map is your best guess on how to get from where you are now to where you want to be. And because it is a guess, it is likely not perfect.

Feedback is one of the road signs you can use to guarantee you are heading in the right direction.

Self-Feedback

Let's experiment a bit.

Ask yourself: Am I tracking toward my outcome or not? How would I know?

One way to track your progress is to check where you are as compared to where you want to be. This is **self-feedback**. For example, if you want to lose weight, you can easily get feedback from the scale or a measuring tape.

Feedback is simply information. Feedback is the guidance system on the airplane to your goals. As you learned in Day 25, the plane's computer and pilot are constantly adjusting course according to the information they are getting. If your goal is to start a new business and achieve gross sales of $100,000 in the first year, how far along are you? Have you started the business? What are your sales?

Self-feedback is great for checking your location on the roadmap. It can also be great for verifying how we feel about our progress - if we feel we could have done better.

Ponder: How specifically could I have done it better?

Ponder: What sort of person could make these adjustments easily?

Frequent self-feedback checks help keep you on track, inspired, motivated, and taking action. If one of your self-feedback checks was daily checks to track if you accomplished your three steps for the day, you probably wouldn't miss a day. Right? If you only check once a week, you might have already missed a day, or two, or (gasp) a whole week! We call these “misses” a **self-induced setback** caused by a lack of appropriate self-feedback.

Self-feedback is personal accountability based in inspired discipline. When we check for feedback from ourselves, we ask ourselves if we did what we said we would do. If we didn't, we can address it. However, if we never ask, the entire goal-achieving project may wither away and die. Ever had this happen?

External Feedback

External feedback from others on how we are doing is also very valuable, especially if we have been taking three steps each day and not achieving the results we want.

For example, if you have changed your eating plan to lose weight, and those pounds just aren't falling off, first look for self-feedback. Have you actually eaten the portions you said you would? Did you sneak a few snacks? However, if you are sticking to your plan and still not moving toward your outcome, then ask for help. Maybe you need more information. Maybe adding activity is the answer. Maybe the type of exercise you are doing is not burning as many calories as you thought. Maybe you need to drink more water.

Asking for feedback from an outside source - from a mentor, inspirational model, your Mastermind Group, or an open, honest and direct friend - is the sign of really wanting to achieve your goal and live your best life.

Get Expert Help

While we are each geniuses about our dreams and values, it is unrealistic to expect that we know everything about every topic. And outside research and feedback can sometimes show you a whole new roadmap to success.

Ask an expert how you might change your plan. In our weight-loss example, maybe you have a body type that needs a different type of exercise. Perhaps you were mistaken about the exact calorie count of some of your favorite foods, and you need to change your portion sizes. And a few people actually eat too little, so eating a bit more might speed up the metabolism so they can lose weight.

Suppose you thought the way to financial freedom was through working hard for over 100 hours per week at a low paying job. Then someone showed you how, with just a few educational upgrades, you could work fewer hours at a much better paying job. Wouldn't you change your plan?

Embrace New Information

Feedback is valuable. However, the truth is, most people don't ask for it. In fact, most of us go out of our way to avoid it because we are afraid of feeling like a failure.

The problem with the avoidance strategy is that if we don't ask for feedback, we may never know what we are doing wrong. New information helps us make the corrections that support us in reaching our goal.

So how do we avoid that fear of failure? Consider that it is absolutely possible and important to become detached from feedback and avoid taking it personally. We can just look at feedback as a way to learn. Consider taking the best and leaving the rest. It's up to you **how** you take it. Even something intended as criticism can be taken as loving feedback, depending on how you frame it in your mind. You can look for the kernel which might be helpful for you, or you can decide to let the criticism collapse you - your choice!

Choose Feedback Sources Wisely

Toxic people freely offer criticism, so choose your sources of feedback wisely. When you seek feedback, ask people who have succeeded at the goal you want to achieve or people you trust to support you, rather than those who are still struggling. Successful people are not still struggling.

So how should you solicit feedback? There are a number of ways:

- In person
- By mail
- By phone
- Through email
- Any other method that supports you in getting the information you need.

To help you ask for feedback more effectively, answer these questions:

PONDER: In what areas might I need feedback?

PONDER: What feedback do I need to ask for that I am not asking for now?

PONDER: Who might I need to ask?

PONDER: When will I ask?

PONDER: How will I ask?

Asking for Feedback

INTEGRATION CHECKLIST

Things you will need

Your journal

A quiet space to think and write

Integration-Related Activity

The goal of this activity is for you to learn to actively and purposefully ask for feedback. With this knowledge, you can learn to be detached from the outcome and learn how you can improve your plan to move forward to Enlightened Internal Leadership.

ANSWER THE QUESTIONS IN AN OPEN, HONEST, AND DIRECT WAY.

Asking For Feedback Strategies

When you solicit feedback, it is important to be detached from what is said. Remember the information is available for you to learn and grow, so you can do more of what works best in getting the outcome you want. Choose to take the best learning, and leave the rest.

ASK YOURSELF: In what areas might it be useful to ask for feedback that I am not presently asking for?

Ask yourself: What specific questions do you want answered?

For example, if you were future focused, perhaps you might want to know:

- Will this idea work?
- How do I add more value?
- Will this sell?
- What are all the possibilities beyond what I have currently created?
- What will have to happen for me to be extremely successful?
- What do I need to do more of in the future?

If you were past focused, perhaps you might want to know:

- What was missing from what I did?
- How can I be better than I currently am?
- What do I need to improve before I move forward?

Now consider these questions.

Ask yourself: Who do you need to ask and why?

Ask yourself: How will you ask?

Ask yourself: When will you ask?

Ask yourself: How will you best interpret the feedback?

Ask yourself: How can you listen for the truth and receive the feedback effectively?

Ask yourself: What will you do with this feedback?

Ask yourself: When will you do it?

Check-In Time

Okay, let's check in again on your current commitment and progress.

Ask yourself: On a scale from 0 to 10, what has been my level of satisfaction with the quality of my commitment and progress so far?

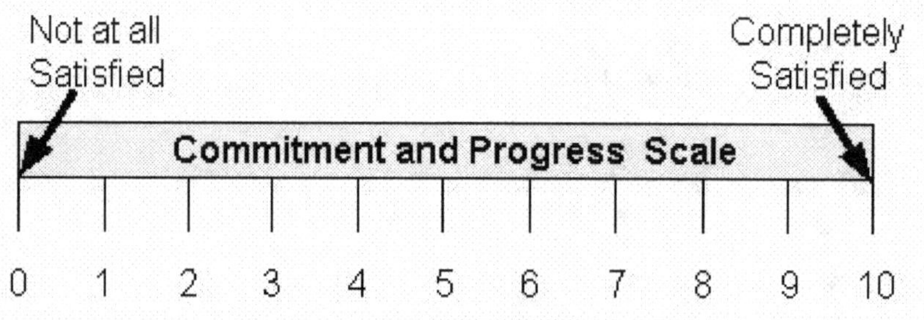

Ask yourself: If my satisfaction level was to move up one number, what would I do differently?

CONSIDER: It's Day 28 and you will soon be completing the program - of course, in a very powerful way. In the spirit of feedback, please consider visiting our web site - www.powerfulchoices.net - and emailing us feedback on your level of satisfaction with the value of this workbook for you. Also, let us know what we could do differently to increase your satisfaction.

Ask for Feedback NOW

Imagine if you accepted feedback as merely information on how you could live your best life sooner.

Knowing that detaching and accepting seemingly critical feedback as information leads you to your goals sooner, what are you be willing to do now?

What action might you take to remind yourself to go solicit feedback as a way to learn - taking the best and leaving the rest - so your future is filled with a life you love?

Part 8: **Completion**

You have built a strong foundation, created a vision, made a powerful choice to go for it, and planned how to reach your goal. You started your plan in action, found some challenges, learned some techniques for continuing your success, and discovered how to check your satisfaction and correct your course when you are drifting away from achieving your goal.

The next phase of the 30-day program is two days during which you learn to finish strong and powerfully.

The architect has a solid foundation, has designed the home, begun construction, anticipated possible obstacles to reaching the completion date, sought support in overcoming obstacles, took action towards building momentum to reach the completion date, and examined the level of satisfaction with the progress. It's now time to complete the project.

As you continue to be the architect of your life, creating the blueprints for success, seeking help and using all your resources to keep your momentum going, it is useful to stay on your path, avoid obstacles and surround yourself with people who help you succeed, collaborating with others who know your challenges and strengths, and seeking feedback on how to succeed in the most efficient and effective manner possible. But the most satisfaction comes from crossing the finish line and arriving at your destination.

Journals

Your journal continues to fill up. Your blueprint is complete and you are taking actions to reach your goal. You have momentum and can see the structure being built on the strong foundation.

What should be in your journal now? Check out your blueprint and make certain that you have completed all the details - done the exercises you might have skipped and put extra effort into ones you might have found challenging.

Review your plan and tweak it as you receive feedback and more information. Make certain that you are getting the support you need and staying focused on what you want. Write down how you plan to create your mastermind group for support now and in the future and who you can contact to build win/win relationships in your life.

Now plan to finish strong - and get your own gold medal of success!

2-Day Completion Overview

The first five days of your journey were about building a foundation. The next two were about inspiration and vision, learning to live **your** dream. Then you spent four days learning how to make your decision powerful and compelling. After three days of planning, you spent two days getting started and five days continuing your successful journey. You then spent seven days checking your level of satisfaction and finding successful people whom you could ask for input and collaborate with to reach your destination powerfully. It's time now to land at your destination and cruise into completion.

In **Day 29** you learn what it means to live with integrity. You are near the end of your journey and it is important to see how the journey meshes with what you truly want in life. You learn to listen to your voice within when you state "I am deeply committed to my goal."

Day 30 is about extending your success. You made it to the end of your journey, so witness the changes in your life. How are you different than when you took your first step onto your staircase? We invite you to take your new skills and incorporate them into other areas of your life so you can truly live a life you love.

Notice the view of your life from this place of completion. Remember **Day 1** and recognize how far you have come. And think of how far you can go by repeating what you now know how to do.

Are you ready?

CHECKLIST

- Be sure you have your journal.
- Set a time aside each day to do your life's work.

Day 29 **Live With Integrity**

This session is about being in integrity with your word and making certain that each action you take in your life aligns with your values.

There is a wonderful movie called **The Notebook** that is worth seeing. The story is of a promise kept through time and across great distances. While we don't want to spoil the movie for you, something happens in this movie that is relevant to this lesson. A young man makes a promise to a young woman. Years later she discovers that he has gone to great lengths to keep that promise. The result - his choice to be in integrity with his word won him the love of his life.

As we come to the close of our 30-day program, one thing to talk about is staying in integrity. How do we define integrity? If you did what you said you would do - this is having personal integrity. If you didn't do what you said you would do, that is not having personal integrity!

Some people think integrity has to do with ethics. Yes, it does, but not in the sense of good or bad, evil or good. Living with integrity means staying true to your values, no matter what your values are.

If you're not living your life in integrity with your values, you're what we call **out of alignment**. When an action or a goal is not in line with your values, you're not living your life in integrity.

Live with Integrity

Living life with integrity is something to check on a regular basis. It's really easy to get off track if we don't really know what our deepest values are.

Right now, stop and evaluate how close you are to reaching your goal. We know you've made progress. The degree of progress you've made is in direct relation to the amount of integrity you displayed over the last 29 days.

If you said you wanted to start saving for college, but made no effort to change your spending habits, you are obviously **not** living with personal integrity. And you won't have made any progress towards your goals! This does not mean you are **bad**, it is just the observable truth of what is so.

If you made massive efforts to change your spending habits - writing up a new budget, following a prepared shopping plan, making payments on your credit cards as you said you would, you are living with personal integrity. And, you likely made progress towards your goal - in fact, if you did all that, you've made a lot of progress.

Our integrity is challenged when we are not very committed to our goals.

Let's suppose that Joe and Marlene, brother and sister, both decided that they would save 10% of their income for a future business partnership. Marlene carefully plans her spending and she sticks with it. Joe starts off well, but soon decides spending just a little bit more than he planned would be okay. Two weeks later, Joe spends a little bit more, and a little bit more; and a few weeks later he goes back to his old habits of spending as much as he likes. Joe is not living with integrity. He is not truly committed to his goal of saving money so he can open a business. There is something more important to him.

Does that mean Joe is a bad person? No, it means he just has to take another look at his true values, his unconscious commitments, and what he really wants.

So how do we make sure that we keep moving forward on our road to our best year yet, when it's so easy to lose sight of our goals? In today's world it is easy to change directions and **go with the flow**, yet this is not living a life on purpose. Either Joe is not committed to his goal, or the goal is not the right goal for him.

Test Your Commitment

Here's an easy way to test your commitment.

Say, ***"I am deeply committed to my goal,"*** and listen for a quiet voice within you. The voice will answer, if you listen for it.

For example, if your goal is to lose weight, what does the voice say when you say, ***"I am deeply committed to losing weight. Of course I will reach my ideal weight."*** If the answer is a passionate ***"Yes!"***, and you haven't lost the weight you planned, then you know it's not your commitment that's the problem. You need to change your approach, to one that might work better for you. Remember, if it isn't working, don't do more of it. Do something different!

If the small voice within said ***"not really"*** or ***"I'd really rather watch TV instead"***, you know you're not very committed, and you've got the wrong goal. Perhaps it wasn't the wrong goal all along. It could have been something you were deeply committed to when you started this program, but for whatever reason, your priorities have shifted, and the goal is no longer a real goal for you.

Review Your Integrity

It's time now to review your level of integrity for the last 29 days.

Have you done what you said you would do?

If not, what got in your way?

- Is it the wrong goal?
- Are you unconsciously committed to something else?
- Was your plan for achieving the goal not workable?

Circumstances change. What may have been a very good plan can become obsolete very quickly as you gather new information. So is the goal still the right goal for you or is it the plan that needs adjusting? Only you can tell - just like only you know if you are living with personal integrity.

Hiring a coach may be the perfect way to help you improve your level of integrity. Good coaches help you be accountable for what you say you want and will do. It's very easy to lose sight of our goals when we haven't shared them with a supportive person. And it is much easier to stay true to ourselves and our dreams when we have the support of a coach.

Coaches help us stay focused on what we want. Consider that living with integrity is much simpler when you have the passionate support of the right coach.

Living with Integrity

INTEGRATION CHECKLIST

Things you will need

Your journal

A quiet space to think and write

Integration-Related Activity

The goal of this activity is for you to examine your current level of integrity. With this knowledge, you can create a masterful plan that meshes with your values, thus helping you to more effectively move forward to Enlightened Internal Leadership.

Evaluating Your Personal Integrity

What is your definition of integrity?

How do you know you are living with integrity?

Let's play a bit and explore what it looks like to have complete personal integrity.

Take a moment to relax, and then, as if it was really easy to do, remember a specific time in the past when you had integrity in a way that you would like to carry forward into your future.

Revisit that moment and notice how you enjoy it.

Take a mental step back and look at the picture - view yourself in action experiencing that moment. Appreciate your face and its animation, your gestures, your voice, your breathing, and the quality of all of your movements.

Now enhance the inner quality, by intensifying the colors on the screen of your mind. See your whole body.

How did you look in this moment?

See the aura of certainty that demonstrates you living with integrity.

How were you breathing?

What is the look on your face?

How was your posture?

Ask yourself: How is my focus? My inner alignment?

Now, take all the integrity of this moment and make a shift.

Bringing Integrity Forward

See yourself taking action after this 30-day program - thinking and acting with integrity in the way that you remember from your earlier experience. Exaggerate the visual aspects of integrity as you take action.

Notice how living with integrity immediately enhances your ability to naturally achieve your goal. You have naturally given yourself the gift of staying true to yourself.

As you hold this image, notice that, to ensure that you stay in alignment and live your life on purpose, you naturally create an **integrity practice** for yourself. An integrity practice is daily, weekly or monthly activities that you create and maintain so you feel good about yourself and stay connected to your inner truth and your vision. The elements of your integrity practice keep in the spotlight what is most important to you.

When you are ready, come back to the present moment.

Ask yourself: In my visualization, what were the two main personal integrity practices I did each day to ensure that I stayed on track toward the fulfillment of my vision?

Ask yourself: What other practices did I create on a weekly or monthly basis that also supported me?

Ask yourself: How did I keep these practices alive through time so I always did them - even when the unexpected events of life presented themselves?

Live With Integrity NOW

Imagine if you lived with inner alignment and personal integrity every hour of every day. What would your life be like then?

Knowing that living with integrity brings you closer to living your life on purpose by achieving your goals, what would you be willing to do now?

What action might you take to remind yourself to live every moment with integrity and move forward to a future filled with a life you love?

Day 30 **Extend Your Success**

This session is about extending the success you built throughout this program.

"I thought I could not catch Loroupe. She was too far away. But some energy came back and I was flying. I think it was the crowd and the smell to win, even with the problems I had."

Pippig was in so much pain, she considered dropping out of the race.

"I had some problems with my insides," she said shyly. "I didn't expect it would become this bad - diarrhea. After 4 miles, I was thinking several times to drop out because it hurt so much. But something deep within me kept me going."

Imagine the scene: Pippig was gaining on Loroupe. Without breaking stride, Pippig grabbed a water bottle, ripped the plastic yellow top with her teeth, tossed the cap to the pavement, and took a sip. She kept running and gulped again. She raised the bottle to her lips for one final drink, gaining ground with each step.

Her thirst quenched, Pippig spiked the bottle to the ground and then sped past Loroupe! She had made up 30 seconds in less than a mile.

"It was amazing for me because so many people screamed even when it was not possible to win anymore," said Pippig. "They said, `You can catch her.' And I said, `Come on, guys, it is such a big gap.' It was like a connection between us and I just started fighting and I imagined I could fly."

Smiling through the pain, Pippig flew across the finish line. Overcoming intestinal difficulties and being behind by nearly a quarter of a mile, Uta Pippig out finished Kenya's Tegla Loroupe and won her third consecutive Boston Marathon in a time of 2 hours, 27 minutes, 12 seconds.

You have done it! You have worked through the thirty days of the Making Powerful Choices program. You stuck with it, even when it was hard, and now you're here, thirty days later.

Looking Back

How has your life improved? Yesterday we evaluated what you learned by living with personal integrity to maintain momentum. Today let's look at how your life has improved, and celebrate.

Over the last thirty days, you've worked hard, and learned new skills. The journey began with you defining a clear vision of what you wanted and where you wanted to be at the end of these thirty days - a vision that aligned with your unique purpose.

You set your foundation by looking at what it means to take 100% responsibility at each of the four stages of your life:

- Development
- Intensity
- Forward Motion
- Enlightened Internal Leadership

Where are you now? Are you in the Intensity stage - conscious of how hard you're having to work? If so, remember that it gets easier as you integrate what you've learned and continue to work towards living your best life.

Have you built habits that support you? Are you building forward motion and feeling consciously competent, leading your life naturally from your newly integrated habit system?

Or, are you now at the stage of unconscious competence, where what was once so hard now seems like an everyday accomplishment?

Can you own that you now have the capability to be an Enlightened Internal Leader in any area and at any stage in your life?

Time to Celebrate

Where ever you are on your journey, take time today to celebrate. In a world of instant gratification, you spent thirty days making conscious movement towards your goal, towards living your best life. You made powerful choices over and over again, even when it might have been easier to quit. Not everyone chooses to play the game of life in this way! You have and it's time to congratulate yourself.

Take a moment to feel proud of where you are on your journey and that you have chosen to live your best life.

If your best friend were with you right now, what would your friend say you should be really proud of?

Say it aloud, just as your friend would, and let yourself receive the truth about who you are and what you have done.

Play a Big Game

Your life really matters and we are grateful for your full-fledged participation in your life. Why? Because when you play a big game, you inspire others to do the same and if everyone played this game, the consciousness of the planet would be enhanced. Believe us when we say, you living your best life really matters to us and to everyone else on the planet, whether they know it or not.

Transfer Your New Skills

It is now time for one last push to transfer your new skills into other areas of your life.

Have you ever heard of 'rolling 30-day goals'? Some people call them New Month Resolutions. This concept helps you build a new life using a series of 30-day goal achievements. Each month you choose a new goal. Some people choose something simple, like adding in one thing that supports you, or letting go of one thing that doesn't support you. Maybe you can look at your do, delete, defer, or delegate list. These small changes add up over time.

Other people choose rolling thirty day goals that build up to a predefined point. This is similar to goal setting - you make a plan, and set up landing points where you can check for feedback. Your thirty day rolling goals are short staircases, with the built-in evaluation point at the end of each month.

To live a full life of greatness and achieve what you want to achieve, take frequent note of where you are, how far you've come, and where you want to go. As Alice in Wonderland was told, if you don't know where you want to go, then anywhere you get at all is okay! We'd rather get to where we want to go, so we examine where we want to be, then choose goals to make sure we get there.

Master's Tip Rolling thirty day goals keep you focused.

Look at your goals each month. Creating small steps each month makes the goals achievable and keeps you **living alive** all year long. Many people bite off too much with massive long term goals and New Year's resolutions. A simpler, more powerful approach is to commit to building your best life by learning the skills of goal achievement, and then using them over and over to accomplish your goal in small bites that you can easily handle.

The New You

You are not the same person who started this program. You have new skills, new wisdom, and probably some new desires. You can take your new skills and wisdom, and use them to build new areas of your life. This is definitely cause for celebration!

Ponder: What did I learn that made the most difference for me?

Ponder: What areas would I like to build upon?

Ponder: What achievement - small or large - brought me the most happiness?

Ponder: How have I expanded my vision of what is possible for myself?

Ponder: What other areas of my life would I like to improve?

Ponder: How can I build upon what I have learned with thirty day rolling goals or New Month Resolutions?

Finishing Strong

INTEGRATION CHECKLIST

Things you will need

Your journal

A quiet space to think and write

Integration-Related Activity

The goal of this activity is for you to celebrate your progress and accomplishments. With this knowledge, you can continue to create many more masterful plans and move towards living a life you love every day.

★ **IMPORTANT INSTRUCTION** **GET READY TO FINISH STRONG!**

Celebration Time

It is time to celebrate!

What does it say about you that you had the quality of perseverance to work towards your dream, your vision for the last thirty days?

ASK YOURSELF: How would I compliment someone else who had stuck with the goal for the last thirty days?

Ask yourself: What is something that you have accomplished in the past weeks that you are really proud of?

Ask yourself: If a friend was to congratulate you on what you did, what would he or she say?

Ask yourself: If a friend was to compliment you on what it took, what would he or she say?

Ask yourself: If a friend was to cheerlead who you are, what would he or she say?

Ask yourself: If a friend was to champion what it means and why it matters, what would he or she say?

Ask yourself: What do I want to accomplish next?
Do you want to reach another landing? Or do you have another dream to bring into your life over the next thirty days, or over the next year?

Ask yourself: What could I start to do **now** that would add significant value to my life twenty years from now?

Ask yourself: How can I set up my life to start to do this now? How can I maintain it through time so everyday I will 'of course' do what adds to living a life I love?

Ask yourself: What's the long term value of having learned the skills in this workbook that I practiced during the last thirty days?

Ask yourself: How can I use the skills I learned to continue to get what I want in life?

Ask yourself: What's the long-term value of achieving the movement towards the big life that I just achieved?

Finish Strong NOW

If you have not yet done so, imagine if you finished this 30 day program saying, ***"Of course I will reach the goal I chose"***, or ***"Of course I will start a new goal every 30 days to work towards a life I love."***

Of course you are committed to living your best life, so what action might you take to remind yourself to continue to create goals and finish them - working every day to increase fulfillment of your life's purpose?

Epilogue

We've enjoyed being your partners in success! Consider that to maintain forward motion you need to get the ongoing support and nourishment you need. Please go to www.powerfulchoices.net and sign up to become a member of Powerful Choices. There are many tools and great discounts to keep this information alive through time. Also, please write or email us and tell us of your success. We'd love to celebrate with you!

We would like to make you a deal. If you email us a description of how you worked towards your dream and what your wins were in participating in this program, and we will send you a special gift.

Please email it to us at choices@powerfulchoices.net because we care about supporting people live their dreams, and because you'll enjoy reading your wins over and over, and reading it will likely propel you towards your next dream.

When you send us the outcomes you had from this program, we will send you a very powerful bonus gift that will support your conscious and beyond conscious minds aligning around this body of work fully. This is a very powerful bonus track that you will love, we promise.

We are waiting to hear from you here at Powerful Choices. We believe in you and are grateful for your participation. We look forward to you becoming a member of our Powerful Choices community. We are excited to support your deeper level of integration through time.

Bibliography

Andreas, Connirae and Tamara Andreas, **Core Transformation - Reaching The Wellspring Within,** Moab, Utah. Real People Press, 1994.

Arbinger Institute, **Leadership and Self-Deception,** San Francisco, CA. Berrett-Koehler Publisher, Inc., 2002

Burns, David, **Feeling Good,** New York, NY. William Morrow & Co., 1980

Canfield, Jack Mark Victor Hansen and Les Hewitt, **The Aladdin Factor: How to Ask For and Get Anything You Want in Life,** Deerfield Beach, FL. Health Communications, Inc., 2000.

Canfield, Jack and Janet Switzer, **The Success Principles – How to Get From Where You are to Where You Want To Be,** Harper Collins, New York, New York, 2005.

Chopra, Deepak, **The Seven Spiritual Laws of Success,** San Rafael, CA. Amber-Allen, 1994.

Covey, Stephen R., **The 7 Habits of Highly Effective People,** New York, NY. Fireside/Simon & Schuster, 1989.

Ford, Debbie, **The Best Year of Your Life,** New York, NY. HarperCollins, 2005.

Goleman, Daniel, **Emotional Intelligence: Why It Can Matter More Than IQ,** New York, NY. Bantam Book, 1997.

Harris, Bill, **Thresholds of the Mind,** Centerpointe Press, Beaverton, OR, 2002.

Hawkins, David R., **Power vs. Force: The Hidden Determinants of Human Behavior,** Carlsbad, CA. Hey House, 2002

Hill, Napoleon, **Think and Grow Rich,** New York, NY. Fawcett Crest, 1960.

Katie, Byron and Stephen Mitchell, **Loving What Is: Four Questions That Can Change Your Life,** 3 River Press, New York, New York, 2002.

Maltz, Maxwell, **Psycho-Cybernetics,** Markham, Ontario, Canada. Prentice-Hall, Inc., 1960

McGraw, Phillip C., **Life Strategies: Doing What Works and Doing What Matters** by New York, NY. Hyperion, 1999.

O'Connor, Joseph, **NLP Workbook,** Hammersmith, London. Harper Collins, 2001.

Robbins, Tony, **Unlimited Power,** New York, NY. Simon & Schuster, 1986.

Tolle, Eckhart, **The Power of Now - A Guide to Spiritual Enlightenment,** Novato, CA. New World Library, 1999

Wieder, Marcia, **Making Your Dreams Come True,** New York, NY. Harmony Books, 1999.

Zanders, Rosamund Stone and Benjamin Zander. **The Art of Possibility: Transforming Personal and Professional Life,** New York, NY. Penguin, 2000.

Human Development and Coach Training

Erickson College International offers, from our perspective, some of the best human development courses on the globe. Courses are currently offered in 11 countries and can be researched on www.erickson.edu. Founder of the College, Dr. Marilyn Atkinson, has one of the world's greatest minds. Her training is known to offer transformation on many levels.

Erickson College International, The Art & Science of Coaching, Modules 1-5 (International Coach Federation – Accredited Coach Training Program), 2021 Columbia Street, Vancouver, BC, Canada, www.erickson.edu, 1-800-665-6949

About Powerful Choices

Our Purpose

To be the spark that lights the fire within by providing training and coaching, to awaken universal principals, and to deepen life's conversations.

Our Vision

To light the fire within people so that eternal embers burn so intensely they spark the desire to share and teach about knowledge and inner purpose.

Our Mission

To provide high-quality, affordable, and accessible training and coaching, and a community that supports living a life you love.

Our Leadership Team

In case you would like to get to know us a bit better, here's the Powerful Choices Leadership Team.

Cara Beckett

Solution Focused Coach, Trainer, Radio Show personality

Cara's commitment to human development and facilitating personal growth has been honed through years of training in such diverse fields as Core Belief Engineering, Polarity Therapy, Reiki, NLP, Silva Mind Control, Educational Kinesiology, Touch For Health, The Art & Science of Coaching, and more. She's passionate about helping humans to grow and develop past what they might have previously considered their full potential. Her commitment to helping others develop has been the base for a popular and highly regarded, weekly one-hour radio talk show on CFBX radio, Kamloops, BC Canada. She's also developed the Carajaz Stress Resiliency

System, presented in workshops and in working with private clients. Other products developed by Cara include the Focus! Book, the Results! Journal, and "The Greatest Self-Help Tool In The World", due for publication this fall.

Renee Choice

Solution Focused Coach, Facilitator, Coach Trainer, Curriculum Designer

As an ICF Professional Certified Coach, a member of Erickson College's International Training Faculty, Neuro-Semantic Practitioner, and Life Long Learner, Renee uses her motivational psychology degree to enthusiastically stand for inner and outer transformation on all levels. With over 12 years combined experience in coaching, facilitating, coach training, seminar and product design, Olympic Games planning, human resource management, and other event coordination, employee motivation, customer service training and personal training, Renee focuses on facilitating empowerment & positive change. She known as a transformational coach and facilitator with the ability to support clients, participants and fellow coaches to get to the root cause of challenges, breakthrough them, and sustain the change through time. Many of her clients and training participants says their lives are never the same after working with Renee.

Anthony Choice

Solution Focused Coach, Trainer, Entrepreneur

Anthony has been in the "people business" for more than 25 years. Supporting groups and individuals to become 'more of who they are' has been central to his life. Anthony offers a lifetime of rich experience to his coaching clients and training participants. He has extensive coach training and a diverse entrepreneurial background that includes entertainment management, hosting a national television show, organizing events, leading training seminars, real estate finance, and Olympic Games planning.

Larrye-Marie Heyl

Solution Focused Coach, Technical Consultant, Trainer, Curriculum Designer

Larrye-Marie has a Masters Degree in Mathematics and Engineering, and brings more than 35 years of training, mentoring, and consulting - with diverse populations on all levels including graduate work - to coaching style communication and processing. She is sought after by the business world for her ability to help executives embrace and apply cutting-edge training, curriculum development, and management processes. Due to her ability to exceed expectations, she has contracted with a number of Fortune 500 companies as a project manager, curriculum developer, process expert, marketing editor, and technical trainer. Yet, the truth is – coaching and human development training is her true love!

To Find Out More

For more information about Powerful Choices coaching and training programs, please connect with us in one of these ways:

- **Email:** *choices@powerfulchoices.net*
- **On the Web:** www.powerfulchoices.net
- **By Phone:** (503) 628-6310 (United States)

www.ingramcontent.com/pod-product-compliance
Lightning Source LLC
LaVergne TN
LVHW061236100826
845148LV00008B/970
* 9 7 8 0 9 7 6 9 0 0 3 0 6 *